CONCEPTS
OF GOD

OTHER BOOKS BY KEITH WARD PUBLISHED BY ONEWORLD

God, Chance and Necessity
God, Faith and the New Millennium
In Defence of the Soul

CONCEPTS OF GOD

Images of the Divine in Five Religious Traditions

KEITH WARD

ONEWORLD

OXFORD

CONCEPTS OF GOD

Oneworld Publications
(Sales and Editorial)
185 Banbury Road
Oxford OX2 7AR
England

Oneworld Publications
(US Marketing Office)
PO Box 830, 21 Broadway
Rockport, MA 01966
USA

ISBN 1–85168–064–0

Cover design and illustration by Design Deluxe
Printed and bound in Finland by WSOY

Contents

Acknowledgements

I am grateful to Friedhelm Hardy and Peter Clarke, of the Department of Religion at King's College, London University, for reading parts of the manuscript. I was immensely pleased to find that their keen critical scrutiny occasionally even registered some approval. Needless to say, they cannot be held responsible for what remains. But I would like to record my thanks for their very helpful comments. I would also like to thank John Todd, who encouraged me to write this book; and my wife Marian for her unfailing support and inspiration.

Preface

For many years I have been intrigued by the question of the relation between different religions. There have been thousands of religious beliefs in the history of the human race; and if they laid no claim to truth, there would be no great problem. But there are a number of worldwide religious faiths in existence today, each of which claims to have a final and absolute truth about human nature and destiny and the real nature of things. The problem is not only to discover which one, if any, is right; but what one is to say about the 'other', wrong, ones. Are they simply false? Or are they aiming at an extremely elusive truth in different ways, all equally valid in some sense? Can one learn anything from them? And if so, what?

In this book I have adopted, so far as I can, a phenomenological method.[1] That is, I have tried to look at five major religious traditions as sympathetically as I can, using terms acceptable to those traditions themselves. I have tried to bracket out my own beliefs; or at least not to let them intrude judgementally upon the traditions I am considering. Where I have criticized, I have sought to let the criticisms arise from within the traditions themselves, so that they rather pose difficulties within a tradition than reasons for rejecting that tradition altogether.

So that my task would be reasonably manageable, I have selected one standard work written by an acknowledged master, which has the status of a classical text within each tradition I have considered. And I have sought to elucidate the doctrine of ultimate reality – Brahman, Sunyata or God – as it is found in those texts. My purpose was to compare or contrast these doctrines. But what I found was a quite remarkable similarity in the basic structure of faith explored by each author; in the advocacy of a certain basic attitude, which I have termed the 'iconic vision'; and in the appropriateness of a response of self-transcendence to that vision. Each tradition has its own matrix of revelation, which gives a distinctive character to the way these attitudes are specified in detail. Yet I have sought to show by simple and detailed exposition that there is a common core of belief about ultimate reality – which I have termed a dual-aspect doctrine (or, with apologies to Buddhism, dual-aspect theism), present in each tradition. Moreover, the differences in emphasis and interpretation of this doctrine do not just exist between different religions. They are to be found *within* religious traditions, as diverse strands. Of course, different religious views of the Real are not identical or even compatible in all respects. But I think one can defensibly say, from the evidence I adduce, that there is a convergence of thought among at least the most reflective theologians or philosophers of the great religious traditions.

This does not mean that every tradition is equally acceptable. I have refrained from asserting my own view (though it would be dishonest to disguise the fact that almost all of my own religious practice has been within Christian traditions). I have, however, tried to elucidate briefly the sorts of considerations which are relevant to forming a view, and to show in what respect religious faith is, and is not, susceptible to rational inquiry. I think that the most important conclusion to be drawn from this study is that the great traditions are not just different and incompatible; they exhibit deep convergences of thought and practice and many overlapping strands of particular similarity. With this in mind, I have attempted to sketch the outlines of what might be called the religious form of life and the dual-aspect doctrine which lies at its heart. I believe it is quite possible that many ordinary religious believers are unaware of the deepest orthodox doctrine of God present in their own tradition, as it is so often overlaid by the minutiae of piety or the latest morsel of theological controversy. A recovery of these beliefs might lead to an increase in understanding and tolerance, as one recognizes convergences between faiths at the deepest level; a clearer acceptance of the infinity and mystery of the divine Being; and the possibility of a conversation with other faiths which might enrich one's own.

If, finally, I write this with a hope, it is that it might encourage a patient, painstaking and particular study of religious doctrines and practices in the light of which the very broad and polarizing questions of my opening paragraph may simply cease to have any further relevance or point.

KEITH WARD

1

The Vedantic Philosophy of Sankara

This is an exploration of one tradition of human thought about God. There are many ways of thinking about God, and many ideas of God. They range from full-blooded personalistic ideas of a cosmic superperson who is constantly interfering in the affairs of the world, to very vague ideas of an 'absolute reality' or ultimate force which has very few practical implications at all. They may be primarily concerned with grandiose metaphysical investigations or with intensely personal religious experiences. They may be taken to refer to a disembodied spirit or they may be accepted as projections of a mythical character whose true function is to regulate or specify human attitudes or ways of life. It is not by any means my intention to investigate all these ideas, much less to provide an accurate or exhaustive catalogue of them.

I am only concerned with one sort of approach to the concept of God. But it is an approach which is of major interest. For it lies at the heart of some of the major religious traditions which exist on this planet. It has a good claim to represent the orthodoxy of the Semitic religions – Judaism, Christianity and Islam. And, as I shall seek to show, it is embedded in the Vedantic schools of Indian religion and even in some major forms of Buddhism. If it is true, this means that there is a tradition at the very heart of these faiths which is held in common. It is not that precisely the same doctrines are believed, but that the same tendencies of thought and devotion exist, and are expressed within rather diverse patterns of thought, characteristic of the faiths in question. Nor is this tradition tangential. For it is formulated definitively by central figures who are accepted as pillars of orthodoxy within their own communities.

It is not my purpose to suggest that all religions really believe the same things. Religions generate infinite differences. They often come into existence precisely as a reaction against other existing religions. Nevertheless, I do hope to show that impeccably orthodox figures within major religious traditions, as they reflected upon and elaborated in a more or less systematic way the ideas of God or of the ultimately real within their own tradition, exhibit remarkably similar directions of thought, and a convergence that is as clear as it may be unexpected. It makes sense to say that the same God is worshipped in many diverse faiths.

My purpose, then, is to expound and clarify what this orthodox notion of God is, and to show in what way it occurs in diverse religious traditions. I will try to bring out some implications that may reasonably be taken to follow from this for our understanding of the phenomenon of religious faith and for the notion of truth in religion. The fact that I am using the term 'God' shows that I am speaking from within a certain tradition. I do not believe it is possible to speak from some supremely objective viewpoint about religions. While trying to understand as broad a range of them as possible, as sympathetically as possible, one's own ways of thought will inevitably colour one's judgements to a large extent. My standpoint is that of a twentieth-century Western European, trained primarily in classical Greek and recent Anglo-Saxon philosophy. My religious practice has been within various forms of the Christian faith; but I have tried to present the views I consider here without making very broad preferential choices between them.

The views I consider are primarily those of philosophers; and this may be thought to be a rather restrictive approach. Philosophers, however orthodox, are not necessarily very important to most religious believers. Yet in the end reflection of a critical and synoptic sort – reflection which tries to elicit and respond to informed criticism and to build up a general, integrating pattern from widely disparate data – is important to rational religious belief. To look at what philosophers have said about their own religious faith is thus one way of trying to bring out the structure of religious belief, considered from an intellectual point of view. It is certainly an important fact, if, as I claim, a common structure can be discerned in apparently widely diverse religious traditions, even a common doctrine of the Real and of the nature of the religious response to it. Such claims will need to be made out in detail. But even the possibility of their truth opens up exciting ways of increasing religious understanding by a greater awareness of what religious traditions, at their most reflective, have in common.

Lack of such knowledge has led to disastrously naïve ideas of God, and to a misunderstanding of what is at issue, when one talks of worshipping God. For worshipping God is not telling some very powerful, invisible person how good he is, in the hope that he will pat you on the head and give you eternal life. It is the reverent awareness of the Being of God, as it truly is. But that is what is so often forgotten.

God is not a wise and powerful person, watching us balefully from some Olympian height. God is a unique, infinite and eternal reality, beyond all human power to describe adequately, yet expressed in and through the finite things of space and time. There can be no question of proving that such a reality exists in the sense that we might one day come across it, like some extremely remote object in space. What needs to be done is to develop a sense that the world of finite things is able to express an infinite reality beyond and yet also infusing it. We need to learn to see things as pointing beyond themselves, as sacramental of a supreme reality and value, as visible images of eternity, in what I have called the iconic vision.

What can help us to evoke such a sense is not science or philosophy, but poetry or music. The language of religion is like the language of poetry; and it is a major heresy of post-Enlightenment rationalism to try to turn poetry into pseudo-science, to turn the images of religion, whose function is to evoke eternity, into mundane descriptions of improbable facts. In a sense, atheism is right – but only in its rejection of a God who never was, and of a belief which never touched the heart of religious faith. Traditional theism seeks a contemplative awareness of the Unlimited, beyond name and form, the just perception of what most truly is, standing far beyond our analytical understanding. One key term Aquinas uses for God is *esse subsistens:* Being existing of itself alone, entire and underived. Or, in another evocative phrase, *pelagum substantiae infinitum:* the ocean of unlimited existence.[1]

This is certainly not an objective existent, understood as one finite object among others in space – time. But to deny that it is existence at all, that it is a form of reality before which human existence is disclosed as poised, trembling, between being and non-being, is to cut off religious understanding at its root.[2] Of course, this idea of God is difficult to grasp; it is the fruit of the practice of contemplative prayer and self-transcendence. But to forget or discard that tradition is to close ourselves off from some of the most profound discoveries of the human spirit. To learn to appreciate it is to transfigure our vision of existence. The contemporary religious problem is not to decide whether or not God exists. It is to learn again, patiently and sensitively, what the great theologians have *meant* by the concept of 'God'.

I shall begin with a consideration of some main Indian traditions. This is partly because, for a Western thinker, it can be illuminating to approach the familiar by way of the unfamiliar. But it is also because the Indian Scriptures themselves embody a much more explicitly reflective and speculative approach to the question of ultimate reality than is to be found in the Semitic religions of Judaism, Christianity and Islam. They are therefore of special interest if one is setting out to reflect on the nature of God.

It is still common in the West to treat Hinduism as a radically polytheistic system, opposed at its root to the ethical monotheism of the Semitic religions. The Hindus, it is said, have many gods, very few of them with any moral attributes. With their idols and huge number of strange rites, the Hindus have thus been often seen just as superstitious pagans, with whom Christians or Muslims have nothing in common. If one does press beyond the appearance of village worship, and attends to the more sophisticated doctrines of the Indian philosophers, it is pointed out that the Hindus are monists with a very impersonal view of the Absolute Reality. God and the world are one, and God (or Brahman) is not a personal being, but some sort of vague impersonal principle which does not really act in human history at all. So again the contrast with Semitic ideas seems total.

All these opinions, however, are based on a fairly deep misunderstanding of that very complex set of religious traditions which are to be found in India. Hinduism is not one monolithic organization. It is a word for almost any religious tradition in India which, broadly speaking, accepts the authority of the Veda and the customs and rites associated with the Brahmin priesthood. Hinduism is not one thing; and there are many different sorts of religious ideas which we tend to include in that very wide and perhaps misleading term. It would be an almost endless task to explore all of them; what I shall do is to discuss what is probably the best-known theological system in the West, one which is sometimes regarded as 'the' Hindu philosophy. That is the school of Vedanta, which became a fully elaborated system in the seventh and eighth centuries CE. As I have stressed, it is incorrect to regard it as the theology of Hinduism; properly speaking, there is no such thing. Vedanta is only one of the six main orthodox schools of philosophy in India; and, as we shall see, there are many important divisions even within Vedanta itself.[3] Nevertheless, Vedanta is the school of thought which has become most widely disseminated outside India, due to the work of many able expositors, from Radhakrishnan, President of India from 1962 to 1967, to Julian Huxley, in his book *The Perennial Philosophy*.[4] It is an extremely sophisticated and subtle system, well worth studying both for its own sake and for the light it can shed on thinking about God in other traditions.

Vedanta is a Sanskrit term which means 'the end of the Veda'. It takes the form of a systematic exegesis of the Upanishads, which are the so-called hidden or secret teachings added to the original collection of hymns, ritual ordinances and charms which comprise the Veda, the primary revealed text of orthodox religious traditions in India. Vedantic philosophers usually begin by commenting systematically on the Brahma Sutras, ascribed to the teacher Badarayana, and probably dating from the first century CE. This is a cryptic work, written in a very elliptical Sanskrit style, which sets forth an interpretation of the Upanishads. It is only one interpretation of these complex and diverse texts; but it does claim to be the definitive and correct one. However, it is so cryptic that it is possible to interpret it, in turn, in very different ways; so that there are different schools of Vedanta, all claiming to give the one correct doctrine and to refute the errors of the other schools.

The starting-point of Vedantic philosophy is thus rather complex and probably seems strange to Western philosophers of more recent years. It is important to see that it takes its stand on the supreme authority of Scripture, not on human reasoning. The Scripture in question is the Veda, which is taken to include not only the four main collections known as 'samhitas' but also and mainly the Upanishads, which were added later. There is a very strong doctrine of direct verbal inspiration. The Veda itself is eternal and changeless. It is not created. As one major Vedantic philosopher, Ramanuja, puts it: 'Veda is eternal; Prajapati [the creator] causes Rishis [seers] to see them, perfect in all their sounds and accents' (333). The words of the Veda are put directly into the mind of the original seers, in correct order and even sound and accent. Moreover, even the gods are bound by the Veda: 'When one Indra perishes, the creator . . . from the Vedic word 'Indra', creates another' (331). That is to say, the Vedic words are changelessly enshrined in the supreme being, Brahman, itself; and when the time comes to create a world, the Vedic words form the pattern on which that world must be formed; and they will be revealed to the sages directly and infallibly when the time is ripe.

The Veda is infallible, revealed truth; and, as Sankara says, 'The fact of everything having its self in Brahman cannot be grasped without the aid of the scriptural passage' (23). What is said of God in Vedanta is said solely on the basis of revelation, which is a verbal communication of propositions directly from the supernatural realm. A similar doctrine of revelation exists also in Orthodox Judaism and in Islam. So one common theme of these traditions is the existence of a revealed, propositional text which communicates truths unknowable by the human mind or reason alone. Orthodox Vedanta is just as dogmatic in making this claim as any orthodox Jew or Muslim is. In that sense, Vedanta is not really quite as tolerant or as capable of adapting itself to include other religious traditions as is sometimes thought. Of course, modern Vedantins could amend this claim to propositional revelation; but if they do, it must be clearly seen as a recent amendment, very different from what any of the classical philosophers would have said.

In fact, the widespread idea that Indian religion is somehow omnitolerant can barely survive even a little detailed knowledge of particular religious traditions. Ramanuja says of Sankara, 'his view rests on a fictitious foundation of hollow and vicious arguments' (39). And Sankara says of the Buddha, 'The Buddha either was a man given to make incoherent assertions, or else a hatred of all beings induced him to propound absurd doctrines by accepting which people would become thoroughly confused' (428). All good stuff, but hardly the essence of tolerance. In India, as everywhere else, religion breeds endless arguments, though at least there is no one official religious body to declare all others to be heretics.

Since the Vedic hymns do speak of many gods – Indra, Agni,

Rudra, Vishnu and a host of others – it may be thought that the Vedic revelation really is wholly different from that revelation alleged to be given in the Hebrew Bible or the Koran. But in fact these hymns are interpreted by Vedantins at least in the light of the Upanishads, for which all the gods are facets or appearances of one ultimate reality, Brahman, which is either identical with one Vedic god (Vishnu, in the case of Ramanuja); or beyond all the gods.

The Sanskrit word Brahman is untranslatable into English. Etymologies abound, explaining its connection with the word for 'breath' or 'prayer' or 'causing to grow'; it is most often explained as a word for the ultimate, abstract and impersonal Absolute.[5] It is certain that the central concern of Vedanta is the inquiry into Brahman. That is the explicit subject-matter of the Brahma Sutras. So, by a study of the later commentaries on this work, it is possible to see what Vedantins mean by Brahman. Do they really think it is an abstract impersonal Absolute, quite different from the living personal God of the Hebrew tradition?

Let me begin with a quote from Ramanuja, the twelfth-century philosopher who is the founder of the philosophical school known as 'Qualified Non-dualism' or 'Non-dualism of the differentiated [Brahman]' (Vishist-Advaita): 'We know from Scripture that there is a Supreme Person whose nature is absolute bliss and goodness; who is fundamentally antagonistic to all evil; who is the cause of the origination, sustenance and dissolution of the world; who differs in nature from all other beings; who is all-knowing; who by his mere thought and will accomplishes all his purposes; who is an ocean of kindness as it were for all who depend on him; who is all-merciful; who is immeasurably raised above all possibility of anyone being equal or superior to him; whose name is the Highest Brahman' (770).

For Ramanuja, Brahman has knowledge, thought and will; it is kind and merciful; it is supremely happy and perfectly good. That does not really sound like an abstract impersonal Absolute. It is very clearly a God with personal attributes. Indeed, Ramanuja stresses again and again that God, described as the highest Person (*purusa*), possesses 'numberless classes of auspicious qualities of unsurpassable excellence' (4). In holding this belief, Ramanuja does differ from Sankara, a philosopher probably of the eighth century

7

CE, whose system of pure non-dualism (*advaita*) is perhaps best known in the West. But Sankara's system, too, is extremely complex.[6] The most fundamental distinction Sankara makes with regard to Brahman is the distinction between *saguna Brahman*, God with attributes, and *nirguna Brahman*, God without attributes. Ramanuja rejected this distinction entirely, holding that Brahman is truly 'an ocean of infinite qualities' (324); and there is no higher or truer Brahman which transcends qualities absolutely.

It is this doctrine of *nirguna Brahman*, held by Sankara, that leads commentators to speak of an impersonal and abstract Brahman; but it may be doubted whether this really captures what Sankara was trying to say. For Sankara, too, writes that 'Brahman is all-knowing and endowed with all powers, whose essential nature is eternal purity, intelligence and freedom' (14). If Brahman in its essential nature possesses knowledge or intelligence, then it is hardly without any qualities at all. Furthermore, Sankara writes, 'Although intelligence only constitutes the true nature of the Self, [that is, Brahman in this context] . . . lordly power . . . with a view to the world of appearances, is not rejected' (410). Brahman really does stand to the world as its Lord, and may rightly be worshipped, at least in one aspect, as a personal Lord.

But does not Sankara say that this whole world is illusion, is not real, and thus that God as the Lord of this world is also an illusion, to be transcended by the reality of *nirguna Brahman?* He does indeed; but one needs to look with some care at the way he uses words like 'real', 'unreal', 'identity' and 'difference' before one can be sure of what he means by saying that. Thus he says that the Real and the Unreal are 'absolutely distinct' (4). The Self, which belongs to the realm of the Real, is pure intelligence, and is not itself an object. In a clear sense, then, Brahman, as the Real, is quite distinct from the world, which is the realm of the Unreal.

The world, of course, is not completely unreal. It exists in a sense, as Appearance. Appearances have their own proper form of existence; but the appearance does not show the true, essential nature of what underlies it, of that which is appearing. Why should the manner in which the world exists be called appearance? Because it arises from *avidya*, wrong conception or ignorance. By *avidya*, 'the self, which in its own nature is free from all contact, becomes a knowing agent' (7). The self, through its ignorance, does *become* something; it becomes an appearance. It is deluded about its true nature, and believes itself to be other than it truly is. Yet this appearance has being. Sankara says, 'The Lord differs from the soul . . . as the real juggler differs from the illusive juggler, or as the free unlimited space differs from the (limited) space of a jar' (70).

It is well known that Sankara maintains that the world is illusion; but what does he mean by that? He produces a number of analogies, which have slightly differing connotations. His favourite is that of the juggler or magician with his illusion. Here, we are made to think something happens by magic, when it is really a trick. We see something which leads us to come to a false conclusion. What we think we see does not exist at all; it is an interpretation placed by our mind upon certain sights and sounds, which is mistaken. The mistake here lies wholly in the perceiving mind, which is cunningly misled. If the world is an illusion in this sense, then our minds cause us to have false beliefs about it; it is not what we think. Similar analogies used by Sankara are: a post which is mistaken for a man; a rope seen as a snake; and a mirage of water in the desert. In all these cases, we see what is not there. But it is worth noting that we only fall under illusion because of causal factors in our environment which objectively mislead us. We have seen men, snakes and pools of water before; and have some reason for thinking we may be seeing one now. But what could mislead us into thinking the world is other than it really is? Where could we have seen similar phenomena before? And who is it that falls under the spell of illusion, if we ourselves are also, as finite selves, parts of the illusion?

Perhaps partly because of these and related difficulties, a number of other analogies are used by Sankara. He compares the world to a dream. Dreams do not have the character we think them to have, so again we are, or may be, mistaken about what we think we see. Yet dreams have a form of existence; they are not just nonentities. Again, he speaks of seeing a transparent crystal which is seen as coloured when the light shines through it. We may make a mistake in believing that it really possesses the properties of colour intrinsically. Yet of course it does really show colour. The mistake lies in ascribing the colour to the crystal, as its intrinsic property. There is no mistaking the fact that the colour exists, and is seen in the crystal. Sankara also speaks of the world as like the reflection of the sun on water. That reflection exists outside our minds; and our mistake, if we make one, lies in being wrong about some of the properties of that reflection – that it is the real sun, perhaps. These analogies are significantly unlike those of the first class, where the mistake was solely in the mind. This second set of analogies ascribes a form of reality to the 'illusions'; but suggests that we may be mistaken in some of the properties we ascribe to them – especially, in ascribing to them independent existence.

There is a third class of analogies, quite often used, but even more obscure. One, already referred to, distinguishes empty space from the apparent limitation of space by the form of a jar. In this case, space is really there in both cases; but if we believe that space itself has the form of the jar it happens to be in, we are mistaken, since space in itself is limitless. Here, the appearance and the reality are just the same; because of certain conditions of perception, limitations of our situation, we mistakenly ascribe limitedness to what is intrinsically unlimited. Once more, we need to ask where our notion of limitedness comes from; and of course it comes from the perceived jar, which is perfectly real in its own way; so there is a quite objective basis in reality for our mistake, and the important thing is to distinguish properly the jar from the concept of the space around and within it.

Then there is the analogy of waves, foam and bubbles. These are said to be distinct from each other, and yet all aspects of the same thing. In this case, it is one and the same thing, the sea, which takes on different forms. A similar analogy is with the substance of clay, which is modified in the form of pots, jars and so on; or of many threads which, woven together, form a cloth. In these cases, the one thing really does take on different forms; there is real modification of form, even though we might say that the underlying, essential substance, remains the same. In a similar way, Sankara compares Brahman to the light of a fire, hidden by wood and ashes. In all these analogies, the 'appearances' are perfectly real and objective, but they fail to show the inner character which underlies and gives rise to them. They are nevertheless real modifications of it, from the point of view of the observer.

These three rather different sets of analogies are paralleled by rather different ways of expressing the relation between Brahman and the world. In its most extreme form, 'the fiction of *avidya* originates entirely from speech only' (352). This implies that we simply misperceive what is there, or come to have false beliefs about it. If the world is a fiction, then it is a projection of mind only, with nothing objective corresponding to it. And even the mind does not contribute real, dreamlike, images. It simply has false beliefs; it describes things wrongly. The difficulty with this view is that of explaining how one could come to have these false beliefs. *Avidya* is defined by Sankara as the mutual superimposition of self and non-self. And superimposition (*adhyasa*) is 'the apparent presentation to consciousness of something previously observed in another thing' (4). But when and how did this 'previous observation' take place? What he seems to have in mind is that one ascribes the properties of the phenomenal self to the real, changeless, eternal self whose nature 'consists of intelligence' (157), in a simple, non-differentiated form; we think that the apparent self is the real self. The mistake is one of mistaken ascription of the properties belonging to one thing to another thing. But the implication of this definition is that the properties which one ascribes do exist, in some sense, though they do not properly belong to the subject one is ascribing them to. And if phenomenal properties do exist, they can hardly be said to originate entirely from speech or verbal activity alone. And indeed, we find Sankara saying that the phenomenal world 'cannot after all be denied altogether' (379). 'For the phenomenal world . . . we may admit the relation of sufferer and suffering just as it is observed' (381). He even rubs this point in with some force – 'Those things . . . of which we are conscious in our waking state . . . are never negated in any state . . . we certainly cannot allow would-be philosophers to deny the truth of what is directly evident to themselves' (425).

The phenomenal world, then, has some form of reality, which should not be denied. Common sense is not being overturned by Sankara. It is quite in order, at its own level. But what is that level? 'By the fiction of *avidya*, characterized by name and form, evolved as well as non-evolved, not to be defined as the existing or the non-existing, Brahman becomes the basis of this entire apparent world . . . while in its true and real nature . . . it remains unchanged' (352). The phenomenal world is still the product of ignorance; it is a fiction; it lies between being and non-being; it has a sort of half-reality. Our ignorance, it seems, is to live in a world of dreams, and to take the dream for reality; whereas the true reality is a changeless substratum of pure intelligence, limitless and free.

So he says again, 'In reality, the relation of ruler and ruled does not exist . . . on the other hand, all those distinctions are valid, as far as the phenomenal world is concerned' (330). On the one hand, 'Brahman is, owing to its manifold powers, able to transform itself into manifold effects' (347). In this respect, 'the world was evolved . . . under the rulership of an intelligent creator' (268); and the world originates from desire and command (170). The highest Lord, 'by means of *avidya*, manifests himself . . . as a magician appears in different shapes by means of his magical powers' (190). All this implies an active self-manifestation of Brahman, under the forms of space and time. But on the other hand, 'His omniscience, omnipotence and so on all depend on *avidya;* in reality none of these qualities belong to the Self' (329). And again, 'These modifications or effects are names only . . . in reality there exists no such thing as modification' (320). Brahman is unchanging and not in real contact with anything (187).

It should be clear that the words 'real' and 'apparent' are being used in a special, and even technical, sense. The three sets of analogies which I have set out suggest three rather different models. The first one suggests that we simply have false beliefs about what the world is like, though what the foundation in reality for such beliefs might be we are not told. The second model suggests that there is something objective, outside ourselves, which leads us to form false beliefs about what is real. Our mistake is one of interpretation, a failure to see what is truly real. The third model suggests that reality and illusion are in some sense one thing, appearing under different conditions – the sea appearing as bubbles, foam or waves; or pieces of thread appearing as a solid surface of cloth. The part the individual mind plays in this illusion is now very small; and the illusion is a character of the thing itself, as it appears in certain conditions. These are what Sankara calls 'limiting adjuncts'; and he says: 'name and form cannot abide in the soul . . . but abide in the limiting adjunct and are ascribed to the soul itself in a figurative sense only' (279). Brahman itself is not modified; all modifications belong to the limiting adjuncts, the conditions of appearance, themselves.

I do not think much point is served by trying to make these

analogies consistent, in a literal way. As analogies, they rather point to something which is itself quite unique, and which they all hint at rather inadequately or obscurely. What underlies them all is the thought that there is a level of reality deeper than that of the sensory world, which is the true substratum of all appearances, and which can be realized in the experience of enlightenment, itself beyond description. When it is said that the real Brahman is without form; that it is 'one mass of knowledge' (281); and that it is devoid of qualities, this is said purely on the authority of the Upanishads; it 'rests exclusively on the holy texts' (350). Yet Brahman, even in its unqualified form, is not a total blank. It is described as intelligence, and also as 'a self of bliss': 'the word bliss is rightly understood to denote Brahman' (76). Bliss, however, is not a property of Brahman; for there are no qualities or distinctions in Brahman. Rather, Brahman *is* bliss and the cause of all bliss.

I believe that the only way to render these texts consistent is to say that certain things are truly affirmed of Brahman; but those things characterize Brahman so inadequately that they must also be denied; it must then be said that Brahman is so far beyond our linguistic resources that it must be spoken of as without qualities. There is here an underlying doctrine of language, as a system of words and concepts which are essentially fitted to categorizing and describing finite things. Thus substantive nouns pick out classes of finite object, which can be assigned into discriminable classes. Verbs are essentially temporal, speaking of the activities or changes in finite objects. The particular ways in which words divide up the world are largely pragmatic and determined by our perceptual and bodily needs. Our language is best fitted to material objects in space, which our sense-organs can discriminate and pick out, which we can identify and re-identify. All this is quite in order, for Sankara, at the level of phenomena. One is reminded of Immanuel Kant's claim that, though he was a transcendental idealist, he was an empirical realist.[7] That is, he did not deny the reality of the material world at all. He denied only that it had in itself, and out of relation to any perceptual organ or observer, the properties which we perceive it to have. What we perceive is a function of an interaction between our minds and an objective reality. If we substracted the contribution our minds and perceptual structures make to the real world, we could no longer speak of what was left – our concepts just would not be applicable to it.

A strange confirmation of this view seems to exist in contemporary sub-atomic physics, in which probability-states, states of potentiality, are actualized only by the interaction of an observer with the system.[8] It is not being said that there is no physical reality there; but that our concepts are inadequate to describe it, except in so far as it relates to us, by means of some experimental or observational interference by us. We can see here a way in which our concepts could be said to give a false view of reality. They are suited to dealing with a world of physical objects, with which we interact by means of our senses; that is, a world of things as they appear to us, under the conditions of observation which our minds contain. The knowledge they give is quite adequate, at its own level, the level of physical existence, of moving as a physical object among other physical objects. But suppose we ask, 'What is the reality underlying these appearances?', then our concepts have nothing to gain a purchase on. We have a reason for saying that it is not as it appears to us; for we can in many cases isolate the contribution made by our minds – in ascribing colours, smells and so on to objects. And we can see how our concepts break down in fundamental physical theory.

That may leave us with just an underlying 'I know not what'; and Sankara never claims to have intuitive insight into that reality; he relies solely on the Upanishads to reveal what the nature of reality in itself is. But of course this is not a purely speculative doctrine. Its function is to delineate the goal of a particular way of life. The inquiry into the ultimate nature of the physical world, for a physicist, may be an interesting intellectual pursuit. But, Sankara says, 'The inquiry into Brahman . . . has for its fruit eternal bliss' (11). It has certain preconditions – the renunciation of any goals to be attained by action; the attainment of tranquillity, self-restraint, patience in suffering and concentration of mind; and the desire for release from the wheel of birth and death.

There is a very definite evaluation of the physical world here, and of what is to be expected of human life. So he says, 'All agents . . . are impelled to action by some imperfection' (435). And again, 'As long as man has not freed himself from activity he cannot obtain his highest end, since activity is essentially painful' (53). In such a tradition, the search for a highest being cannot lead to a supremely active being. It must lead to a being beyond action and change, with nothing to be accomplished, resting in itself alone, a being of pure intelligence and bliss, free from all imperfection. One can see how, in the practice of yoga, renouncing all goals of action, one may come to apprehend within the 'cave within the heart', that which is inactive yet blissful, a calm and unchanging consciousness which is both at the deepest level one's own self and also the root of all finite things. Why is activity denied of Brahman? Because activity implies imperfection and need. Where there is no need or dissatisfaction there is no point in action.

How, then, does the world of illusion spring into being? How can the manifestly perfect give rise to the imperfect? This remains a wholly unsolved problem, for Sankara. Again he offers a spread of views, which are rather different in their implications. At one end of the spectrum, Brahman remains unchanging, unmodified. The world of finite objects is born and decays by some inherent power of its own. There is a realm of being, or half-way between being and non-being, known as 'the Undeveloped'. It is the seminal potentiality of names and forms; it 'contains the fine parts of the material elements, abides in the Lord and forms his limiting adjunct . . . being itself no effect' (140). This is perhaps reminiscent of Leibniz' view that there is a realm of potentiality which, by its own inherent power, presses towards existence.[9] We might say, then, that Brahman has two distinct aspects: one perfect and unchanging; the other consisting of a realm of potentialities, which realizes itself in successive ages in exactly the same way. Sankara believes in the eternal recurrence of the universe. 'The phenomenal world is the same in all world-periods (*kalpas*) . . . and there manifest themselves, in each new creation, individuals bearing the same names and forms as the preceding creations' (215). The perpetually recurring existence of the finite universe, without beginning or end, is in some sense necessary. When it is said that it is 'unreal', what is implied is that it is unreal, as an independent series of existent beings. In fact it is totally dependent on the eternal Brahman, which is self-existent, being alone fully real. Brahman in itself does not change; but it appears under the forms of space and time, which are like veils, hiding its true nature. This appearing is not something that Brahman *does*; it is rather like the reflection of the sun on water, which the sun does not intend to bring about, but which happens in dependence upon the sun, because of the nature of water. But where does the water, i.e. the 'limiting adjunct', come from? Does it exist independently of Brahman? Or is it some sort of necessary emanation or overflow of the being of Brahman? Or is it created?

Strangely, Sankara is committed to a doctrine of divine creation, though he often speaks of the world as an unavoidable procession from the divine nature, without any motive (357). He says: 'Brahman is that from which the origin, subsistence and dissolution of this world proceed . . . an omniscient, omnipotent cause' (15). Further, 'the world originates from Brahman by thought' (48). 'He wished, may I be many' (Taitt. Upanishad 2, 6). Then, 'entering into the beings which it had emitted, Brahman stays inmost' (68). It is important to recognize that Sankara is not thinking of Brahman as being able to do absolutely anything, without any constraints at all. It is rather as if its thought 'releases' the already defined and existing world of possibilities into actuality. There is no alternative to what exists; for the Vedic words are eternal. They 'became manifest in the mind of Prajapati the creator . . . and he created things corresponding to those words' (204). So the eternal plan of the universe is eternally and necessarily in the mind of Brahman.

There is a further complication in the doctrine; for the Vedantins hold that, in general, 'the effect is in reality not different from the cause' (94). It is for this reason that, unlike Western philosophers, they assume that Brahman is the material cause of the world. That is, it is the stuff out of which the world is made. 'The cause virtually contains all the states belonging to its effects' (145); and so 'the creator is non-different from the created effects' (265). 'The Self modifies itself into the self of the effect' (287). And yet, at the same time, 'the changeless Brahman cannot be the substratum of varying attributes' (327). The only way of making these statements consistent is to say that there are two Brahmans: the higher and the lower. The higher is changeless and unmodified; the lower modifies itself so as to give rise to the transmigratory world. Sankara says: 'The Self, although eternally unchanging and uniform . . . appears in forms of various dignity and power' (63). In fact, there is a threefoldness in Brahman. *Nirguna Brahman* is the utterly simple being, intelligence and bliss, eternally unchanging. *Saguna Brahman* is 'the eternally perfect highest Lord', the object of devout meditation, who may 'assume a bodily shape formed of illusion . . . to gratify his worshippers' (80). Thus he may appear as Indra or Vishnu. And there is Brahman, who enters into all things as the Self of all – 'Brahman, without undergoing any modification, passes, by entering into its effects, into the condition of the individual soul' (30).

But how are these three aspects related one to the others? It is clear that Sankara holds that *nirguna Brahman* is the only truly real. *Saguna Brahman* belongs to the realm of illusion, of play and half-reality. What is the point of making this distinction between reality and illusion? I suggest it is because, if anyone thinks their phenomenal selves are ultimately real, they are mistaken. To overcome illusion, one must realize one's inner identity with Brahman – 'The man who has once comprehended Brahman to be the self, does not belong to this transmigratory world as he did before' (43). For him, there exists no longer anything to be desired or avoided. 'From the mere comprehension of Brahman's self . . . there results cessation of all pain and thereby the attainment of man's highest aim' (23). The distinction Sankara makes between the real and the apparent is meant to evoke in people a vision that they can transcend the phenomenal world, overcome desire and realize unity with the pure blissful intelligence, free from all interests, which is the source and goal of all.

For Sankara, therefore, devotion to a personal and glorious ruler of all is quite proper; but better than that is knowledge of the God without form, which comes only when all desires, even the desire for heaven in the presence of God, have ended. Even then, however, Sankara accepts that devotion is enough for most in this life. For those who reach the qualified Brahman world, by their devotion, do not return to the world of *samsara*, of birth and death. 'In the end they have recourse to eternally perfect nirvana' (419). By this release, all causal potentiality is 'destroyed by perfect knowledge' (243), and no subsequent rebirth will follow. This doctrine makes it difficult to hold that every new world-period will be exactly the same as the last; for, if some souls obtain release in one world-period, their causal residue is destroyed entirely, and in the next world-period they will never exist at all. That in turn means that all the causal chains with which they are connected cannot occur.

So in fact there will be quite a few changes in each world-period, if any souls really obtain release at all. On some later versions of Vedanta, the world-periods continue until at last every soul has been released from rebirth; but that is not part of Sankara's view.

There are some major problems with Sankara's view, which were pointed out quite sharply by Ramanuja. But it would not be an adequate presentation of Advaita Vedanta to say that it is a form of pantheism which makes God and the world identical; or that it views Brahman as abstract and impersonal. For Sankara, it would be false to say that there is no personal Lord and ruler of the universe, an intelligent creator of the world, omnipotent and omniscient. There is such a Lord, in just the same sense that there is a world of physical objects and finite souls at all. In another sense, of course, the world is an illusion; and in that sense, the personal Lord is an illusion too. But as long as we take the phenomenal world to be real, we must take God to be real, in just the same sense. The realization of knowledge of unqualified Brahman is far beyond most of us, and could not even be known about, 'even by divine beings of extraordinary power and wisdom' (307), except on the ground of scriptural revelation. What the doctrine of *nirguna Brahman* says to us is that our highest thoughts are quite inadequate to the reality of God. We can say, on the basis of revelation, that God in itself is without properties, is changeless and simple, is self-sufficient and 'one mass of intelligence'; that it is free from all difference, and is not in real contact with anything; that it is pure intelligence and bliss, the witness of all things, untouched by all. We can say that in some sense we are one with Brahman, and may come to realize this unity, by renouncing desire and action.

This is not pantheism, for Brahman alone is real, and is quite distinct from the world of illusion. And it is not really saying that the impersonal is higher than the personal, as is often said about Vedanta. Naturally, Brahman is not a person, in the sense of being a finite rational agent. Yet Brahman is all-knowing and consists of perfect bliss. So it must be conceived by analogy with consciousness and feeling, however refined and heightened. And Brahman emanates or originates the world by thought, and is thus the cause, and indeed, the causal agent, of all things. In other words, it is more correct to think of it as a conscious agent than to think of it as a non-aware and non-rational power or force, as some other

Indian traditions have done. The fact that 'Brahman' is a neuter word, in Sanskrit, is certainly helpful in not ascribing any sex to the ultimate cause and reality; but it does not imply that consciousness is to be denied. On the contrary, that is an agreed description of Brahman by all Vedantins; though they disagree about exactly what 'consciousness' is.

It must be said, in the end, that *nirguna Brahman* is spoken of in two contrasting ways by Sankara. On the one hand, there is the purely negative way, by which qualities are denied of it – it is even said to be 'non-being', as contrasted with the sort of being finite things have. But, on the other hand, some positive things are said, on the basis of Scripture; and the most important of these are that it is pure being, consciousness and bliss. It is also primarily defined as the cause of the world in the Brahma Sutras. Evidently some things can be truly said of Brahman, though we cannot know in what sense they are true of it – since we have no idea what knowledge or bliss might be like, in a being which is utterly changeless and simple. In what sense can a finite soul be identical with Brahman? Only in the sense that it casts off its individuality and personal characteristics, and itself becomes that simple eternal Self. But then again, nothing can 'become' Brahman, since everything already is Brahman, at its centre. It is more a matter of casting away the illusion of individuality, and leaving only the pure Self, which is one and the same in all things.

The way of life which these notions delineate is one of progressively casting off desires and attachment to the world and to one's own character, so as to leave nothing but the changeless Self, which has always been there, as it were diguised by the illusion of individuality. How did that illusion arise? Because of the karmic potentiality in the limiting adjuncts of Brahman, necessarily emanated in each world-period. We are born in a world of illusion; and our final destiny and goal is to escape altogether from the realm of rebirth, and realize unity with the changeless and eternal being of bliss, which is true reality.

The reason this Brahman is called the Real is because it is that on which all things depend; and, even more importantly, it is that to which we should be seeking to return. The desiring agent and enjoyer which we commonly call the self has to be transcended and cast aside, by ascetic discipline and meditation. Then, we achieve a state akin to that of deep sleep, when consciousness of particular objects vanishes, when we no longer have desire for or aversion from anything; and we achieve release from the cares of the world – 'the practical world vanishes in the sphere of true knowledge' (135). The finite world is unreal because it is unsatisfactory and cannot give us true happiness. The finite self must be negated, in order that the true Self may be manifest, which is 'the state of absolute isolation and rest, enjoying full ease'(55).

Sankara's doctrines have their sense only in this context of the ascetic life, which is seen as a release from the unreal, from darkness to light, and – as the *Brihadaranyaka* Upanishad explains – these are equivalent to a release from the mortal and transitory to the immortal.[10] All this presupposes that rebirth is a thing which is in the end undesirable; and that individuality possesses no unique value, worth preserving. For Sankara, personal immortality is not really to be desired; for the whole of my personal self, with its character, desires and interests, is to be set aside. Then the self that remains, though it is said to be my inmost Self, is not particular to me; it is 'the witness, different from the agent that is the object of self-consciousness'(37). My character is to be cast aside as illusion; and I am to be merged into that one undifferentiated Self which is beyond time and change.

This form of spirituality is clearly quite different from one which takes each individual to have an enduring and unique worth, precisely because of its own distinctive personal characteristics; and which regards the world of finite things as good and of worth on its own account. For Sankara, the world itself is beyond redemption; and the best thing is to transcend it utterly, to cut off the causal nexus which keeps one alive and find a higher, truer reality beyond the personal self. This is no doubt why Brahman is often called impersonal; and yet it must be seen that one cannot cut off *samsara* just by committing suicide, nor by ceasing to exist. Moreover, it is eternal bliss which is sought and omniscience, not mere non-being. So it is essential to Sankara's doctrine that Brahman really is my true self; it is the real 'I', though it is different from my finite ego – 'the connexion of self and mind depends on wrong knowledge'(47).

The whole question of the relation between my finite self and Brahman is peculiarly complex; and I have to confess that in the end I find it incoherent, as Sankara propounds it. I do not doubt there is an important truth somewhere in that area; but Sankara seems hampered by his own interpretation of the Veda, which allows him little leeway. His problems, however, are very largely those of theologians in the Western traditions, too; they are not peculiar to him or to Vedanta. We shall see them occurring again in the Semitic traditions in a very similar form.

The first main set of problems is concerned with the doctrine of Brahman without form. At times he writes as though all properties must be denied of Brahman – 'his omniscience, omnipotence and so on all depend on ignorance; in reality none of these qualities belong to the self'(329). Yet he also says that 'Brahman is bliss'(76) and also 'one mass of knowledge'(281); and is 'that from which the origin, subsistence and dissolution of this world proceed'(15). We might say that these are not to be regarded as properties possessed by Brahman, but as denoting its simple and non-complex nature, which is 'not composed of parts'(29). But huge problems remain. If Brahman is omniscient, does that mean that it depends, in respect of what it knows, upon the existence of the illusory world? If it is without illusion, presumably not. But if it does, then it is not without contact with anything. Is its bliss quite unaffected by all the sorrows of the world? And, if so, is that really compatible with its being perfect? So the first problem is: can Brahman be characterized in any way at all? If not, then it cannot be spoken of; we could not even have any inkling of what the word 'Brahman' means. But if so, then it cannot be wholly devoid of form, since it must have some nature that we can describe in some way, however inadequately.

Sankara does undoubtedly say that there is a higher and a lower Brahman; and these must be forms of one and the same thing. So perhaps Brahman can be spoken of in its qualified form, which truly belongs to it; though not in its unqualified, essential form, which is beyond description. That seems to make sense; but can Brahman truly have a qualified form? If it is devoid of change and contact, how can it manifest itself, or appear, even less enter into the world? The paradox is at its strongest in such propositions as this: 'Brahman, without undergoing any modification, passes, by entering into its effects, into the condition of the individual soul'(30). We might say, Brahman is essentially unchanged and remains always what it is; yet there is a manifestation of its character in finite forms, which does not change it at all. But this is not really satisfactory: 'The holy texts declare that not the entire Brahman passes over into its effects, and . . . Brahman is without parts'(351). If Brahman is without parts, then there cannot be part of it which is unchanged and another part which manifests itself. Perhaps, then, like Aristotle's Prime Mover, it does not actually do anything, but is, as it were, reflected or imitated in some other medium.[11] There is a hint of this view, when Sankara writes: 'Belonging to the self, as it were, of the omniscient Lord, there are . . . the figments of ignorance, not to be defined either as being Brahman nor as different from it'(329). But the trouble even with this carefully indeterminate status is that Brahman has to be the material cause of all things, not only the operative cause (284); and 'the effect is in reality not different from the cause'(94). There is no reality independent of Brahman; so there is really no alternative than to say that Brahman is both wholly free of all contact and change; and also manifests itself in various forms, known by the ignorant and termed limiting adjuncts of its essential being. But this is to erect a vast dualism at the heart of a doctrine which is committed above all to non-dualism at any price.

One way to save the situation is to distinguish between a dualism of substance and a dualism of attributes. One could then say that there is no substantial dualism; Brahman is the one and only self-existent being. But there is a dualism of attributes. For, as well as the utterly simple and eternal intelligence and bliss, there is the dynamic Lord, the ruler and intelligent creator of the universe; and these two are one – the former perceived in its true essence, the latter perceived only by a form of ignorance. What is ignorantly known is indeed known, but not in its essential character. It might be better to speak of 'defective or incomplete knowledge', which does lead us to know something, but not the real nature of things. But how can such different attributes belong to one being? Is this more than a verbal unity? And would we not be better advised to distinguish Brahman altogether from the world, and say that it is that to which we must escape from the world? However, this view comes near to some forms of Buddhism, which Sankara resolutely opposed; he insists that Brahman is that from which all worlds originate; it is the creator, even if only from the point of view of relative truth.

The attempt to define Brahman purely by negatives is bound to fail. For if every phrase is negated, one is left with sheer self-contradiction; that is, with saying absolutely nothing. Thus one might say, 'Brahman is not describable'; but one would also have to say, 'Brahman is not indescribable'. That would convey no information. Thus Brahman cannot be defined merely by negation. The point of negative assertion is then to say that Brahman is not in itself as it is conceived by us. Nevertheless, some of our concepts are less inadequate than others. It is more adequate to say that Brahman is intelligence than to say that it is stupidity or unawareness. It possesses knowledge, though we cannot say what its knowledge is like – it may be an unimaginable form of non-object-bound consciousness. But how do we know which concepts are adequate? Sankara appeals simply to propositional revelation. But of course we still have the question, how do we know the Scripture is inerrant? It is clear that appeal is often made to the great seers who have known Brahman. By ascetic practice they have overcome desire and attachment, and found within themselves a source of joy and enhanced awareness which seems more real than the ephemeral things of daily life. In the light of this experience, all finite objects seem unreal or apparent only; and their longing is to be immersed in the immortal, the deathless, the truly real.

Thereby arises the idea of the world as the sport of Brahman, a sort of cosmic dream. When we awake, we will find that we are one with, lost in, Brahman the changeless. So the doctrine is that there is a changeless Brahman, in which we can participate, underlying all the changes of the finite world. It alone, in its changeless form, can give peace to the soul, ending the chain of illusion. The difficulty with this doctrine is that *my* release does not end the chain of illusion; for other selves carry on in the round of *samsara*. Nor can it end the chain for *me;* since I do not 'really' exist, so there is nothing to be released, nor anything which can be said to *have achieved* release.

What determines Sankara's view is a very negative assessment of the finite world. It exists without motive; it is simply illusion. There is also a very negative view of individual existence, which brings only a manifold chain of ills and is not to be desired. Given these beliefs, release from individuality and from the finite is the goal of life. The paradox is that release cannot be achieved in fact; for the world eternally recurs; and since my self was always an illusion, there is nothing to be released, nor anything which can release it, nor anything which can enjoy the sense of 'having been released'.

Advaita Vedanta is thus caught in a number of seemingly irresolvable difficulties. Brahman without qualities seems to be an incoherent concept; some qualities must be ascribed to anything that can be spoken of at all, even if one goes on to say that these are not as we understand them, and that they are not really qualities belonging accidentally to God. There is no coherent explanation of how illusion can arise in a changeless and all-wise Brahman, or of how the higher and lower Brahman can form one being – we can say the words, but no explanation is forthcoming of how such duality can exist in what is supposed to be a wholly unitary being. And there is no explanation of what it is that suffers delusion or obtains release, of how God and the soul can be absolutely distinct and yet truly one.

Nevertheless, despite these problems, it would be misleading to say that for Sankara Brahman is a completely impersonal principle, or that he identifies the individual soul with this principle directly. Though he speaks of a Brahman devoid of form, he always characterizes it as omniscient, blissful and cause of all through will. This, it seems to me, is a personal reality in the end. It is true, however, that this Brahman is free from all real contact, is changeless and free from all difference. It is primarily characterized as 'the witness', not concerned with the finite; emanating the world of necessity, without motive, and not truly related to it. Union with this god is possible, however, and indeed is the proper goal of the meditative life; and such union gives eternal bliss. A rather passive god, it may seem, then; but one which can be known, knowledge of which gives bliss and which is alone truly real, or self-existent.

Moreover, however complex the doctrine, Sankara undoubtedly holds that Brahman emanates the world from itself by thought and enters into it, as the Self of all – it is omnipresent. *Saguna Brahman* really is Brahman, manifesting itself as object of devotion, as intelligent creator, as 'the golden person in the sun'.[12] It cannot be said that the individual soul, just as it is, is identical *salve veritate* with this Brahman. The notions of unity and difference are pressed to their limits in this area. Sankara is quite clear that the individual soul is as distinct from Brahman, as the unreal is from the real. Yet there is a unity, for the soul could not exist even for a second

24

without Brahman, which alone is truly real, in that ultimate sense where 'real' means something like 'real in an unqualified, changless, self-existent manner'. So Sankara can say, 'The Lord differs from the soul . . . as the free unlimited space differs from the (limited) space of a jar'(70); but he can also speak of 'the false notion that the Lord and the transmigrating soul are different'(51). Even more strongly, 'There is in reality no such thing as an individual soul absolutely different from Brahman'(104). And yet 'the conception that the body and other things . . . are our self, constitutes ignorance . . . from it arise fear and confusion . . . an endless series of the most manifold evils'(157). The difficulty here is that the self as agent and enjoyer, as conjoined to the body and enfleshed in the world, is something which results from ignorance of our true nature; it is illusion. Yet at its own level it has reality; even illusions have a sort of being. This individual soul, then, is a half-reality, and to that extent distinct from the full reality of Brahman. The soul, being an appearance of Brahman, is both identical with that of which it is an appearance, and yet distinct, in being *only* an appearance. If this is to be called non-dualism, it is a very subtle from of non-dualism. It is not saying that the phenomenal world, just as it is perceived, is really part of God, much less the whole of God. The world as it is perceived is so far from being part of the Real that it does not even possess reality in the true sense. Thus it is wholly other than the real. The self that is identical with Brahman is the self purified from illusion, merged in the pure consciousness which is alone real. Is this pure consciousness any longer 'me'?

This is perhaps the greatest difficulty with Sankara's doctrine of *moksa* (release). If I desire release from the cycle of rebirth, from the karmic consequences of my acts, then what is it of this 'I' which can remain, to be released? Suppose the chain of karma is terminated, so that there is nothing further to be undergone or enjoyed. Does anything remain? In what sense can *I* be released, if nothing remains of that agent and enjoyer which I have until now called myself? There may remain a pure infinite consciousness; indeed, that was always existent; it is unchanged. But then, how can one suppose that I have realized anything with regard to it? One can only say that, on the one hand, this chain of karma has been brought to an end; and, on the other hand, that the changeless Brahman remains, as it always has done, unmodified in any way

either by 'my' release or my transmigratory progress. There seems
no purchase for the concept of self here, to enable me to say that I
become one with Brahman.

Brahman is always blissful and omniscient. I am presently
unaware of this; but that makes no difference to Brahman. However,
by austerities and meditation I overcome desire and cease to be, as
agent-enjoyer. This still makes no difference to Brahman. So in
what sense have I attained release? One needs to add, and it is an
essential part of the doctrine, that, as I overcome the desiring self,
so there arises, within me, bliss and tranquillity. But is this 'my'
bliss? Is it a bliss felt essentially and distinctly by me, which
previously I did not feel? I think we are compelled to say that it is;
though one wants to say that this bliss is not self-generated. It
seems to arise from a source other than the desiring self, to which
one becomes gradually transparent, until that bliss fills one's own
being. As desire fades, so bliss pervades.

Sankara uses the model of unity here to convey the thought that
this bliss is in itself from a self-existing and unchanging source
beyond the individual self; and yet it is realized in the self, as that
self overcomes attachment to worldly consequences. We might say
that I realize my true self only when I am wholly permeated by
that greater self, when it becomes the heart of myself; and yet 'I'
experience it, and so in a way remain distinct. In putting it this
way, I am certainly qualifying Sankara's terminology in a fairly
radical way. That is because I find the notion of the release of the
soul incoherent, as he puts it; since there is no real self to be under
illusion, and no self which endures the passage from illusion to
release and immortality. My suggestion is that his doctrine arises
partly from a particular interpretation of the Upanishads, which is
not compelling; and partly from a determination to see Brahman
alone, in its purity, as real, and all else as *maya*. In any case,
Sankara's doctrine is not monist, in the commonly understood sense,
that there is only one thing, and we are all parts of it. Though he
says there is only one thing, we are not *parts* of it; we are appearances; and as such, quite as distinct as any creature is from its
creator. The sense of 'oneness' he is concerned with is, I have
suggested, that for which the self-existent bliss so fully permeates
the finite centre of consciousness that the finite self finds itself
interpenetrated by the Real. This concept of 'unity' is a very

stretched one, and I would have to say, on my proposed interpretation, that it misleads Sankara into dividing the Self into 'phenomenal' and 'real' aspects in an incoherent way.

Sankara says, 'He who knows Brahman . . . in whom all desires
and works have become extinct . . . has become the omnipresent
self'(375). Yet, 'The soul, as long as involved in *samsara*, has for
its essence the qualities of its limiting adjuncts'(45). As long as
individuality remains, plurality and distinction remain; at that level,
the world is as it seems to be. Thus the operative force of Advaita
Vedanta is the recommendation to a way of renunciation of desires
and works; the renunciation of the world and of individuality. Only
when this is accomplished, does there arise the notion of that which
cannot be spoken of, since it is simple, changeless and without
properties. Its character can only be known on the basis of Vedic
revelation, not by reflection or argument, much less by experience.

Thus we can say that even for Advaita, the least theistic form of
Vedanta, there is a recognition that the ultimate basis of all things
lies in a reality which, though indescribable, may yet be characterized as bliss and knowledge; that is, in a personal way. Moreover,
we may relate to this reality under the form of a personal Lord;
and that is no more an illusion or fiction than the whole of the
material world itself is. God is as real as the world; and, on the
level of speech, that is as real as you can get. It is only by meditation
and insight that you may move to a stage beyond personal devotion,
when it seems right to speak of a cosmic unity of bliss, beyond
individuality. But that experience, it must be stressed, is so far
beyond description that only revelation can tell us what its nature
is. We might think it better to say, then, that devotion to a personal
Lord, and the pursuit of selflessness, patience and restraint, may
lead us to the realization of a wordless state, which we may speak
of only as a form of awareness and of supreme bliss, which in some
way unites us to a reality beyond the finite and temporal.

I have considered Sankara because he is perhaps the best-known
Vedantin philosopher. I have tried to show that his view is very
subtle, and can only be taken as a form of impersonal monism, as
it is often misleadingly described, if one neglects his own stress on
the relative reality of the finite world of *maya*. Nevertheless, a set of
evaluations is built into his interpretation of the Veda, the most
important of which are the negative evaluation of the values of the

finite world, of individuality, of any thought of a point or goal in history, and the building up of any social form of life, as a worthwhile human endeavour. It is true in the end that his system is 'world-denying', in that it looks to release from this world as the highest good; he can look for no hope in this world, with its doom of eternal return and its train of manifold ills. So God is a self without action; and the finite world is an incoherent but necessary appearance, with no positive point, created 'without motive'. In the end, God cannot explain the world, for Sankara, since it has no explanation; it must just be accepted. The major difficulty in Sankara's thought is that of relating *nirguna Brahman* and *saguna Brahman*. It remains unclear how a perfect and self-sufficient reality could give rise to a world of illusion and desire; and it remains unclear what is meant by the 'limiting adjuncts' which seem in some way to be part of Brahman, even though Brahman is simple and without parts.

Nevertheless, despite these difficulties and differences from the Semitic religious traditions, a number of clear and important similarities emerge. First there is the founding of religious doctrines on revealed truth, rather than on sheer speculation and argument. It is believed that ultimate reality discloses its own nature to human beings, who are incapable of working it out properly for themselves in its hidden character. Second, there is the belief that there is a highest Lord and creator of all things through will; a doctrine which Sankara is at pains to assert as fully acceptable at the level of ordinary human thought and action. Third, there is a dual-aspect doctrine of the unconditioned and its appearance in the names and forms of the finite realm. The same Brahman is unqualified and qualified in different aspects; and though that relationship remains unclear, it is definitively asserted to exist. Fourth, and associated with this, is the view of the finite self as both one with and distinct from the Self of all. Brahman, as the cosmic self, is hidden and distinct from the self; the appropriate relation to it is one of submission or devotion. Yet Brahman, as manifest in its qualified aspect, is one with the self; and the self finds its true fulfilment and identity in becoming the conscious vehicle of that Self; finding it within the secret cave of the heart.[13] Fifth, human life is seen as limited by ignorance; and its true character is to be found only by turning from desire to find eternal bliss by unity with an inner reality, concealed from ordinary view.

These are themes which will be found in each major religious tradition as we now go on to consider them in turn. They suggest a similarity of structure and of basic vision and response which underlies all the differences of particular doctrine. They suggest a picture of the religious life as one which turns from the concerns of the world to find eternal bliss in a source beyond the finite and temporal, which yet manifests in personal form, possessing supreme bliss and knowledge. This is a structure I shall seek progressively to articulate as I examine succeeding traditions.

2

Ramanuja and the Non-Dualism of the Differentiated

I have noted that it is a major theoretical problem for Advaita Vedanta, as represented by Sankara, to say how one can assert the existence of a Brahman which is wholly devoid of any properties whatsoever. It is equally difficult to say how finite selves come into being or how they can achieve liberation if they are illusory. And it is hard to see how and why the finite world could ever have come into existence at all; for how could the perfect originate the endless train of ills which is the samsaric world? In considering these problems within the Vedantic tradition, the work of Ramanuja, the twelfth-century teacher of the Sri Vaishnava sect, is of special interest; for he does take a much more positive view of individuality and the finite world. It is not only that he likes them more; he does seek to provide some sort of rationale for their existence, and not just leave them as an inexplicable appearance, lying between reality and unreality; created and permeated by a God who yet is not changed or modified by anything. Ramanuja's concept of Brahman is immediately more theistic. He says: 'Brahman denotes the highest Person [*purusa*] . . . free from all imperfections and possessing numberless classes of auspicious qualities of unsurpassable excellence'(4). There is no Brahman devoid of form. Brahman has an infinite number of properties; plurality is not unreal. He points out that if the distinction of Brahman and *avidya* is real, then there really is distinction in reality; so non-dualism, in its strictest form, is false. But if the distinction is unreal, then Brahman and *avidya* must be one and the same thing; and so *avidya* must be Brahman; and so must be real. The argument is compelling, logically; one cannot both believe that the world is appearance only, and that there is only one non-dualistic reality. Thus his view is termed qualified non-dualism, or non-dualism of the differentiated [Brahman]. There are many real distinctions; but they are all distinctions within one basic reality. In this way, Ramanuja is ironically more of a monist than Sankara, who retains the basic dualism of reality and appearance. His most basic and famous doctrine is that the world is the body of God. 'The entire world is a body the Self of which is constituted by knowledge abiding apart from its world-body'(95). Just as each human body is controlled by a self, so the universe as a whole is the body of the world Self, which yet has a substantially distinct existence.

To speak of the world as the body of God is a metaphor, and it must not be thought that Ramanuja means that the universe has feet, hands, brain, sense-organs and so forth. What, though, does he mean? He says: 'To stand in the relation of a body to something else, means to abide in that other thing, to be dependent on it and to subserve it in a subordinate capacity'(262). He amplifies this later: 'Any substance which a sentient soul is capable of completely controlling . . . and which stands to the soul in an entirely subordinate relation, is the body of that soul'(424). A body, for Ramanuja, is any substance which is under the complete control of a soul, and which depends upon it entirely. This is a very unusual sense of 'body'; since human bodies are certainly not, or do not appear to be, under the complete control of their souls; nor do the bodies depend upon the souls. It often appears quite the reverse. But what Ramanuja has in mind is that the body is the place where my will can operate directly upon material things. I can raise my arm, while I cannot move a chair in the next room without using my body in some way. Now God can directly cause anything in the universe; so in that way it may be said to be his body.[1] However, there are major difficulties with the view. A body is generally taken to be an inert physical substance. But Brahman 'has the individual souls for its body'(132). That is a much more difficult proposition. For are individual souls not distinct existences, with at least a measure of freedom, and suffering from many imperfections? How, then, can they be under the complete control of Brahman?

The reason why theists make a distinction between souls and God is that souls are finite centres of consciousness, whereas God is infinite; souls fall into error and sin, whereas God is omniscient and perfect; souls suffer the consequences of their deeds, and so what happens to them is largely due to their own karma, whereas God is beyond karma and cannot suffer in that way. These are major problems for Ramanuja; but he does not hesitate to tackle them, and remain within the Vedantic scheme, as outlined by Badarayana.

First of all, he insists, as against Sankara, that 'consciousness is the attribute of a permanent conscious self'(56). It does not make sense to speak of a pure consciousness, without a subject or object. However, he stays within the Vedantic concept of the self as essentially a knower – 'To be a knowing subject is the essential character of the self'(551). Action and enjoyment are still seen, in the end, to have the character of imperfection; and so release from *samsara* is still the definitive aim of religious practice. 'Not a shadow of imperfection, such as ignorance, attaches to Brahman, the absolutely blessed'(229). Thus Brahman is not involved in the pleasures and pains of transmigratory existence; it remains essentially apart. In a sense, then, Ramanuja can say, 'Brahman is in itself altogether devoid of form . . . does not share pains and pleasures' (610). But he is not speaking of a Brahman without qualities. He is speaking of Brahman, apart from its connection with the world. As such, it has unlimited knowledge, non-contracted intelligence and absolutely non-conditioned existence. It is the only Real, if real means without change or tendency for some of its qualities to become non-existent, through the passage of time. Ramanuja speaks of a higher and lower Brahmam (313); but the higher Brahman is the highest Self, not subject to pleasure and pain; and the lower Brahman is Brahman as causal and effected.

Brahman is seen as the cause of the world through will – 'the highest Self evolved names and forms by entering into matter by means of the living souls of which he is the Self'(141). 'Though entering into the effected condition, it remains unchanged; its essential nature does not become different'(142). So, on the one hand, Brahman can be spoken of as simple, changeless, impassible and perfect. But this same Brahman has also another aspect, in which it expresses itself in the finite world. 'The combination of matter, souls and the Lord is the material cause of the world . . . matter and souls have being only as modes of the highest Self'(142). 'The material world has its being in Brahman. Matter (*prakriti*) during a *pralaya* (between world-periods) unites with Brahman and abides in its subtle state, without distinction of name and form – the Unevolved. At the time of creation, it divides itself'(368). As with Sankara, we are not to think of God as being able to choose, in a rather arbitrary manner, which possible world he might bring into existence. Rather, there is an eternal and unevolved aspect of his own nature, which contains the potencies of all things; and which divides itself when the time is ripe. '*Prakriti*, the material cause . . . is Brahman only . . . the effect is the cause itself which has passed into a different state'(398).

Dr Julius Lipner, in his book *The Face of Truth*, argues that the Lord's creative action is intrinsically unnecessitated, according to Ramanuja. That is, the production of the world depends on the will (*samkalpa*) of the Lord. It is not constrained by nature to create the world. It is quite true that Ramanuja declares, in accordance with Scripture, that Brahman originates the world through will: 'May I be many, may I bring forth' (Taitt. Up., 2, 6). But does that entail that the Lord is free not to create? It does not; for if the Lord is necessarily what it is, and if its will is part of its nature, then it may originate the world through will, desiring that it should be manifest, even though it is not free to desire otherwise. It could, of course, be said that it is free not to create, in the sense that nothing external to it compels it to create. Creation arises out of its own nature. The point of referring to will is that the world does not proceed from Brahman unconsciously, or by mischance. Brahman desires it to be what it is, and consciously brings it to be out of Brahman's own potential nature. But that in no way implies that it might have chosen not to desire the world or bring it about.

Dr Lipner also suggests that the Lord is in no way subject to karma. Again, that is indisputable, for Ramanuja. He is in no way bound by past meritorious or sinful acts of himself. He is beyond karma, in the sense that the released souls may be embodied and manifest themselves in finite forms while being beyond karma – beyond the further influence of the fruits of meritorious action. Yet, as Dr Lipner points out, 'the Lord may be said, in Ramanuja's reckoning, to be extrinsically constrained by karma in so far as he chooses freely to create each new world after first having considered the unmatured karma of the previous worlds'(90). But the question is whether the Lord is free to consider the potencies of karma present in his undeveloped state and then decide not to create them.

The reason I think he is not, according to Ramanuja's view, is that each new world-period is said to be the same as the previous one; and this process is without beginning or end. It seems unrealistic to suppose that the Lord makes a new decision every time he creates a universe, but always decides the same way, even though he is, on each occasion, free to do so or not. It seems to me a more satisfactory account, in the absence of a clear statement from Ramanuja to the contrary, to say that the creation of worlds is necessitated by the nature of Brahman itself, in its unmanifest state. It is, however, important to remember Dr Lipner's main point, which is that the Lord, for Ramanuja, has a total sovereignty of will over the world, which is wholly dependent upon that will (*samkalpa*) for its existence. So the world cannot be seen as just an illusion, or as a rather regrettable mistake, as Plotinus, for example, seems often to interpret it.[2]

The Vedantins' doctrine of causality is that the effect must be contained virtually in its cause (the doctrine of *satkaryavada*); and indeed, cause and effect are in a sense one. Thus, 'Prakriti, as eternal and material cause . . . denotes Brahman in its causal phase, when names and forms are not distinguished . . . when they are evolved, distinct, Brahman is called an effect and manifold'(399). Why does Brahman emanate a world? 'The motive which prompts Brahman to the creation of a world . . . is nothing else but sport, play'(477). In fact, 'The reason for a particular creation . . . may be 'Brahman's recognition of Prakriti having reached a certain special state'(487). Or again, 'Its own potentiality leads it into a condition of being'(478). One must conclude, I think, that the being of the world is necessary. It presses into being from the inner nature of Brahman itself, in its causal state. Moreover, if you ask why particular things are as they are, Ramanuja says, 'Each soul has a material body corresponding to its karman'(328). However, each soul is beginningless, and has not originated. It has existed in an infinte number of previous worlds, and in each of them what happened to it was due to its own karman. But how did this karman originate? If it is literally without beginning, it is very hard to say that what happens to it is always, at every stage, due to its own past acts. If something has a beginning of existence, then we might say, what happens to it later is due to what it does from that point. But of course it begins with a specific nature which is given to it, and is not its own responsibility. Responsibility has to start some-where. But if it is beginningless, how can one distinguish what is given and what is self-made? It does not seem logically possible to say that everything that happens is due to some past act of the self, when that past never began. So is the nature of each soul due simply to Brahman, in its eternal though causal nature? But then in what sense does Brahman completely control the finite, if it necessarily flows from what Brahman is, and there is no alternative to its being thus? In a sense, Brahman is at the mercy of its body, since it is unchangeable and it constitutes the effected state of Brahman.

Is the possession of a body a good or bad thing, for Brahman? When Ramanuja asks what ignorance consists in, he answers, 'The consciousness of the I which has the body for its object is ignor-ance'(72). Ignorance is the confusion of the self with the body of which it is the self. Plainly, then, self and body are distinct. So the finite souls, as the body of Brahman, are distinct from Brahman; what they must do is to recognize their essential nature as knowl-edge, and not as material things. And indeed he says, 'Souls, matter and the Lord are essentially distinct'(102). When the soul achieves release, it does not achieve substantial unity with Brahman, but only 'the same attributes'(98). 'The attributes of the finite soul do not touch the highest Self, any more than infancy, youth and other attributes of the material body touch the soul'(229). But this is an odd doctrine, that the soul is unaffected by what happens to the body. What is the point of embodiment at all, if this is so? Embodi-ment must be ascribed simply to ignorance – and yet Ramanuja is not content to say that embodiment, even in the state of release, is simply put aside.

Of the released soul, he says, 'The released soul, freed from its connection with works . . . i.e. the body and the rest, abides in its true essential nature'(756). So it may seem that the released soul is essentially disembodied. And so, in a sense, it is. But he also says that 'in that state, the soul can realize all its ideas and wishes'(760): 'The released may at his liking be with or without a body'(763). 'The released soul may have experience of different worlds created by the Lord engaged in playful sport'(764). Ramanuja wants the best of both worlds – both a complete freedom from the exigencies of karma, and also the pleasures which embodiment alone can give.

In its liberated state, the soul is no longer bound by its works; it has ended the chain of becoming, and can rest in pure knowledge. But it can also manifest a body of play, wherein all wishes are immediately realized, without any admixture of pain, decay or death. This parallels the way in which Brahman itself may take on an individualized body: 'Brahman possesses a divine form suitable to its nature, with infinite, supremely excellent and wonderful qualities . . . he individualizes that form to gratify his devotees . . . as a shape human or divine'(240). The release the souls seek is not necessarily complete disembodiment, then, but freedom from the attachment of desire which binds them to the wheel of rebirth.

What, then is the reason for creation, according to Ramanuja? First of all, it is mere sport – which implies a positive element of enjoyment. Yet this hardly accounts for the existence of so much suffering. So then there is an element of necessity – Brahman, in its causal and effected state, must manifest itself and become many: 'The wonderful worlds springing from the mere will of a perfect and omnipresent being cannot but be infinite'(750). On the other hand, each soul is beginningless, and is bound by its own inherent karman. If Brahman is said to have complete control of souls and matter, this does not mean that it can do anything logically possible with them. They are bound by their inherent nature to certain actions and events. In what sense, then, are they one with Brahman? They are not substantially one with the highest Person, who, being free from all imperfections, is untouched by the sufferings of finite souls. Indeed, to escape from ignorance, one must learn to make clear distinctions between the Self of all; the finite knowing subject; and material objects, which are quite distinct from the self, and do not belong to its essence.

Now, however, it becomes hard to see what can be meant by Brahman being the Self of all, when it is substantially distinct from souls and matter. We have seen that having a body is not essential to Brahman, and it would be an error to think that Brahman was substantially identical with the world, as its body. Nevertheless, that Brahman whose essence is unrestricted knowledge takes the world as its body. 'The relation of bodies to the Self is analogous to that of class characteristics and the substances in which they inhere; the Self only is their substrate, final cause, and they are modes of Self'(136). This seems to mean that the world could not exist without Brahman; that it depends wholly upon him at all times. Further, the world manifests the Self, and enables it to enjoy the fruits of karma. Of course, in the case of the supreme Self, there is no karma to be worked out. Yet by analogy the karman of all beings is contained in it, as all effects are contained somehow in their cause. So the world does manifest the nature of lower Brahman, working out the potentialities eternally inhering in it.

The second half of this view cancels out the first. That is, Brahman was first of all said not to need a body, to be wholly self-sufficient. But then it is said to have the necessity of manifesting itself, as all things originate by will from its own necessary nature, 'the Undeveloped'. The relation between the perfect and untouched Brahman and the manifester of a very imperfect world stands in need of clarification. Indeed, this view turns out to be remarkably like that of Sankara. If the real is the unchanging, and free from any shadow of imperfection, then the higher Brahman alone is real. Its relation to the world is like that of a soul to its body; that is, any identity is *avidya*, and release from all contact with the world is to be desired. What is this Self which enters into matter and evolves name and form, which 'constitutes both effect and cause'(142)? Ramanuja insists that it is Brahman; and yet Brahman remains free from all imperfections. Whereas Ramanuja insists on knowledge having a substantial self; and on the substantial difference of the highest self and finite selves; like Sankara, he is unable to resolve the basic duality between the higher and the lower Brahman, by which one is free from contact, and the other (and yet somehow the same) is the Self of a finite world. Souls and matter are 'modes'(142) of Brahman; yet 'the highest Brahman, though entering into the effected condition, remains unchanged'(142). All one can do is to say that there is an essential nature which remains unchanged; yet a manifestation in action, a dynamism of finite manifestations of that nature in time, which can be seen as a 'joyful play', the objectification of a changeless nature.

Moreover, Ramanuja stresses that 'cessation of bondage is to be obtained only through the grace of the highest Self'(145); so Braham plays an initiating role in releasing the soul from the realm of desire and decay, into a world wherein all its purified desires can be realized. Finite souls come to be by a self-manifestation of Brahman; yet they remain substantially distinct; and their true destiny is to come to know Brahman, and thereby obtain release from ill, and entrance into a paradisal world of bliss and heightened knowledge of what is real. On this view, the action that is painful is action with attachment; there is a form of action, the joyful play of the bliss of Brahman in finite form, which is beyond pain; and that is the goal of devotion and religious ritual.

Thus, in saying that Brahman is the Self of all, Ramanuja seems to mean that all things depend wholly on it, and are manifestations of some part of its qualified nature; further, their final end is to come to know it as the highest reality, and achieve a sort of recognized unity – though not of substance, only of likeness of attributes. If this is so, then the statements that the world is the body of God, and that we are parts of the body of God do not have the alarming implications some Western thinkers may have imagined. Indeed, they are operationally identical with the classical Semitic doctrine of creation.

The differences are perhaps that Ramanuja stresses how 'the infinite number of manifold beings' are manifested endlessly from Brahman, and by some form of necessity – though still through the will and desire of Brahman. This may not be an important difference, however, for in the Bible there is simply no account of how or why God came to create; there is just the statement that he forges the future by will, and that from him proceed good and evil alike.[3]

Brahman is unable to experience pleasure or pain, because 'the cause of experiences, pleasurable or painful, is not the mere dwelling within a body, but subjection to the influence of good or evil deeds; such is impossible to the highest Self'(265). Brahman cannot feel the pain which results from our evil deeds, since it is perfect, and does no evil. Yet it has complete knowledge of the world. Ramanuja suggests that 'To him who has freed himself from ignorance in the form of karman, this same world of pain presents itself as essentially blissful . . . a plaything of Brahman, whose nature is supreme bliss'(306). This is perhaps not fully satisfactory; for suffering still exists; and it is hard to think that Brahman, whose knowledge is perfect, should not have knowledge by acquaintance of pain. It is common Upanishadic doctrine that 'the world is each time created to the end of souls undergoing experiences retributive of their former deeds; otherwise the inequalities of the different parts of creation would be inexplicable'(392). If one gave up the doctrine of rebirth and of the beginningless existence of each soul, one might have to adjust the view to a large extent. It would be much harder to take the view that 'the highest Self, desirous of providing himself with an infinity of playthings . . . so modifies himself as to have those elements for his body' (405). It is not so easy to think of the world as a collection of playthings, if the suffering in it cannot be blithely ascribed to previous acts of each individual soul, even if those acts are cases of specific ignorance, or conscious rejection, of Vishnu's grace. How can Brahman find sport in a suffering world? The doctrine that 'all imperfections and sufferings belong only to the individual souls' (406) has just a hint of a sadistic God about it, rather than of one who truly cares for what, is, after all, in some sense his own Body. If the souls are a manifestation of Brahman, then can one quite so confidently ascribe all suffering to their own fault, and not to the necessary self-manifestation itself? And can one talk of the Lord blessing and punishing, that is, reacting to specific events in time, while yet he 'is in no way touched by imperfections and changes' (406)? But it must be remarked that the same difficulties apply to Christian theology of the same period; they are not peculiar to Indian philosophy. The paradoxes of divine determination and human freedom; of divine perfection and human suffering; of divine changelessness and human temporality, remain in all theistic views of this period, East and West.

The supreme goal for which Ramanuja hopes is that 'intuitive knowledge of Brahman, which is supreme unsurpassable bliss' (681). It is clear that Brahman is other than the individual self, even though 'the subtle elements of the soul on release are incapable of being thought and spoken of as separate from Brahman' (738). So one may unequivocally speak of the relation between Brahman and the self as one of relationship, and not mere identity; as a state in which the released soul is ruled by its own will, and has not lost its individual identity in Brahman. Ramanuja has not, then, such a negative evaluation of the world and of individuality as Sankara. He looks rather for a transfigured world, in which the continuing self, knowing Brahman and bliss, will have its capacities expanded; it will have 'freedom from all evil and sin . . . intelligence, bliss and the other essential qualities of the soul which were obscured and contracted by Karman' (758). All the same, the world of *samsara* is one in which 'an infinite mass of sins [negative karma] accumulates in endless aeons' (489); so freedom from its present state is much to be desired. There is no thought of a historical goal; the released soul in its liberated world has passed beyond space and time as we know it. In that sense, one can understand how there is no clear demand for social justice or for a real transforming action of God in the world. Grace remains inward, known in the hidden places of each individual soul.

Ramanuja agress with Sankara in thinking that action with attachment, motivated by desire, bringing karmic fruits in its train, is an imperfection. Yet he allows in a more positive way for action as a sheer joyful expression of creative freedom, and is thus probably nearer to the spirit of the Bhagavad Gita, which enjoins action without attachment rather than simple renunciation of all action.[4] Ramanuja also agrees with Sankara and with the Vedic tradition in general in believing in the cyclic recurrence of the created world; in the absence of any final social goal in the world; and in accepting a basic duality of aspect in Brahman, though conceived in a rather different way than that of Sankara. But Ramanuja's doctrine permits of a much greater value in individual existence; in the continued immortality of the released souls; and in giving a positive role to creation in being the manifestation of the infinite joy of Brahman. His central controlling metaphor of the world as the body of the Lord helps to determine his view of the way in which the finite self is one with and yet distinct from the Real. But the relationship between the free actions of finite selves and the all-controlling will of the supreme Self is not worked out in detail, and perhaps not greatly helped by this metaphor in the end.

Ramanuja's doctrine of God is a complex and fascinating one which shows many similarities to Semitic doctrines. In his hands, Vedanta comes even closer to the Semitic tradition and is capable of throwing much new light on that tradition by showing the way in which basic controlling metaphors and underlying views of the world influence one's working-out of the basic structure of the religious life. There are other strands of Vedantic thought, of course. In particular, Madhva represents an even more overt form of dualism between Brahman, conceived in a personal form, and individual souls. But the main themes are, I think, sufficiently well brought out in the commentaries of Sankara and Ramanuja to make possible some assessment of the constellation of themes present in the Vedanta. In seeking to do this, I shall also attempt to bring out what I shall term the basic fiduciary structure of religion, a structure which reveals the common themes which link major religious traditions at a fundamental level. If I can do that, the claim to discern a common underlying doctrine of God in these traditions will gain in precision and plausibility.

Attempts to achieve one all-embracing definition of religion have notoriously failed to find universal assent.[5] But that is not to say that we have no idea of what a religion is, as opposed to, say, a piece of art, a philosophy or a moral system. Anthropologists, psychologists and philosophers can all study the phenomena of religion; and they know fairly well what sorts of things they can study and what sorts of things they can ignore. Naturally there are borderline cases; but there are also central cases; and it is by reference to the central and clear cases that one can best get an idea of what religion is.

There are many forms of religious life. They begin in many ways – with ancestor reverence, fertility rites, oracles and rituals for persuading or controlling demons or spirits. Underlying most of these forms is a desire to be appropriately related to those forces which control human destiny, so that harm can be avoided and well-being achieved. What most obviously characterizes religion is the activity of worship and devotion. Viewed by the sceptical, this activity may seem to be an attempt to gain magical control over one's destiny, by mental techniques which are conspicuously unsuccessful, in general. Viewed more sympathetically, one may discern the attempt to give reverence to embodiments of specific ideals and to aim to embody those ideals oneself. Religion is not, however, just a quest for an ideal of human welfare. It is such a quest; but it is typically pursued by means of a relation to those greater powers which condition human existence and which may influence it for good or ill. What is sought, the sympathetic observer will say, is true human well-being, by the discovery of the proper or appropriate relation to that which is most truly real. One of the most basic claims of religion, appearing in many different traditions around the world, is that human well-being can be achieved by being rightly related to how things are. It lies in the adoption of an appropriate set of reactive attitudes to the world at large, or to its ultimate but perhaps hidden or ambiguous character. Thus the believer does not just focus on a subjectively chosen ideal for his own life. He seeks to find this ideal embodied in the real world, as its most fundamental character, and to give it due reverence and worship. The varied images and rituals of religion are ultimately focused around this theme, of the reverence of those ultimate powers, by right relation to which true well-being can be achieved.

But how does one come by an idea of true well-being? How can one discover what the ultimate conditioning powers of human existence are, and what form of relationship to them can bring well-being? It is characteristic of most religions to say that the real character of things is hidden to ordinary perception, and needs special techniques to discern it. Thus there arise prophets, seers or shamans who consider themselves to be specially chosen to say what is true of the hidden but ultimate reality and how we should find fulfilment by relation to it. One may have inspired teachings or writings; special experiences of a psychological sort; miracles and fulfilments of prophecy in the objective world; or reflective meditations on the nature of things. Each of these can give rise to a revelatory matrix upon which a religious tradition can be formed. A revelatory matrix is a paradigm metaphor which encapsulates a particular vision of the world. An example of such a matrix is the Upanishadic statement, 'Those who see all beings in the Self and the Self in all things, will never doubt It'.[6] To 'see the Self in all things' is to react to the world *as if* it expressed a Self, in a way analogous to that in which human bodies express human consciousness and purpose. And to see all things in the Self is to regard ourselves *as if* we were parts of one inclusive awareness, prepared to carry out its purposes as required. The phrase does not really attempt to describe, in any straightforward way (in what we might call a 'literal' way). It seeks to evoke a way of life which is regulated, in its most general forms of apprehension and action, by a controlling metaphor. We are given an 'as-if' model for regarding and reacting to the world. The term 'matrix' seems appropriate for it, because it is a basic mould or pattern which forms our most general perceptions of things and our reactions to them.

A revelatory matrix has a threefold regulative function. It is regulative for human understanding, providing a paradigm by which an explanation can be given of how things are and of how they came to be as they are. Thus one might say that all things arise from the Self; and this, if it is plausible, explains how things have come to be. It is regulative for human feeling, providing a metaphor in terms of which one can react to the events of life – as manifesting a gracious and compassionate Lord. And it is regulative for the will, in providing a hope and a goal of effort and self-discipline, in a full union with and knowledge of the Supreme Self. The matrix thus shows what reality most truly is; how it has come to be; and what our future is, in relation to it. It gives a basic pattern of understanding in terms of which we can develop a view of our place in the universe and the central purpose we can give to our lives.

The source of the matrix is revelation; either the claim to omniscience, as traditionally with Sakyamuni and Jesus, or a claim to inspired knowledge given by a suprahuman source to a chosen person, as with the authors of the Veda, Torah and Koran. But it is evident from the first that religion is not just concerned with a speculative account of what reality is like – though it usually involves such an account. Its concern is primarily a practical one; a concern with how to achieve well-being, or liberation from the limitations placed upon us by existence. Thus the revelatory matrix does not simply, or even primarily, tell us what the Real is like; it proposes to us a way of liberation from the Unreal to knowledge of the Real, and so it speaks of the Real in ways which are conducive to liberation. This way is usually to be completed after earthly death; but it can be begun during life; and its fulfilment can perhaps be assured then. We can then see the structural configuration of a religion as the framework it gives for understanding human life as ordered to an objective goal of fulfiment (objective, because it is not chosen by human persons and it remains what it is, even if no one believes in it at some time). One begins with a statement of the human condition, with all its limitations. Some account is offered of how this condition came to be as it is. Then the goal of freedom from these limitations is specified, together with the means to attain that goal. Finally, an account of the nature of the ultimately Real is given, and a particular understanding of the mode of revelation which discloses this nature. These factors provide the main outlines of the structure of a religious form of life.

I make no claim that this account is complete. But it may be helpful in articulating in an ordered way some of the key themes of a religious understanding of the world. In the case of Vedanta, the chief *limitation* of the human condition which needs to be overcome is ignorance (*avidya*). The *cause* of ignorance is the desire for action and finite experience, which leads to the existence of those karmic chains which bind every human soul. The *way to release* from karma and from ignorance is strict self-discipline, through good works, devotion and meditation, leading to the ending of desire and the breaking-off of all attachments to the world. The *final goal* is eternal bliss and union with the Self of all, which is the unconditioned and only self-existent Real. That *Reality* is understood as pure Intelligence and Bliss, beyond any attachment to action. And the *teaching of this way* originates with the Vedic Scripture and with those ancient seers who show the way to release, by their own accomplishing of liberation.

The structure is quite a clear one, and we shall find it reflected in the other major religious traditions which we are examining. The existence of such a common structure is important, in view of the fact that each religious tradition needs to arrive at some explanation for the existence of other traditions. In so far as each one makes a claim to discern the ultimate truth about human existence and the final liberation for human beings, a problem arises as to why these facts are not more widely known. Why are they apparently confined to only one religious group? And why do very different traditions exist, in sometimes quite radical conflict with the preferred tradition of the believer? If there is a common structure to religious forms of life, one is able to see different faiths as different, culturally conditioned configurations within that structure. The arguments that exist will be the quite natural and healthy sorts of argument that exist in any sort of human intellectual endeavour – say, in physics or biology. They will also be complicated, of course, by the very unhealthy and perverse sorts of argument that arise from human pride and jealousy, as rife in religions as anywhere else. The way to liberation will not then be confined to one group only; it may take many forms, but with a discernibly similar structure, in very different contexts.

This does not imply that all faiths are equally true; that is absurd; and where there are genuine disagreements, at least one position must be mistaken. But it does remind us that intellectual and even moral mistakes, as long as they are genuine errors, arrived at in good faith, are quite compatible with having a firm grasp of the basic structure and intention of the religious life, as one of turning from the world to submit the self to what is conceived as a self-existent Ideal. More will be said about the structural configurations of religion in the next chapter, about its polarities, paradoxes and ambiguities. But at this stage it may be helpful to compare the Vedantic configuration with the basic Semitic configuration of Judaism, to illustrate how the common structure points up some key similarities and differences between them.

A major theme of Vedanta is the relative unreality of the world. It is not that the universe does not exist; but that it is less than real, compared to that which is changelessly and self-existently real. Another way of putting this is to say that God has a form of reality by comparison with which the world fades into insignificance. God's reality is beyond change and time. It is a form of existence which seems quite unique, which may properly be called 'immortality'. It is beyond duality, beyond pain and passion, beyond decay and death. Again, in Sankara, it is not conceived very personalistically; but it has the character of being, consciousness and bliss. It is supra-mental, not sub-mental. There is a problem for Vedantins of accounting for the origin of the world, if it is appearance only. If Brahman is perfect and changeless, why should it create a world? Indeed, how could it create imperfection? And how can the fully real give rise to the merely apparent? To whom would it appear? And why should ignorance ever arise, where only perfect knowledge exists?

At this point, ironically, a fundamental dualism arises in advaita (non-dualism); the dualism between the highest Self, simple, impassible and immutable; and the Self of all, which originates the world through will and enters into it. One possibility is to say that the world overflows from changeless Brahman, actualizing itself from the realm of potency which also clings to Brahman, as its limiting adjunct. It is like an overflowing of the divine Being into the abyss of nothingness, without intrinsic point or motive. But another possibility is that Brahman actually wills to become many, to explore the infinite number of finite manifestations of its own being, in sport, and thus to realize the potentialities which are immanent within it. It creates infinite worlds of bliss; and these worlds have a true reality, which is, however, always wholly dependent on Brahman for their being. Vedanta vacillates between these views, of the world as the illusory reflection of infinity and the world as the sacramental self-manifestation of infinity. The common underlying theme is the dependent reality of the finite world; and its basis as lying in a changeless realm of bliss beyond it.

The biblical picture is spelled out very differently. The Book of Genesis asserts that the world is good, or was good when it was first created; so it seems to have a relatively independent and valuable existence. Moreover, the world is not said to be in any sense a part of God; on the contrary, it is quite distinct from God, who remains transcendent to it. The world neither overflows from Jahweh, nor does he manifest himself in infinite numbers of worlds. Rather, the picture the Bible gives is of God deciding to create this world, not by some inner necessity and not in mere playfulness, but for a specific and freely chosen purpose. The picture is different; the revelatory matrix is not of the Self of all, hidden in the finite, but of the Almighty Will, commanding all things to be and to obey. Nevertheless, both traditions agree that this world depends wholly upon a self-existent reality beyond it. Though the Jewish tradition does not speak of God as unconditioned bliss, it is not likely to deny that Jahweh has such bliss, that 'in thy presence there is fullness of joy'.[7] And we have seen that even Sankara is as happy to speak of Brahman as the Sovereign Lord as he is to speak of the world of finite things and events, and to give each of them equal reality – indeed, to give the Sovereign Lord more reality, since he is the direct appearance of the Unconditioned Self.

Vedantins speak of the goal of life as union with the Self, whereas Jews speak of an obedient love of God. Again, there are clear differences here; early Judaism, especially, had no belief in life after death at all; whereas Vedanta always assumed the view of reincarnation. Yet it is again not unreasonable to speak of a similarity of structure; of a turning from selfish pursuits to an obedient union with a higher personal being, which can be consummated in an experience which seems to convey an increase of understanding, wisdom and joy or bliss.

The Bible does not speak of the condition of human beings as one of ignorance, but as one of sin or disobedience, which causes death, both in the physical sense and in a more subtle spiritual sense of lack of vitality and creativity. God is seen as the Judge who condemns man to death because of disobedience, but who offers him life on condition of repentance and good conduct. Again, however, it is clear that most people are ignorant of the presence of God; and that disobedience is very closely connected to selfish desire, which is the cause of the fall into *samsara* in the Indian traditions. Vedanta does not at all have the same sense of impending moral judgement, or of a divine demand for justice and mercy. Yet one of its deepest underlying themes is that of the moral government of the world.

The belief in rebirth is fundamental to all Indian religious schemes; it both accounts for the perceived inequalities of life and enables one to argue that there is a basic moral causality in the universe. Whatever you do, for good or ill, will have its return; earthly life is a working-out of the consequences of past actions, until one transcends the sort of desires which lead to attachment altogether. This moral scheme does not require any intervening personal agency of a retributive sort. So God is not seen as a Judge, who hands out punishment or rewards on a Judgement Day. Rather, there is an inherent causal law, in virtue of which deeds inevitably bring on their due consequences to the agent, without the need of externally imposed punishments. Goodness produces pleasure, and evil thoughts produce pain; no personal agent is required to set up this form of causality, to correlate happiness with virtue and pain with vice. Nevertheless, it is essential to see that the law of the universe is a moral law; it is not just a mechanistic law of physics.

There is no further account of how this law came to be as it is. Indeed, at the most basic level, Indian thought tends to say that there is no ultimate explanation. Good just produces pleasure, and that is how things are. This belief clearly does not arise from the way things are perceived to be. It is a basic belief in justice; that things are ultimately as they should be; the universe is justly ordered. So, although Vedantins and, more especially, Buddhists, do not attribute these karmic laws to a personal God, they are far from thinking that they are blind, purposeless or amoral. There are, in their view, fundamental principles in the structure of the universe which are principles of justice. Things go as they ought – that is, as a moral agent who was wholly impartial would choose them to go. The universe meets the moral demands people make of it – that is a statement of faith. Thus one must think of the karmic laws as bringing things about as they ought to be; and that is very closely akin to the belief that there is a divine judgement on good and evil.

These Vedantic and Jewish ideas are similar in structure, though not in content. They both see human life as suffering from a defect which is due to selfish concern and ignorance of the divine Being. They see human life as condemned to a long chain of ills, from which, however, there is a possible release. The desirable goal is a relation of knowledge and joy with the personal origin of the world; and that personal being himself reveals the goal and the way to it in revealed Scriptures, given through rare and spiritually gifted teachers of wisdom. What of the means to achieve release? Here the Jewish view may seem to be much more activist, social and this-wordly than the Vedantic; for what is recommended is obedience to the Law, the Torah, in its communal form, whereas Vedantins stress much more the lonely ascetic practices of yoga wherein release is found in what Plotinus called 'the flight of the alone to the Alone'.[8]

Those differences do indeed exist; yet for both traditions sacrificial ritual and rites of praise and devotion have an important part to play. As so often in Brahminical strands of religion, sacrifice is felt to have an efficacy of its own, but it does not do so without the appropriate mental attitude on the part of the sacrificer. It represents a giving-up of something in acknowledgement of a higher power, to which devotion is appropriate. There is a return; and this can vary from material blessings such as money and cattle, to the grace of the presence of the god. As so often in religion, there is a whole spectrum of attitudes possible on the part of the faithful, from gross transaction, by which my gift binds the god to bless me, to a wish for union with the personified god.

It is quite clear that in Vedanta the ritual is not regarded as having the highest degree of worth. Pious practice is encouraged; but chiefly as a means to a growth in knowledge of Brahman. The ritual is a way of preparing the mind for that knowledge; but what really counts is the achievment of unity with the Self of all. It is, however, important to note that, while union with Brahman may be beyond description (beyond duality), it is saved from being a mere blank by the fact that it is prepared for by the practice of sacrifice and devotion. Thus the rite of sacrifice shows the right way to approach Brahman – namely, as a suppliant or devotee; as one coming before an overwhelmingly greater, more powerful and valuable reality, which is capable of bringing good or harm to the suppliant. When one goes on to say that Brahman is beyond duality, one is relativizing these practices and the conceptions that go with them. One may even discountenance them, and say they must be transcended. But one is decidedly not saying that they should never have been undertaken, or that there is a better way to Brahman. These constitute the way to the wordless; and, if one is indeed going to throw away the ladder in the end, at least one must first of all have climbed it. To throw the ladder away without having climbed it is to remain firmly on the ground, and not to achieve what there is to be achieved. In other words, sacrifice and devotion retain their reality and their necessity; but they are not the final word. Beyond them, but not without them, there is that which is beyond speech, which can be realized but never adequately spoken of. The theme of the ineffability of the Real is very basic in Vedanta; but it is always balanced with the theme of the necessity of pious practice and devotion to the gods, who show forth Brahman in forms suited to the needs of the worshippers. The way to Brahman is through self-renunciation, meditation and ritual practice. These things train the mind to achieve a state which may no longer be spoken of; and which both Sankara and Ramanuja agree is only known by the revealed authority of the Veda.

That the role of sacrifice is very similar in Judaism is seen in the fact that sacrifice ceased to exist with the destruction of the Temple in Jerusalem, and Judaism survives with the memory of it and a spiritualized interpretation of it which makes its intermediary character even clearer than in Vedanta, where it survives in many sects in modified form. With all the great differences of content between these traditions, a common structure can be discerned, which enables us to speak of both as central and incontestable cases of forms of the religious life. Within that structure, each tradition has a typical configuration of themes which are centred on a particular matrix, a dominant revealed metaphor for the Divine. The Vedantic matrix is the idea of the Self; and it is articulated in different ways by different schools of Vedanta. I have considered only two major philosophers; and one can see how Sankara stresses much more the final ineffability of the Self and its character as pure Intelligence; while Ramanuja stresses the possession by the supreme Self of innumerable excellent qualities and the substantial and distinct character of the great mass of selves which constitute the finite world. Even within a common structure and a shared matrix of revelation, a whole range of possible differences of interpretation exist; and that is why it is in the end misleading to lump whole religious traditions together in opposition to other traditions, as if they were monolithic blocks of clear agreed doctrine or practice.

In expounding the Vedantic doctrine of Brahman, one main concern has been to explore the degree to which there is affinity with accounts of the nature of God in other religious traditions. I have referred to orthodox Judaism as a contrasting tradition which seems to be very different in its major themes, in order to test any claims to similarity. My conclusion is that it is not straining the evidence to say that there are affinities between this Indian tradition and orthodox philosophical accounts of the Semitic traditions of Judaism, Islam and Christianity. To put it more strongly, the Vedantic doctrine of Brahman is operatively similar to the orthodox doctrines of God in Middle Eastern traditions which I have briefly characterized here, and shall be looking at in more detail in subsequent chapters. By an 'operative similarity', I mean that the concept functions in the same way in the life of the believer; or, to be more exact, in the same set of ways. It functions in a similar way to a similar purpose; and the diversities of interpretation within the tradition reflect similar diversities in other traditions.

Indian views often seem to be wholly different from the theistic faiths deriving from the Hebrew Bible, and that there are important differences is manifest. But, I have tried to show, it would be wrong to characterize 'Hinduism' as simply polytheistic, or impersonal and unconcerned with morality and judgement. In the philosophical schools of Vedanta the notion of Brahman, the ultimately Real, is developed in a complex and subtle way. First of all, the idea of Brahman functions not as a purely speculative doctrine, but within a conceptual structure outlining a way to liberation from the confining restrictions of human existence in the world. When it is seen within this structure, one can see how it operates to define an objective goal of human life and the way to it. It is essential to see that it is not a dispassionate appraisal of what the basis of the real world is like, as it might be in post-Cartesian Western philosophy. What is important is its operative force: that is, the difference it makes to conduct (and that includes the conduct of knowing) if it is believed to be true. We might say that a description of Brahman is adopted because it is conducive to liberation, because it brings eternal bliss. What the description does is to specify a way of life in relation to an unconditioned reality, depicted in the model of a supreme awareness and bliss, an unrestricted intelligence.

In the philosophy of Sankara, this operative account is particularly clear; for he insists that *saguna Brahman* is in the end subordinate, in respect of reality, to *nirguna Brahman*. When we speak of Brahman as without qualities, we are not describing a mere nullity; we can hardly be *describing* anything, if we say it has no properties we can describe. But, as I have pointed out, it is logically improper to say both that Brahman has no qualities whatsoever, and that it is cause, bliss and unrestricted intelligence at the same time. The solution to this logical impasse is to see that we are not using these terms descriptively, so as to say: Brahman both has properties and has no properties at the same time. What we are doing is to loosen the hold of all descriptions of Brahman; to show that the seeming description actually functions to specify a way of life in relation to that of which we cannot properly speak. We need the models if we are to have any operative force at all, to take the way to liberation. But we need the negative qualifiers to profess a final agnosticism about the adequacy of our descriptions.

The temptation is, then, to say that these models for the unconditioned are merely pragmatic; that they are psychologically helpful, though false descriptions. Then it is important to say that these are not fictions; they are not invented and they are not adopted because they make us feel happy or useful. Indeed, that at which one is aiming ('liberation') cannot even be comprehended independently of the proffered descriptions. We may understand roughly what bliss is; but eternal bliss can only be understood in relation to the Eternal; it needs a special form of perception to see it as desirable; even to see what it is. That 'special form of perception' is what the doctrine of Brahman seeks to evoke; and independently of it one cannot understand what liberation is.

But is it not circular to say that liberation is only to be defined by a doctrine of the Real; yet the Real is known to us only in so far as it conduces to liberation? No; it may be compared with seeing an object from a distant point – say, for instance, seeing the planet earth from far out in the solar system. At that point one sees something which can guide one to move to a nearer viewpoint – perhaps into the earth's atmosphere. From there, one sees much more clearly – continents, seas and even cities come into view. Again one moves towards a specific continent, and to a city in that continent, and views it from a height of a few hundred feet. Now one can see streets and people; and one can move further, to identify a particular person. At each stage, one sees something which guides one's subsequent action. And then, that action having been completed, one sees something new, which will guide one further towards the goal. So one might say that at each stage of our spiritual journey, we can discern something which is able to guide us a little further. Then, from that new viewpoint, we see further again. At each stage, we see what is conducive to further progress; and when we make that progress, we see a little more. At each stage, the goal is liberation; but how we conceive that goal depends upon what we see of that reality which defines the goal; at each stage, our idea of liberation is defined by our doctrine of the Real. Yet as we move on, we discover that what we discern as the Real depends upon our progress towards liberation, which enables us to see more (or, unfortunately, sometimes less) clearly. At every stage, what we see is only appearance; and it always has the function of guiding our actions in response. When we speak of the Real beyond appearance, we are making an ideal construction of the imagined terminus of our journey. And at that stage, Sankara in effect refuses to speak, since speech can only encompass appearances.

For Sankara, the Real truly appears, yet it always transcends. The paradigm matrix spells out a way of life in relation to that which appears and moving towards that which transcends, the asymptotic goal of liberation. Thus he can say, 'That person yonder in the sun, I in truth am He'.[9] And yet the Real, formless and without qualities, is absolutely distinct from all things finite. This is the special form of perception which Vedanta is based on. We might call it the iconic vision, a term which derives from the Greek word '*eikon*', meaning 'image', which has the connotation of mediating the reality it expresses. The iconic vision is a response to the finite world which sees it as veiling reality, but also as manifesting reality when the veil is rendered transparent. It is to take the world as an appearance, which manifests the underlying reality and yet can place a barrier between the observer and the reality. There is a double movement of the mind involved in this response to the world. First, there is the unitive sense, by which one sees all things as manifesting one reality, and oneself as permeated by that reality. So all is one; in the famous phrase of the Upanishads, '*tat tyam asi*'.[10] Secondly, however, and inseparable from the first aspect, is the sense of absolute difference; the sense that the finite and the infinite are distinct in kind, so that the Real and the Good is wholly other than the world of appearances. When these two aspects are held together, then one sees the Real in and through the appearances, within and yet always beyond them, as far as reality is from illusion, knowledge from ignorance.

In one sense, the notion of the Real wholly beyond appearances, self-sufficient, unchanging and complete, is an ideal construct, the imaginary terminus of an uncompletable spiritual quest towards liberation. What is misleading about this way of putting it is that people think of an ideal as non-existent, and of imagination as the construction of falsehoods. It is important to see that an ideal, in the sense I am using it, is not a purely subjective idea, with no reality outside human minds; and it does not state something to be true which is actually false. The question is one of *what it means* to say that there exists an infinite, immutable, eternal reality. We can certainly imagine some object existing for a long time without changing; but can we really imagine a timeless object or an object without any limitations at all? The very idea seems contradictory; for all objects are finite by definition. Brahman, then, is a non-object; but how can one say that a non-object exists, that there is one?

The short way of dismissing this notion is to say that it is senseless; but this is where I have tried to show the sort of sense it has by placing it in its proper context of the structure of a religious form of life. The negations lead one to loosen the grip of descriptions of Brahman; whereas the insistence on existence, causality and perfection lead one always to assert that *there is* something beyond what we can say. Of course these terms do not correspond one to one with some external reality; what could be meant by such a reality? What is being said is precisely that God is not a finite, limited object which can be imagined just being there, like a solid lump of rock. So the question is of what it means to assert the existence of an unlimited reality. And at least in this case it seems correct to say that what it means is given by how it is used in religious discourse[11] – to say that there is an endless development and growth of knowledge, understanding and love possible to finite creatures; that an actual full comprehension will never be achieved; for God is a mystery which is beyond all actual, finished comprehension, yet always capable of a further development of comprehension.

The force of saying that God is infinite is, at least partly, to say that God is not a completed reality in the way that any bounded being is. He always stands beyond, whatever stage of response we have arrived at; yet he is always present at every stage, offering further reaches of understanding and love. Of course such a concept of God is an imaginative construct of our minds; what alternative exists? It is an ultimate postulate which cannot be conclusively verified; but which can, in a sense, be confirmed by our successive apprehensions of him and by the occurrence of the same structure of thought and apprehension in so many diverse cultures and societies. It is felt to be given by revelation, as the Upanishads testify. That is to say, it is a concept which forms in certain minds which are attentive to the supreme reality and receptive to its interaction with them. They become the seers whose words, formed in response to the object of their devotion, are then felt to be 'heard' by them rather than just made up laboriously.

It is entirely artificial to divorce revelation, experience, reflection and the interpretation of particular events or phenomena from one another wholly. From one viewpoint, one can trace the development of Upanishadic doctrines of the Self through the development of sacrificial rites and yogic practices. One can discern primitive cosmological speculation and see how particular gurus have been taken to be manifestations of a higher divine principle to their disciples. Revelation has a natural history; it has its influences and sources in ordinary human faculties.[12] Yet from another viewpoint it can be taken to be prompted and guided by a transcendent source, shaping all those materials to create a new perception of things. The extent of this shaping is a matter of dispute among believers; but the orthodox of most traditions tend to magnify it as much as possible, so that the texts become infallible or free from error. That is certainly a possibility; and it is not irrational to accept such a thing if one is prepared to allow the existence of a supreme guiding Self underlying all things. Yet the exact form revelation takes, and whether it is indeed infallible – whether that really is the best possible form of revelation, must be decided by further reflection. It cannot be taken for granted that a God would give an infallible revelation. There may be good reasons why all revelations should be partial and fallible. While the notion of authoritative revelation lies at the heart of the structure of faith, there is a whole range of possible positions on the nature of that authority.

Orthodox Muslim accounts speak of a direct verbal transmission by God; while Buddhists rely on very old traditions recalling the teaching of the enlightened one, whose own experience is the guarantor of truth. Within each tradition there is the logical possibility of a continuous range of positions between the two poles of propositional dictation and enlightened experience. While the orthodox tend to make claims for infallibility as strong as possible, other believers allow for the possibility of such an element and degree of personal experience and developing historical context that a degree of partiality and fallibility is introduced. It may be argued that this allows revelation to be considered as much more a personal interaction between human and divine, whereas infallibilist accounts treat revelation in a rather mechanical way, as the passive reception of information. Moreover, a stress on factors of personal temperament and cultural context may help one to appreciate the rich diversity of different traditions, and make possible a more tolerant and appreciative attitude to other traditions than one's own.

It is possible to develop a view of revelation which allows for the guiding role of God while also allowing for a growth in knowledge and a gradual correcting of earlier views by later ones in some respects (note the the way in which the Koran 'corrects' some elements of the Hebrew Bible, for instance). Thus those who feel intellectual difficulties about the cosmologies of both early Semitic and Indian streams of thought; and about some moral judgements about retribution or the meritorious efficacy of ritual action to be found in the Scriptures, may maintain an acceptance of revelation together with an acceptance of the findings of well-established and responsible Critical scholarship.

For such views, all words might be the words of men and women, and yet be partial discernments of God, both prompted by God and building on past traditions of disclosure. One could give authority to great sages and poets who have written works of power and insight, extending human vision. One could give authority to saints, mystics and visionaries, whose personal experience of God seems especially vivid and intense. Great moral reformers and people of psychic and charismatic power might also be given a certain authority – not indeed free from error, but capable of showing us what we could not have seen alone, and what we ignore only at the cost of a restriction of vision. On such an account, authority would lie in the notable exercise of certain human excellences, as responses to divine disclosure. It would be personal, developing and always to some extent incomplete. One might support the view by developing the thought that revelation is primarily a matter of personal interaction between God and human beings; and that a creative, explorative human response is an important virtue which God might wish to encourage and not repress.

It must be said, however, that most traditional believers will wish rather to stress the unalterable given-ness of revelation, on the grounds of its supreme importance for human salvation and the weakness and even idiosyncrasy of the human intellect. Thus one can see how there can be fundamental differences about what revel-ation might be expected to be, which will govern what one goes on to accept as authentic revelation. Yet that does not mean that revelation has no important place. It retains a vital place, as testifying to a belief that the source of our deepest religious ideas is not simply human imagination or feeling or intellect; but lies in a transcendent origin. The matrices which constitute revelation, records of revelatory events, states, sacred writings and rituals, may be seen as given data, to be accepted by faith; or as imaginative, creative attempts to discern the meaning of human experience, in response to a partial and developing apprehension of a God who discloses himself in ways suited to particular historical conditions. These two approaches introduce a polarity which extends across religious boundaries rather than within them; they must both be considered, in any attempt to give an adequate account of the fiduciary structure of religion. However, it is enough to record at this point that most traditions do ascribe infallibility or omniscience to their key religious teachers; and so do regard revelation as both a natural product of human abilities and also a supernaturally guided product at the same time.

For Sankara, the attitude to revelation which is appropriate to Vedanta is typically complex; and it illustrates well one application of the iconic vision. For Scripture reveals the Real, Brahman, to be the origin and goal of all. Yet Scripture is also a veil of the truth; and in the end, in the experience of enlightenment, it may be transcended. It mediates Brahman; yet Brahman is also wholly beyond; and both these views must be taken in dialectical tension before one can really appreciate what it means to say that the Veda is the revelation of Brahman. Where all words fail and turn back,[1] even the words of the Veda fail; but they remain true on their own level of *samsara*.

The Vedantic view, in both versions I have considered, leaves some major problems unresolved. First, can creatures be free if they are manifestations of Brahman? Can they achieve release, if the reality of Brahman is unchangeable, and so cannot be added to by the release of any finite self? Secondly, how are the aspects of Brahman, as higher or even without qualities (in Sankara) and lower, or causal and effected, related? How can a changeless Brahman manifest itself in time, an all-wise being become ignorant; or a simple being have two aspects? And thirdly, how can suffering arise if Brahman is perfect? How can Brahman be untouched by it, and yet be omniscient? Such problems are not, of course, confined to Vedanta; we shall meet them again very soon. But they need to be addressed by any view which seriously attempts to achieve a unified vision of reality, capable of effecting human liberation from ignorance and desire.

Despite these problems, Vedanta is an elegant and imaginative attempt to provide a coherent account of the structure of the religious form of life. It takes the idea of the Knowing Self, beyond action and desire, as its matrix for understanding. And it develops this matrix as one formulation of what I have termed the iconic vision, a particular vision of the nature of things which is what gives a matrix its religious nature and power. These ideas are spelled out against a background belief in reincarnation, Brahminical rites of sacrifice and yogic practices of meditation. These and many other historical factors go to make up the distinctiveness of Indian religious life, in those sects which are allied to the Vedanta. Yet for all the difference and diversity, I have tried to draw out one way in which it can be said that there is here a recognizable doctrine of God, capable of throwing light on the views of other religious traditions, and perhaps of fruitful interaction with them to bring about new forms of understanding in religion.

We are not just faced with a total opposition between Hindu polytheism and Semitic monotheism, between Hindu indifference to the world and Semitic social concern and moral earnestness. It is even too easy, I have suggested, to oppose a misleadingly named 'Hindu monism' with Western dualism; for when they are examined carefully, it turns out that modes of description are being influenced by controlling metaphors which say operatively similar things under different forms of description. The Vedantic tradition itself is careful to say that Brahman can be 'indicated indirectly, not described directly' (*Laksyate, na tu ucyate*). There is no point in unifying all religious doctrines to produce one mess of mixed metaphors. Yet neither is it fair to take verbal oppositions as the final sign of difference in religion. Careful examination may reveal operative similarities which may be much more important. That is the task I have attempted. My conclusion is that one may speak of a common tradition of thinking about God; I shall seek to illustrate this further in considering representative philosophers from other religious traditions, and to show how a recovery of this tradition, often neglected in the modern world, may help to advance both an understanding of the nature of religion and, for believers, a deeper form of religious understanding.

3

Buddhaghosa and Asvaghosa: Buddhist
Analogues to God

It may seem very odd to include a treatment of Buddhism in a
study of the concept of God, since Buddhism may be reasonably
defined as an atheistic religion.[1] While there are thousands of gods,
demons, spirits and ghosts in popular Buddhism, there is no great
interest in one personal God. Even less is relationship with such a
personal God taken as a goal of the religious life. Most forms of
Buddhism are characterized by a total disinterest in the idea of
God; and for this reason, definitions of religion which seek to specify
it in terms of a belief in God find Buddhism a difficult case. Some
writers, such as W. D. Hudson, adopt a brusque approach and say
that Buddhism is not a religion.[2] But that, as I will show, is a most
arbitrary procedure, missing out much that is of great interest for
religious belief.

The central concept of Buddhism is not God, but nirvana (in
Sanskrit; nibbana, in Pali). It is rather unfair to begin with a
definition of it, since it is said to be quite indefinable. But there is a
classical account of it in the Udana, a commonly accepted Buddhist
Scripture.

> There is, disciples, a realm devoid of earth and water, fire and
> air. It is not endless space, nor infinite thought, nor nothingness,
> neither ideas nor non-ideas. Not this world nor that is it. I call
> it neither a coming nor a departing, nor a standing still, nor
> death, nor birth. It is without a basis, progress or a stay; it is the
> ending of sorrow. For that which clings to another thing there is
> a fall; but to that which clings not no fall can come. Where no
> fall comes, there is rest, there is no keen desire. Where keen desire
> is not, nothing comes or goes . . . there is no death, nor birth . . .

there is neither this world nor that, nor in between. It is the ending of sorrow. There is, disciples, an Unbecome, Unborn, Unmade, Unformed. If there were not this . . . there would be no way out for that which is become, born, made and formed . . . but there is release.[3]

This seems to be about as negative a doctrine as one can get. Buddhism is indeed a doctrine of extreme reticence about the final goal of human life. Yet it does assert most definitely that there is a final goal; and that there is a way to it which is hard and arduous. There is release. Thus the world of change, of becoming, of birth and rebirth, is seen as finally undesirable, as a realm of suffering. If desires can be extinguished, then there is a state to be attained which is not mere non-existence. Von Glasenapp, in his standard work on Buddhism, says, 'However the ramifications of the nirvana concept may vary, the basic idea is the same. It is an indefinable state, independent of all worldly ties, beyond all earthly passion, freedom from all egotistical, false ideas – in short, it is the exact opposite of everything known to conditioned, individual existence between birth and death.'[4]

It may seem that nirvana is a state of mind, a purely psychological state, when passions have been calmed and an inner freedom achieved.[5] In that state, there is no keen desire, and no sorrow; there is nothing to be wished for or to be avoided. Yet this seems an insufficient characterization; for in that state of nirvana, there is no death, no birth and no form. It is Unbecome; and therefore it cannot be a state of mind which comes into being at a specific point in time. Rather, it must be something beyond the individual mind. But what?

It may seem that nirvana is extinction. Did the word not originally mean 'blowing out'? And is it not the cessation of the round of rebirths, the ending of conditioned existence? Thus it seems to be at least the extinction of the individual self. And how can the non-existent be distinguished from the unborn, unmade, unformed? However, it is explicitly stated that nirvana is not nothingness. It is a state of some sort; and the individual finds in it, not a mere non-being, but a sort of fulfilment – though, indeed, it is very unlike what sensual people would call fulfilment. The standard refutation, from within the strictest tradition of Theravada Buddhism, is to be found in the *Visuddhi magga* of the fifth-century monk, Buddhaghosa.[6] He writes: 'Nirvana has been metaphorically stated as extinction, since in a broad sense it is the sufficing condition of that extinction which is termed cessation without rebirth.' There is a sort of extinction, an extinction of the round of rebirth in this transmigratory world. Yet extinction is only a metaphor; it is not literally so. 'Why is it not so stated explicitly? Because of its exceeding subtlety . . . it can only be reached, not produced, by the Path.' That is, one may show the way to that state; but the state itself cannot be brought into being. It may be entered into by the individual who seeks release. 'Hence it is without source. Being without source it is free from old age and death . . . it is permanent . . . because it transcends the intrinsic nature of matter it is non-material . . . being attainable through special insight effected by strong effort and being announced by the omniscient one, nirvana, as existing in the ultimate sense, is not non-existent.' It may be spoken of as non-existent, in the sense in which finite material things exist. It does not exist in that sense. But it does exist in a more ultimate sense, beyond change and division. And it can be attained. 'For this has been said, "Monks, there is that which is not born, not the result of becoming, not made, not conditioned" (Itivuttaka, 37)' (16, On the Truth of the Cessation of Ill'). The unconditioned, uncreated has being; and that being can be attained by the individual self.

There remains a major problem in this account. If nirvana can be attained, then there is something which has not attained nirvana which can subsequently attain it. But nirvana itself cannot come into being or change; so nothing can be added to it. What then is it which comes to attain that which is beyond change? If the individual self simply became extinct, nothing would be attained. One could only say that the Unbecome remains; while some finite self had ceased to be. But, as we have seen, that is ruled out; in some sense, nirvana is a proper goal of human effort. It must then be that the finite self comes to participate in the Changeless; to enter into a new state, in which the Changeless is reflected fully in the individual self, to such an extent that it seems wholly to fill its being.

Of course, Buddhism is committed to the doctrine of *an-atta*, no-self. All things are impermanent, made of collections of individual fleeting events. There is no enduring substantial self, underlying its fleeting thoughts and feelings and perceptions. So it would seem that there is nothing which could endure to attain nirvana, once the chain of events, caused by desire, had come to an end. That is the case; and so one comes to the central paradox of Buddhist philosophy – that the permanent is to be attained by that which cannot endure beyond the impermanent; and one is to enter into a state which cannot in any respect come to be. Unfortunately, I can only state this paradox, and can see no way of resolving it. It seems to me, that despite the doctrine of nirvana, there is a deep commitment to the view that there exists some self which can pass from the impermanent to the permanent. In that case, one must look to the operative force of *an-atta*, and suggest, perhaps, that it seeks to distract attention from the self which is the origin of desires; that is to say, from the ego which seeks to draw all things to itself as centre.

Buddhaghosa's great work is called *The Path of Purification*, and he says, 'Here, by purity is meant nirvana, which is free from all taints and exceedingly pure. They way to this purity is the path of purity' (Introductory Discourse). So, as it is put 'The cleansing of one's mind . . . is the religion of the Buddhas' (Dhammapada, 183). As a path of virtue, one is to seek 'absence of mental remorse, gladness, rapture, tranquillity, joy, practice, culture, development, adornment, concentration, fullness, fulfilment, certain disgust, dispassion, cessation, quiet, higher knowledge, perfect knowledge, nirvana' (from Patisambhida, i,46). These characterizations are not merely negative. They do not speak only of the cessation of craving. There is also reference to joy, fullness, culture and perfect knowledge. Thus nirvana cannot be seen as a diminishing of personhood. It is, rather, its expansion to an indescribable degree, in the direction of knowledge and joy.

'Monks, I will teach you the unconditioned . . . the Truth and the other shore, and what is very difficult to see; the ageless and the permanent, and that which is without hindrance; the deathless and the auspicious and the secure; what has not been before and what is without calamity; what is without suffering, the pure and the Island, the shelter and the refuge will I teach you' (Samyutta 4, 362 and 369). In other words, nirvana is much to be desired. Difficult to achieve, it is beyond change and conditions; and when all passions and sufferings have been ended, and one has dissolved all connection with impure feelings, then one can be conscious of what the Samyutta-Nikaya (43,1,2,iv) calls 'peace without movement or desire', beyond the three unwholesome roots of greed, hate and delusion.

In all forms of Buddhism, there is agreement that nirvana cannot be spoken of; that it is the unconditioned; that the way to it is by overcoming greed, craving and attachment, by freeing oneself from a sense of selfhood, with all its transient desires; and that it brings to the mind calm, tranquillity, peace, joy and enhanced knowledge. As the Lankavatara Sutra puts it, 'You do not vanish in nirvana, nor is nirvana abiding in you; for it transcends the duality of knowing and known and of being and non-being' (2,1,7). Perhaps, then, the best way to think of it is not as self-negation nor yet as self-fulfilment as this is ordinarily understood, but as self-transcendence – finding one's truest reality in being fully attentive to the unconditioned, which brings bliss and knowledge. It must be said that this is, despite all protestations to the contrary, recognizably akin to theism. It places the highest reality in a form of being which is more analogous to awareness, knowledge and bliss than to matter, randomness and unconsciousness. The distinction from forms of theism is the lack of emphasis on creativity or activity in the Supreme Mind, and the very extreme reticence about its character. 'The eternal-unthinkable is the exalted condition of self-realization and also of highest reality . . . because it has nothing to do with existence and non-existence it is no doer' (Lankavatara Sutra, 2,17). It is a form of being beyond action and beyond conditions; so by comparison with conditioned and impermanent things, it is non-existent.

This reticence about the supreme reality, the unconditioned, is most welcome after some human claims to know the inner workings of the being of God. Buddhists do not accept the inspiration of the Veda; so their comments do not depend upon a verbal revelation, but upon the experience of the Buddha, the Enlightened One. Since he speaks only of what is useful, of what can bring liberation, discourses about the inner nature of the supremely real are not very important for him. Nevertheless, one has to be concerned about what human liberation really is; about what the supreme goal of human action might be, about what Enlightenment is. To that extent, one cannot avoid questions about the nature of liberation. The Buddhist view seems to be that one can speak only of the way to it, not of the thing itself. Yet we must still have reason to think that we really are on the way to something, not just to some intense psychological state. We want to know; can the goal be reached? The experience of Gautama testifies that it is possible. So Buddhism, more than any other faith, does not rely on revelation from God. It relies on a testimony to a particular kind of human experience of the unconditioned; it takes a minimalist view of the creative action of God. We might say that, at least in one school of Mahayana, and in some others implicitly, it is theistic, in that it speaks of Eternal Mind as the truest reality, or at least as the best analogy we have for the truest reality. But it is non-theistic, in so far as it attributes to this Mind no action. It can be achieved or attained; but it does not prompt, help or reveal itself.

The problem of the existence of the finite world remains, however, in Buddhism as in orthodox Indian cults. And there are many forms of Buddhism which do take a more positive view than the extreme reserve of Buddhaghosa of the origination and nature of the conditioned. I will consider one text from the Mahayana tradition, *The Awakening of Faith*, traditionally attributed to the second-century Indian sage Asvaghosha, but completely available only in a Chinese version of about 550 CE.[7] The positive tone comes out in such statements as this: 'From the beginning, Suchness [*tathata*] in its nature is fully provided with all excellent qualities . . . great qualities . . . great wisdom . . . true cognition . . . eternity, bliss, Self and purity . . . immutability and freedom . . . though it has, in reality, all these excellent qualities, it does not have any characteristics of differentiation' (65). This simple, impassible, eternal, immutable being of bliss, wisdom and knowledge is indeed spoken of as Mind, and to it are ascribed numberless excellent qualities. It is, in other words, a state of perfection, far from being non-existent, impersonal or abstract. Moreover, it is in one sense quite other than any finite mind precisely because of its possession of such unsurpassably excellent properties. On the other hand, 'From the beginning corporeal form and Mind have been non-dual'(72). That is to say, 'Mind includes in itself all states of being of the phenomenal world and the transcendental world'(28). It is essential to this form of Mahayana Buddhism that reality is non-dual; that the phenomenal (the apparent) and the transcendental (the real) are two aspects of the same thing. 'Mind has two aspects . . . the Absolute (tathata) and phenomena (samsara) are mutually inclusive'(31).

That means that the attainment of nirvana is not a transfer from the empirical world to the realm beyond; since there is no realm beyond; there is only the one world, seen either as empirical or as transcendental. Thus it is that 'All sentient beings intrinsically abide in eternity and are entered into nirvana'(46). All that is needed is to realize this, and the unsatisfactory nature of impermanent nature (which was always in a sense illusion) will be overcome in the experience of absolute bliss (which is only seeing the same reality in its true nature).

It is accepted that it sounds odd to say that the Absolute and the phenomenal are one, when 'True Mind is eternal, permanent, immutable, pure and self-sufficient'(35); and when 'all modes of mind and consciousness are the products of ignorance'(41). What greater difference could there be than that between the immutably real and the ephemeral illusion? Thus the text says, 'All explanations by words are provisional and without validity . . . all things are equally in the state of Suchness . . . incapable of being verbally explained or thought of'(33).

As with Sankara, whose views were influenced by Buddhism,[8] there is a problem of whether one is going to say that Suchness is completely indescribable, or that it can be spoken of at least as if it possessed properties. So on the one hand, Suchness is 'truly empty (*sunya*) . . . it has never been related to any defiled states of existence, it is free from all marks of individual distinction of things'(34). It is impassible, immutable and simple. Yet, on the other hand, 'Suchness or the Dharmakaya [literally, the self-subsistent Buddha-nature or 'body'] is not empty, but is endowed with numberless excellent qualities'(76). It is at once explained that 'the soiled states of defilement . . . merely exist in illusion'(77); they are seen only by the pluralistic outlook held by defiled minds in *samsara*. Yet they are seen; and in some sense *samsara* does exist. 'Since the Dharmakaya is the essence of corporeal form, it is capable of appearing in corporeal form'(72). The distinction is between essence and manifestation or appearance. The essence is wholly ineffable; but from the point of view of beings in the finite world it can be described as having attributes. We can know that 'the essential nature of Mind is unborn and is imperishable'(32). This knowledge is founded on the experience of those who are enlightened – 'When Bodhisattvas become free from activating mind, they will be free from the perceiving [of duality] . . . the Dharmakaya knows no such thing as distinguishing this from that'(71). To the extent that this is really founded on experience, it must be the case that, in a real sense, what is said to be ultimately real is still spoken of as the object of experience – as, in a way, appearance still. The claim to transcend any form of personal experience at all is not one that can be accepted uncritically. It is true that the enlightened souls claim to have transcended individual consciousness, to have passed beyond duality into an undifferentiated state. But all they can really say of this is that 'If a man is able to . . . understand that Mind is beyond what it is thought to be, then he will be able to . . . enter the realm of Suchness'(73). The difficulty about a person who claims to have experienced the Ineffable is that he cannot really say what he has experienced. Nor can we be sure that he is justified in saying that it is in itself ineffable, rather than that he is unable to describe it. Thus the claim to have transcended duality cannot simply be accepted at face value. What is being spoken of is an experienced state still. If it is an experience human concepts are unable to apply to, and which is therefore beyond our linguistic categories, unable to be divided up in ways which our concepts may in some form mirror, then we are hardly entitled to claim knowledge that it is in itself wholly undifferentiated, simple or unoriginated. There is a peculiar paradox in asserting both that one has entered into a state which is beyond all description; and that one can say one has attained the absolute essential truth, which one *knows* to be simple, unborn, pure and imperishable. How, if it is beyond description, can one know that one has attained true reality; or that it is imperishable and unborn? These are grand claims to make for the completely unknowable – to know that it cannot come into being or perish, that there is no more ultimate reality; that it is truly self-sufficient and changeless. One might make claims about ultimate reality on the basis of experience. But if one does that, one can never be logically certain that what one experiences is in fact the case. Even if one experiences something which seems quite unique and ineffable, one cannot be certain that it is so.

The point of these remarks is not to throw doubt on the experience of enlightenment. But it is to throw doubt on the certainty of any claims, arising out of such an experience, that one has knowledge of ultimate reality, or of a reality which is immutable and simple. I would grant that enlightened souls do claim to have a sort of experience which is one of great bliss and enhanced awareness; and they do feel themselves to have entered into a state which is beyond full description. But there is a great logical and a great epistemological difficulty with taking these claims to express a form of ultimate truth. The logical difficulty is that they do make positive claims, and ones extremely difficult to substantiate, about ultimate reality. To say that something never originated and will never perish; that it is in itself impassible and simple – these are extraordinarily bold claims to make. There is a logical paradox even in saying that one knows that there exists something about which no one can know anything. The claim that one has experienced a reality which is beyond one's own powers of description – 'Mind is beyond what it is thought to be' – all one's efforts to describe it seem to be inadequate – is perfectly comprehensible. But it is quite different from saying that one knows one has experienced a reality which is unborn and imperishable. How could one know such a thing? This brings us to the epistemological difficulty. The logical difficulty was that one was saying important things about the unsayable. The epistemological difficulty is that there is no way of being sure that an object of experience has the qualities one thinks it to have. And since one has not existed for ever and will not continue to exist for ever (or at the very least one cannot now experience such everlasting existence) one could not be in a position to confirm that anything was without beginning or end. One could only make such a claim as the result of argument. And it is therefore by argument that such claims must be assessed.

I suggest, then, that the operative force of the apophatic statements about Suchness (that it is empty, simple and eternal) is that concepts seem to be inadequate to characterize the object of the ultimately enlightened experience. Indeed, it is so unlike the ordinary experience of finite objects in the world that it seems to be even beyond the duality of subject and object. Awareness of a

distinct conscious self (that form of non-thetic consciousness which
is aware of the observing self at the same time as one is observing
some external object) fades away. One is no longer aware of oneself
as observing, being distinct from that object which is observed.
There is, rather, an experience as of pure consciousness, where no
finite object is to be discerned, and no observing subject which is
clearly distinct. There is only a feeling of expanded consciousness.
But one has to remember that it is the insufficiency of human
concepts which is in question here. One can say: that is how it
seems. But any positive claims must be founded upon and supported
by arguments. How can we know there is a simple, eternal, impassible, self-sufficient reality? The Buddhist claim is that when ignorance is dispelled, it becomes clear. But what that comes down to is
that Buddhist meditation-practice teaches a certain way or path to
which that is the postulated goal. Ultimately, its truth depends
upon the authority of the Buddha, the one who is enlightened. In
that sense, Buddhism is a revealed religion, founded on the authority of a particular person, who claims to know what is ultimately
true. Or perhaps it is more accurate to say that he refuses to speak
of such things as 'ultimate truth', and simply speaks of the way to
overcome anger, fear and the ultimate emptiness of desire. That
may be more true to the impetus of Buddhism. It is a way of release
from imperfection. It does not speak of what lies beyond, though
release is possible; there is a further shore.

As Buddhists often say, repeating the teaching attributed to
Gautama, if a house is on fire, we do not stop to analyse the nature
of heat; we get out as efficiently as we can. So if we once perceive
the suffering of the world, and the emptiness of desires, we will not
stop to analyse the ultimate nature of nirvana. We will disengage
ourselves from *samsara* as quickly as we can. And yet . . . the whole
question is, 'Is our house on fire?' Is it true that all is suffering,
and that the way to end suffering is to extinguish desire? That there
is release? However agnostic Buddhist doctrine tries to be, in the
end doctrines are there; and very fundamental and important ones.
Buddhism is a religion, above all, because it is a way of release.
One might, after all, come to the view that all is suffering, and
commit suicide, or just try to make the best of it. For Buddhists,
there is a higher way, a true goal, a knowledge as opposed to
ignorance, a bliss as opposed to suffering, a permanent as opposed

to the impermanent. So we must ask about the nature of the goal. And if that nature connot be settled simply by an appeal to experience or to revelation, then it must be adjudged by argument. Perhaps all that can be established is that there is an important aspect of ultimate reality which is completely beyond the range of our concepts to grasp. What is said of it, then, is said because it seems to be the completion, not the mere negation, of a certain route which meditation progressively reveals.

'The essential nature of reality . . . is everywhere the same and without duality . . . it is, in the final analysis, in the state of quiescence'(84). And again, 'The essential nature of reality is free from covetousness . . . from the defilements which originate from the desires of the five senses . . . without suffering and free from anger and anxiety . . . does not have any distinction of body and mind and is free from indolence . . . is always calm and free from confusion . . . is always characterized by knowledge and is free from ignorance'(86). What becomes clear is that the description is taken as a description of a certain route towards the clarifying of mental states, in meditation. When one is set free from desire, anger and anxiety, then one may be said to be in a state of calm and simplicity. One seems to be in a state of enhanced bliss and awareness; and we may say that this is a state without duality, self-contained, quiescent. It is a state of having passed beyond the impermanent to an enduring centre.

In the Buddhist tradition, this is an entrance into a real state which is not just a matter of my own psychology. In one sense it is other than oneself, for it is not bounded by my desires or wishes. But in another sense, it is not distinguished from what I am, since it is the centre of that awareness which I realize in meditation. Moreover, it is said to be the essential nature of reality, the goal which puts an end to suffering. But is it true that reality is essentially quiescence, simple and eternal?

One thing to be stressed is that this state is far beyond the attainments of most people; it is for supreme Bodhisattvas only. On the way to that state, and below it in the hierarchy of being, is the *sambhoga-kaya*, the 'bliss-nature', which 'has an infinite number of corporeal forms, each form having an infinite number of major marks . . . it manifests itself without any bounds . . . in accordance with the needs of the devotee. Yet it always remains firm . . .

endowed with infinite attributes of bliss'(70). In other words, of the essentially quiescent state we must also say that it has infinite attributes of bliss. It would be false to say that the real is wholly and only simple and eternal; for it manifests also in a body of bliss. To see the attributes alone would be to miss what is essential and self-subsistent about the Real. But to see the quiescence alone would be to miss all the attributes of the Real, and to think of it as virtually non-being. Both must be said, so that when you think of the attributes, you can say: 'But it is not only thus'; and when you think of the Unborn and Endless, you must say: 'But the tathagata womb is endowed with numberless excellent qualities'(29).

The Awakening of Faith expounds a doctrine of a personal saviour quite plainly. It begins with the affirmation: 'I take refuge in the greatly compassionate one, the Saviour of the world, omnipotent, omnipresent, omniscient'(23). This could immediately be called a form of theism without qualification, except that this God is not the creator of the world, and does not personally act within it in distinguishable ways. Or so it might be said. But if omnipotence is taken seriously; and if it is held that the world is not other than Suchness, in phenomenal form, some doctrine of creation, as total dependence of the phenomenal on the essentially and self-subsistently real, is present. And the Buddha-Saviour does act in the world in some ways. 'Because of the compassionate protection of the Buddhas [the disciple] will be able to advance on the path to nirvana'(61). If protection means anything, there is some causal influence of the Buddhas on the disciple. If there were not, the whole notion of a Saviour would lapse into vacuity. 'Suchness is . . . provided with suprarational functions and the nature of manifesting itself'(59); thus it does appear in the world, which entails that it causally modifies the structure of appearances so as to include what it otherwise would not have included. While a doctrine of an active God is not present in this form of Mahayana Buddhism, there is after all a belief that there is an omnipotent, omniscient being which can appear within the world and help people towards liberation. So much is this so, that Bodhisattvas 'take a vow that one will liberate all sentient beings, down to the last one, no matter how long it may take them to attain the perfect nirvana'(84). A Bodhisattva 'can manifest himself everywhere in the universe and benefit all sentient beings'(89). I do not think a theist could wish for much more than that.

We seem to have moved a long way from the utter quiescence of non-duality. A rich devotional strain has a proper place in this form of Buddhism: 'If a man meditates wholly on Amitabha Buddha in the world of the Western Paradise and wishes to be born in that world . . . then he will be born there . . . he will see the Buddha at all times'(102). That may not be the final goal of release for oneself, let alone release for all sentient beings. But it is an acceptable stage on the way; and it is a form of liberation from *samsara*.

How can one reconcile that with the teaching: 'A man comes to believe in his essential nature, to know that what exists is the erroneous activity of the mind and that the world of objects in front of him is non-existent . . . this is called gaining nirvana'(58)? I think it must be said that there is a twofold strain at work. One strand of teaching is that rebirth must come to an end; there must be no return to the unreal. But another strand would teach that, since the unreal is nothing, there is nothing to be overcome. Thus one is entered into nirvana now: 'All phenomena are identical with Suchness'(29); and there is no need for a subsequent release. It is a matter of how one sees one's life now, as bound by the desire for fruits, or as liberated by union with the eternal, which is manifested as the Saviour Buddha now and, more fully, in the Western Paradise beyond death.

As with Vedanta, one can see how it is an oversimplification to say that Buddhism is non-theistic; that it believes in a cessation of individuality; in a finally impersonal reality; and in a denial of any value to the world. All these statements are in a sense true; but they cannot be taken in an unqualified sense. Buddhists do not worship or pray to one personal creator God. And yet 'the Dharmakaya of all the Buddhas, being one and the same everywhere, is omnipresent . . . they reveal themselves in accordance with the mentalities of all the various sentient beings'(91). Devotion can then be paid to the Buddha-nature, which may be spoken of as omnipotent and omniscient. Buddhists do hope for a state in which 'there will be no more rising of the [deluded activities of] Mind'(58). And yet they aspire, not to extinction, but to a perfecting enlightenment and an entry into eternal bliss, by comparison with which the sufferings of this life fade into relative unreality. Buddhists claim that essential reality is 'free from all marks of individual distinction'(34). Yet 'the one and true Mind . . . is endowed with numberless excellent qualities'(76). Buddhists affirm that all is suffering (*dukkha*). And yet, 'All sentient beings, if only they were able to realize it, are already in nirvana'; and thus one can live beyond suffering, as the joyful manifestation of Suchness, and its phenomenal manifestation.

There is, in short, a range of attitudes a Buddhist can take, from total world-renunciation to a life of compassion for all beings or of devotion to a personal Saviour.

It would, of course, be true to point out that these views are historically and geographically distinct, so that the whole range is rarely available to any one individual. And it might well be said that Amida Buddhism is really only one rather extreme side-trend even in the Mahayana. Nevertheless, this range of possibilities does exist within Buddhism.

So it can be positively misleading to separate Buddhism from Hinduism or from Christianity, as though one was distinguishing one monolithic body of doctrines from others. Of course there are identifying features of those who follow the way of the Buddha. They will accept the four noble truths; they will seek for enlightenment, following the path of the Enlightened ones who have gone before; they will embrace a doctrine of non-self, the impermanence of all finite things; and pursue formalized techniques of meditation and self-discipline. These things delineate a framework of life within which a person can construct a personal appropriation of faith. But that framework leaves open many possibilities of interpretation, as we have seen.

To take just one example, the doctrine that all is suffering (*dukkha*) can be taken in a very pessimistic sense, so that all desires and pleasures are to be eschewed, and one seeks only the elimination of attachment.[9] But it can also be taken, quite plausibly, as saying that the sorts of desire which lead one to be unduly concerned with one's own subsequent pains or pleasures (the 'fruits' of action) carry a deep unsatisfactoriness within them. They are indeed to be overcome; but not by a complete abandonment of the world. Rather, what is required is a transformed vision of the world, as the manifestation of nirvana, which one can enjoy in purity when one has overcome the desire for egoic fruits, and takes things just as they are, as the manifestations of what, when most truly seen, is unrestricted bliss.[10] Similarly, the doctrine of no-self (*anatta*) can be taken either as saying that there is nothing beyond the impermanent desires which constitute a certain succession of conscious states, without foundation. Or it can be taken as teaching that beyond the relatively illusory self there is an underlying Mind which is fully omniscient and awake, with which one can be united.

Each doctrinal position has a range of possible interpretations, spread out on a sort of scale from a straightforward, literal, 'hard' or 'pure' interpretation to an elusive, stretched, figurative or 'deep' interpretation. Each individual believer has a number of possible thematic routes he can take, through different interpretations within the structural framework. The general set of possible structural positions exists, whether fully worked out or not, in each religious tradition. Thus it may well turn out that believers in very different traditions take very similar thematic routes of faith. There can in that sense be a deeper kinship between adherents of diverse religions than there is between adherents of the same religious group whose thematic routes are quite different. It is for that reason that it is misleading to group people simply into different, competing 'religions'; and that one cannot generalize to say that Buddhism, as such, is a 'world-denying' faith or that Christianity, as such, is a 'world-affirming' one. The contrast of the world-saving Bodhisattvas with the fourth-century desert Fathers of the Christian Church should make the misleadingness of such generalizations at once apparent.

There is nothing wrong, however, with particularizing further, and saying that a *specific* view is world-denying. One can even say that the conceptual position that the finite world is created without motive is more naturally taken to be less world-affirming than the conceptual position that the finite world is created for the sake of the values it can realize. Nevertheless, by the time these positions have been qualified by other structural elements, the natural or *prima facie* suggestions may easily be cancelled out – as when Ramanuja makes lack of motive a positive affirmation of the playful joyfulness of creation, and a spontaneous expression of the unlimited excellence of Braham. Or, from the Christian tradition, the idea of the world as a vale of tears, in which most of the inhabitants are destined for everlasting damnation, is surely not an unqualified affirmation that creation is, as such, good.

We can find in religious traditions of many different sorts a similarity of structural positions and possible thematic routes of faith. It is partly for that reason that it does make sense to include Buddhism in a study of the concept of God. Though that specific concept is of no importance for the vast majority of Buddhists, it would, as I hope I have shown, be mistaken to think that one cannot trace in Buddhism a similar range of themes to that which can be found in the overtly theistic traditions. In particular, the themes of the ineffability of the ultimate reality; of the relatively 'unreal', or non-self-sufficient character of the finite; and of the possibility of a finite manifestation of the ultimately real in time (in the person of an enlightened one), emerge as strongly characteristic of Buddhist life. In some sense, for the most severe Theravadin Buddhist, the truly real is a fulfilment, and not a negation, of personal being. For did not the Buddha, with the attaining of nirvana, experience the passing away of the perishable and the entrance into eternal bliss?

I am most certainly not saying that all religions really believe the same thing. Nor do I wish to confuse different faiths into one squashy syncretic muddle. On the contrary, I am more inclined to say that no two people can ever agree on matters of religious belief, if they probe deeply enough. What is of interest is that the differences do not always lie where people think they do, in the obvious verbal oppositions between contrasting doctrines. And I am concerned to show that people in very different traditions may quite fairly be said to be engaged in a similar sort of enterprise, and to exhibit similar sets of attitudes and ranges of difference within those traditions. The implication is that one cannot say that one tradition, as such, is true and the others false. But one is not immediately thrown to the contrary view that all traditions must be equally true or equally misleading. One is free to explore the structural configurations of belief and to see how similarities may lie in surprising places; and the greatest differences may lie between those who live within one 'agreed' set of credal beliefs. In the case I am considering, the idea of God, there appears to be a real sense in which many people in different traditions, in virtually every part of the world, may be said to be engaged in a similar set of pursuits. And it would not be unfair to represent this as a quest for God, even when they would not use that conceptual framework for what they are doing. The disputes about the nature of Suchness in Buddhism reflect disputes within Christianity about the nature of God – whether he is a person or the 'Actus Purus', beyond time and change. There is a common quest; though it does not follow that every way of expressing the nature of that quest is equally useful or adequate.

A Christian should not say to the Buddhist, 'Ah, you are looking for God, though you do not realize it'. But he might say, 'My quest for God and your search for nirvana have very deep similarities; and the range of differences between Buddhists on this issue are reflected by a similar range of differences between Christians. From my perspective, therefore, I can fairly represent what you are doing as a quest for God, as long as I am careful to qualify my understanding of God suitably. You can represent what I am doing as a quest for nirvana. From there the discussion can proceed (if we want). But something has been established – there are complex sets of agreements which do not run along the traditional boundaries between the religions. And recognizing that puts us in a new and more fruitful position, as we live alongside one another.'

This is the point at which one may explore a little further the basic fiduciary structure, and see how different thematic routes may be suggested by the basic matrices which are given by authoritative teachers in the various traditions. Most religions depend upon authoritative teaching at some point; and, as has been noted in the previous chapter, the nature of this authority can lie on a scale anywhere between the polar notions of a dictated form of words and of a particularly impressive sort of human experience. We have seen that Vedanta relies on the 'heard' words of the Veda; though the hearers were themselves great sages who had practised ascetic disciplines and were advanced in meditation, before they were fit to hear truly. Buddhism relies on the omniscience of Sakyamuni, by which he comes to know the Dharma, the truth about the inner structure of things. But by the time he comes to know that truth, he has himself passed beyond the finite conditions of human life, to become one with all the Buddhas, the omniscient and compassionate Dharmakaya. In a sense, then, the revelation comes from beyond normal human experience, even beyond humanity itself, as one human life becomes the vehicle of the Buddha-nature.

The fact is that words of Scripture are not just found lying around in the forest. They are uttered by sages and prophets, in particular contexts; and so there is a continuity between the two poles of utterly passive receptiveness to divine dictation and the disciplined and heroic grasping of the final truth for oneself which the Veda and the Buddha respectively represent. Particular forms of belief may select one of a great number of possible places in that continuum; but most of them will qualify their own belief by the incorporation of paradox into their account, which introduces the polar element, as a minor and qualifying strand. For example, Sankara may say that the words of the Veda, in their exact form and inflection, are infallibly true. Yet he will also say that all words belong to the realm of illusion. His dominant image is qualified by the awareness of a contrasting pole of understanding, that knowing the right words is not enough; what is needed is spiritual vision.

A similar polarity exists when one considers representations of the nature of the Real. Here, views can vary from a very active, personalist view of God to the quietist and passive notion of the Void. The Buddhist account is the most agnostic or reticent of all; yet the use of personal terms connoting wisdom, compassion and knowledge, awareness and bliss is fairly common with regard to the ultimately real. The Vedantins explicitly use the model of the Self, though that is construed as primarily knowledge and bliss, without creative action being an essential or fully real part of its being. Nevertheless, both Buddhists and Vedantins speak of avatars or of Bodhisattvas who represent creative and saving actions on behalf of other sentient beings, and so an active element is not completely absent in these views, even when it is only a relatively minor theme in the theoretical structure (though not necessarily a minor one in the practical devotional life of believers).

Naturally enough, the theme of the goal of enlightened endeavour varies in a way proportioned to the account given of the nature of the Real. Here, the poles are, at one extreme, the idea of extinction of the individual self and release from all limitation; and, at the other extreme, the idea of a loving relationship with a personal Lord. Some Vedantin and Buddhist traditions incline to the former pole, though again paradoxical qualifications are present, for the extinction of the self is also the entrance into eternal bliss, not mere non-being. But for other traditions within Vedanta and Buddhism, devotion to a personal Lord, and taking refuge in the Buddha of the Western Paradise, play the key role; and the paradoxical qualification takes the form of saying that such a Lord is not ultimately real.[11]

As for the means to achieve the goal, the two corresponding poles are those of effort and grace. Indian sects are most obviously divided into those which stress the monkey-method of release, whereby one has to work hard, like a baby monkey clinging to its mother, to attain release after many aeons of lives. And then there are sects which offer the cat-method, whereby one is carried by sheer grace, as a kitten is carried in the mouth of its mother, without doing anything first. Again the paradoxes, if properly attended to, prevent exclusivity in this area; it is clear that the Lord saves whom he will, but that also we must respond to him ourselves and work out our salvation with diligence.

The two final strands of the fiduciary structure are that of the condition of human limitation and its cause. Those who incline to stress the huge divide between the infinite and the finite will perhaps incline to a world-denying attitude, which attributes human existence to ignorance or involvement with matter as such. The cause of this ignorance will be the belief that finite reality exists – that is, that it has intrinsic value and goals worth aiming at. Whereas those who incline to envisage the Real in more personal or qualified terms may give more importance to finite reality and adopt a generally world-affirming attitude, for which there are worthwhile values to be achieved by human action. Then the cause of human ills and limitations is liable to be ascribed to disordered desire, to the misuse of responsibility, rather than to finite selfhood as such.

I do not wish to oversystematize these themes; and even within one sect it is possible to find quite a diverse thematic structure deployed, due to all sorts of historical and cultural influences. My only aim is to show that there is a polarity within each strand, and that these polarities form continua which roughly correlate with one another. Paradox is often employed within religion to acknowledge the existence of such polarities, and the insufficiency of any one model to give a fully adequate account of the material it is attempting to deal with.

There is one other factor that is of some importance in the life of religion. That is that every position is ambiguous, in the sense that it can be taken in different ways in the life of the believer. Everyone knows that religion is very often a force for great evil; and it is part of the ambiguity of religion that it allows for this. The point of the whole structure is that it sets out a way of human liberation from the conditions which restrict human existence; so it is an essential part of the structure that it places the normal condition of humanity as one of ignorance or disordered desire. It is hardly surprising then – on the contrary, it is part of the internal logic of religion – that many, or even most, believers will continue to evince their ignorance or disordered desires in their understanding and practice of faith. It may be said that there are three basic ways of using each position in one's own life. It may be used as a way of repressing the self; or as a way of gratifying the self and its desires; or, finally, as a way of transcending the self in relation to self-existent value.

In the case of revelation, it is readily seen how this can be used to repress the self, by taking away human judgement and maturity, and insisting on the passive reception of authoritatively proclaimed truths. Similarly, revelation can gratify the self by giving power and status to those who claim to know the truth and impose it on others. It is difficult indeed to tread the narrow way between these failures of understanding, and find a fully mature response to the revelation of the nature of the Real which is given in Scripture or by an authoritative teacher. The right response is that which brings one to maturity through permeation by a higher Self, not repressing but expanding one's personal powers; and which sees that such a response cannot be imposed on others by compulsion.

Doctrines of Brahman or the Real can also be used to repress the self, by leading one to devalue one's own personality in fear before an oppressing witness and judge of all. And it may lead one to gratify the self by giving rise to a sense that whatever one does is validated by the Real; so that one lives beyond good and evil, with everything sanctioned by a power beyond criticism.

The representation of the goal is repressive when it inculcates a quietistic and self-punishing asceticism – the way Sakyamuni renounced when he chose the 'middle way'. It is self-gratifying when it leads to a sense of spiritual élitism, which places one on a plane above others, and thus leads to a sense of superiority in the most subtle way of all – the way which says, 'I am not proud; but I am worthy of respect because of the higher Self which lives in me'. This too is seen to be a false spirituality by all sages in the

Vedantic traditions; but that does not stop it being commonplace in religious life of all sorts.

The means is repressive when it leads to a hatred of matter, of the body and of the world as such. And it is self-gratifying when it leads to an exclusivism which places one in an elect community while all others are 'unsaved' or without hope or at best inferior beings.

Doubtless there is an endless number of perversions of faith; but it is very clear that being a member of a religious community is no guarantee of morality or wisdom. It is therefore important to be aware of the ambiguities of faith, which arise from spiritual truths being misused to bolster self-hatred or undue self-love. The religious path is one in which one must finally overcome even the selfish desire for paradise, the last desire of the divided self, and live for the Self alone, beyond fear and desire. Thus the Buddhist path can be seen as an unequivocally religious one, whose structure is operatively similar to that of theism, and quite distinct from movements such as Marxism, which offers no path to the liberation of the self, or from purely philosophical theories, which are concerned only with speculation and not with the progressive transfiguration of human life by the transcendence of self.[12] One can discern in the many Buddhist traditions the sixfold determining structure of the religious life; the necessity of the iconic vision to a religious view; and the specification of a set of reactive attitudes by a basic matrix, which is revealed by an authoritative teacher who has discerned the way to liberation. These are themes that we shall be able to trace in the Semitic traditions deriving from Judaism. And in such a context of a lived practice, one can see how concepts of Brahman, of nirvana, of Suchness and of God have an operative similarity which enables one to speak without undue distortion of a common vision of the nature of the ultimately Real and the attaining of the objective goal of human life by relation to it, in the major religious traditions of the world. The clarification and further exploration of this common vision, and the acceptance of its manifold cultural and historical expressions, is one of the most important tasks facing religious believers in the modern world.

The Fiduciary Structure

		A	B
1 Authority	Dictation / Experience	Dictation	Experience
2 The Real	Active person / Passive Void	Active person	Passive Void
3 The Goal	Love Obedience / Absorption	Love Obedience	Absorption
4 Means	Grace / Moral, Ascetic and Ritual Effort	Grace	Moral, Ascetic and Ritual Effort
5 Limitation	World affirmation / World denial	World affirmation	World denial
6 Cause	Sin Judgement / Ignorance Karma	Sin Judgement	Ignorance Karma

4

Images of God in the Hebrew Bible

It may be thought that Judaism stands at the furthest possible remove from the Indian traditions of Vedanta and from Buddhism. The worship of idols and strange gods is consistently condemned in the Hebrew Bible: and Jahweh is said to be a 'jealous God', who has set apart his people for the exclusive worship of him alone. Jahweh is also spoken of, throughout the Hebrew Bible, in an extremely personalistic and objectified way. That is, he is construed as a King, a Shepherd, a Judge and Father of the people: as one who stands over against the whole created order, making moral demands on the people of Israel and having very specific purposes for their role in the world. There is little trace of that one morally demanding and historically acting God in Indian thought. There is virtually no tradition of prophetic teaching which condemns the injustice of the state and calls for a national commitment to one way of life. What, then, could there possibly be in common between these streams of faith? Must they not meet each other with incomprehension and hostility, however veiled in politeness?

The fact that Judaism is unequivocally an ethnic faith has meant that at least it does not try to impose its way of life by force on those of other nationalities. It is a way for one people; and as long as it is permitted to live in that way, it does not threaten the way of life of others. Nonetheless, a Jew can scarcely have complete disinterest in the spiritual life of other peoples. There is, after all, only one Creator of the universe, and it must be of some importance that all creatures can come to know and serve him in some way, even if it is not by obedience to the Torah. There is need for a philosophical account of the nature of this God, which might clarify the way in which other peoples might relate to him, or come to understand what he is.

There is no such account in the Bible itself, which confines itself strictly to the revelations given to the patriarchs and prophets of Israel. Both the Upanishads and the Buddhist Pali Canon contain sections which may fairly be regarded as philosophical or doctrinal, exploring views of the nature of ultimate reality in a reflective and meditative way. In the Hebrew Bible there are virtually no passages of that sort. Philosophical reflection on the nature of Jahweh, the God of Abraham, Isaac and Jacob, is almost entirely absent. It is accordingly very difficult to know what the Hebrews thought about God; that is, how they themselves interpreted the words they used about God. I rather suspect they thought as many different things about God as different philosophers do. But we do have enough material to construct a fairly clear idea of the biblical God, even though its interpretation cannot be decisively established.[1]

Philosophical accounts have been developed within Judaism. Perhaps the most highly regarded is that of Moses Maimonides, the twelfth-century Spanish Jew who wrote the Mishnah Torah, a major codification of the rabbinic law and ritual; and whose formulation of thirteen fundamental elements of Jewish belief has come to be widely accepted as an almost official creed of orthodox Judaism. He is generally thought to be the greatest of the medieval orthodox Jewish theologians; and he is highly regarded within Judaism as one who stands recognizably within orthodoxy, even by those who do not share all his views. His major philosophical work is *The Guide for the Perplexed*, and in it he works out a philosophical account of the nature of God which aims to combine the insights of Aristotelian philosophy with the revealed traditions of Judaism. In examining this doctrine, we shall find a view which has a central place in Jewish orthodoxy, and by relation to which all other philosophical views within Judaism must define themselves.

In this case I think it is important to get fairly clear about the revealed scriptural view of God, since Maimonides assumes its truth, and does not by any means wish to contrast his philosophical view with a different, biblical, one. He wants his interpretation to be taken as a fair and correct one. But the tone and character of Aristotle's philosophy is so different from that of the Bible that we need to look at it rather carefully. For it is the biblical teaching about God which seems so very different from the Indian traditions; and we will need to assess the extent to which this is really the case, and the extent to which Maimonides can fairly claim to present a view of God which is both biblical and philosophical.

I will begin with a text; it is, I think, wholly representative, but spectacularly ornate. It is from the prophet Habakkuk, chapter 3, verses 3–15:

> Was thy wrath against the rivers, O Lord? Was thy anger against the rivers or thy indignation against the sea, when thou didst ride upon thy horses, upon thy chariot of victory? Thou didst strip the sheath from thy bow and put the arrow to the string. Thou didst cleave the earth with rivers. The mountains saw thee and writhed; the raging waters swept on; the deep gave forth its voice, it lifted its hands on high. The sun and moon stood still in their habitation at the light of thine arrows as they sped, at the flash of thy glittering spear. Thou didst bestride the earth in fury, thou didst trample the nations in anger . . . Thou didst trample the sea with thy horses, the surging of mighty waters.

Here is a picture of the earth-shaking warrior god of storm and battle, riding on the clouds, striding over the hills, his robes red with the blood of his enemies, sending plagues before him and drawing death behind, hurling his lightning-bolts from his thundering chariot. It is a dominant picture of God in the prophetic writings. But it is not the only one. Another major image is that of God as the King of Israel, whom Isaiah saw enthroned in or above the Temple in Jerusalem, his robe filling the whole Temple (Is 6:1); who is later described as having his throne in heaven and the earth for his footstool (Is 66:1); and further as sitting on his throne beyond even the highest heaven (2 Chron 6:18). Jeremiah speaks of him as being present everywhere (Jer 23:23). Evidently, this is a King who is no normally embodied being, but who can appear in variously embodied forms. Then there is the picture of God as shepherd of his people: 'He will gather the lambs in his arms, he will carry them in his bosom' (Is 40:10). I suppose it is clear to all that this is a metaphor; God does not look after a flock of physical sheep. But it is just worth remarking that there is no notice saying: 'Beware, metaphor ahead'; any more than there are notices, 'This sentence must be taken literally', in other parts of the Hebrew Bible. It takes no subtle philosophical argument to believe that none of these pictures is to be taken in a literal sense. For this reason, I do not find it wholly satisfactory to say, as is sometimes said, that the biblical idea of God is anthropomorphic. I would prefer to call it anthropophanic, inasmuch as God certainly appears to the prophets in the likeness of a man. The trouble with saying that he has the form of a man is that the central Hebrew prohibition is on making any image of God at all. As Isaiah 40 puts it, 'To whom can God be compared? He is not like an idol.' (40:19). True, this may only mean that he is living and not an artefact. Yet the adherents of other gods did not identify their gods with their idols; their thought was that a god could be accurately represented by an idol or embodied in an idol; that it could be properly expressed in some visible form. So the Hebrew aversion to idols seems to be an aversion to representing God in any visible form at all; as if one could say, 'This is truly what he is like'.

There may not seem to be much difference between making a physical image of a god and creating a poetic verbal image; especially since, for the Hebrew mind, we are told, words themselves carry something of the reality of that which they denote. The controlling notion behind the prohibition is perhaps that one should not worship or bow down to any object which represents anything finite or created (cf. Ex 20:4). One cannot easily worship a poem; and one can say that, while the words denote something real, that reality is not in truth as it is imaginatively depicted.

My own view is that the Hebrews were rather unfair to idolaters; fairness in religion was never one of their more notable virtues. Sophisticated Hindus do not suppose that their god is like their idols; but maybe the very unsophisticated attribute magical powers to these physical symbols. Clearly, the unsophisticated also take the biblical images of God literally, saying that God truly has a real, masculine human form. But at least there is no tangible object to which they can attribute magical powers (though the Ark of the Covenant, despite all these theological precautions, was itself treated as a magic talisman in the early wars).

Perhaps, then, the prohibition on images was an attempt to prevent magical uses of the divinity by giving him tangible expression. But it can certainly be said that Jewish reflection on these passages has consistently stressed the incomparability of God, in the sense that he is not similar to any created thing. I doubt whether this is just a later sophistication; but I do not wish to make too much of this point. I should be content to hold that the prophetic images cannot all be taken literally; and that there are no internal criteria for saying that some of them are literal and some are not, or that some elements of them are literal and some are not. There may be philosophical difficulties here about whether metaphors must have some elements which are translatable into literal terms, if they are to denote at all.[2] Before we sink in that swamp, however, there are two more prominent images from the prophets that deserve a mention.

One is the almost over-familiar image of God as Father. What is not over-familiar is the thought that he is the Father, not so much of all creation, as of Israel. 'Out of Egypt I called my son . . . it was I who taught Ephraim to walk, I took them up in my arms . . . I bent down to them and fed them' (Ho 11:1–4). Sometimes this view seems very crude: God chooses Israel to lord it over other nations, and do to them as they had done to it. At other times, as in Isaiah 19, Israel's vocation is more clearly seen as spiritual leadership of the nations. In both versions, the idea of a special vocation is strong. Even when the tribal God of Deuteronomy 32:8 ('Jahweh's portion is his people') has given way to the one and only God of Deutero-Isaiah, this God retains a unique relation to Israel. He has chosen it to be his servant, his son, his priestly people. Again, the metaphors are working hard. They strongly suggest something to us; we know it is not literally true, as depicted; but we would be very hard put to it to say what it is, in other terms.

The prophets do put it in other terms. But they are no philosophical help; for they offer only another image, one which contrasts strongly with that of the avenging storm warrior, and even with that of the extremely stern, though finally forgiving, father. 'The Lord delights in you . . . and as the bridegroom rejoices over the bride, so shall your God rejoice over you' (Is 62:5). God, the rejoicing bridegroom, finds Israel deeply precious to him, and he sings and is joyful over her return. This is a passionate God, who is filled with sadness by separation and filled with delight by reconciliation. His people make a difference to him and he is affected emotionally by what they do. This is distinctly different from the impassible God of the Alexandrian Fathers: but, of course, they would heartily agree that it is metaphor.

So now, armed with these five prophetic images of God (and we could add others – Judge, Teacher, Liberator and so on), which all would agree to be largely metaphorical, we must return to face the question: what lies behind the metaphors? What is the prosaic reality behind the poetry? It is remarkable that the biblical writers make no attempt at all to answer this question. In particular, they do not offer a superior, more abstract or philosophical concept which discloses a reality hidden behind these very personalistic symbols for the devout. Nevertheless, these are not just poems written for some aesthetic pleasure or imaginative play. These are the images deployed by prophets, men who stood in an established position in the life of Israel and filled a specific set of expectations. They had, and were expected to have, visions, dreams and auditions; they uttered inspired words; they 'spoke the words of the Lord' to his people: or at least they claimed to do so. They do provide information – not about the nature of God or about his cosmic purposes; but about the future of their own tribes, and the explanation of the meaning of their history. The prophets issue specific predictions, which are the guarantees of their authority, if they come true, and an invitation to a public stoning to death, if they do not. God says 'Who is like me? Let him proclaim it, let him declare and set it forth before me. Who has announced from of old the things to come? Let them tell us what is yet to be' (Is 44:7). God is the one who shapes the future, and who tells his prophets what is yet to be. He is a God who acts and speaks. What the images speak of, then, is that power which shapes the future and declares it. I doubt if the prophets would have easily understood the drawing of a logical distinction between a religious language-game and a historical language-game; between uses of language to speak of religion and uses of language to speak of historical occurrences. When they spoke of history, they spoke of the acts of God: and when they spoke of God, they spoke of the one who is known by his mighty acts – the deliverance of Israel from Egypt; amazing victories in battle; and the future return to a transformed Jerusalem. When they speak of Jahweh as 'the living God', they mean that he accomplishes specific things in history.

This element of creative historical action is even stronger in the earlier parts of Scripture, where the miraculous element is greatly heightened. God, or his angel, causes great plagues, throws armies into panic and causes women to conceive in miraculous circumstances. He causes the sun to stand still, rivers to dry up, earth-quakes to destroy walls and towers, and manna to fall from the skies. He walks in a cloud of smoke and fire before the Israelites in the wilderness; he fills the Temple with the dazzling glory of his presence, and he confirms the authority of his chosen prophets by signs and wonders of various sorts. In these early records, Jahweh is constantly and directly acting on behalf of his people to deliver them from their enemies, punish them for their sins and lead them to a land of their own where they can worship him in peace. The great metaphorical images which the prophets use are images for the action of a dynamic, interacting will, bringing things to be for a moral purpose, concerned for the realization of a particular purpose in history by a particular group of people, the Jews.

Believers differ on the interpretation of these historical records. For the more traditional, they simply assert miraculous events which happened. Others will take them to be largely imaginative, poetic accounts which read back into a long past era the concerns of another age, and which bring out the *meaning* of remembered events by portraying them in miraculous form. Thus a poetic metaphor, of God surrounding Jerusalem like a fire, may be turned into an objective historical event in the far past. For the latter group, the recorded historical events are themselves metaphors or images. The element of miracle tries to bring out the spiritual meaning of the event, but is not to be taken literally.[3]

Whether these records are taken literally or not, the images used for the God who is said to be thus acting are clearly metaphorical in large part. There is agreement that God acts, and that is a distinctive feature of the biblical God. But what exactly is one to understand by 'an act of God'? What is the real nature of the God who acts? Did the biblical writers have a view of this?

It would perhaps be anachronistic to look for a fully consistent view. It is not that the Hebrews were logically inept: but that they rely heavily on paradox and hyperbole. I will take just two examples to make the point. Zephaniah speaks the words of God: 'I will utterly sweep away everything from the face of the earth' (1:2). But just a little later he says, 'I will change the speech of the peoples to a pure speech that all of them may call on the name of the Lord and serve him' (3:9). The logical purist will say that God cannot both destroy everyone and get them all to serve him at the same time. Those more inured to the ways of poets will see here a use of hyperbole, juxtaposing extreme alternative views to express powerful feelings in a rhetorical way. Again, according to Hosea, God says, 'I will destroy you, O Israel . . . compassion is hid from my eyes' (13:9–14). But six verses later he says, 'I will love them freely, for my anger has turned from them' (14:4). Either God is extremely changeable, or we have here again a case of poetic excess and of qualification of one view by its opposite almost immediately.

These points are familiar enough, no doubt. But we need to bear them firmly in mind if we are to try to extract a 'biblical doctrine of God' from such texts as these. We must beware of taking any statement at face value, or in isolation from the contrasting exaggerations which will almost certainly be found near at hand. It is perhaps not surprising that Plato did not like poetry. Yet, though we cannot hope to extract one coherent doctrine, I think we may find enough clues to form at least a general picture of the biblical idea of God. Indeed, it is a positive gain to see that the biblical view will be both vague, many-sided and dynamic in its interplay of contrasting and poetically intensified images. We are in the world of mythic story where the imagination is regarded as having its own mode of access to reality. But such a world is not another world, parallel to this; it is a way of representing this world as expressing a meaning and purpose within its temporal structure.[4]

There are three main conceptions of divine action in the prophetic books. I do not suggest these are quite distinct: but they co-exist with a degree of tension which is never wholly resolved. First, there is the view I shall term 'moralism'. On this view, everything that happens is either a reward for virtue or a punishment for sin. It is well put in the astonishingly myopic Psalm 37: 'I have been young and now am old; yet I have not seen the righteous forsaken or his children begging bread' (37:25). And it is rescinded by a puzzled Jeremiah: 'Righteous art thou, O Lord, when I complain to thee, yet I would plead my case before thee. Why does the way of the wicked prosper?' (12:1). The option that all would be put right after death did not really exist for these prophets; so they were never completely content with the view that God arranges history to punish his enemies and reward his friends, even though that is a constant refrain in the prophetic books. Sometimes this moral balancing-out is represented as taking place almost automatically, rather like the Indian law of karma: 'As you have done, it shall be done to you, your deeds shall return on your own head' (Ob 15); 'Powerful men will be destroyed by their own evil deeds' (Is 1:31). But usually a much more personal note is struck, as in Jeremiah 3:3: 'You have polluted the land with your vile harlotry, therefore the showers have been withheld.' God responds to his people's sin or repentance, by controlling the weather or raising up armies to punish them.

The trouble is, this is not true on most occasions. We might reflect, with Kant, that if it were, people would have a very different concept of morality: since moral conduct would be immediately and apparently prudential.[5] The remarkable passage in Isaiah 53: 'And they made his grave with the wicked . . . although he had done no violence . . . he makes himself an offering for sin' (53:9–10) – is a notable attempt to grapple with the problem of innocent suffering. But we have to say that the moralistic view remains, and is even strengthened in the latest books, where the strict observance of the Sabbath, prohibition of all contact with foreigners and devotion to ritual practices are all made into conditions of achieving material prosperity and getting sufficient rain for the crops.

Nevertheless, that view collapses in face of the blood of the innocents; and so there is a second conception, that of interactionism. God acts sometimes, but does not do everything. Thus he allows things to happen which he does not want: 'You shall be far from oppression . . . if any one stirs up strife, it is not from me' (Is 54:14–15). People can act, despite God; and indeed this does seem to be an implication of the fact of sin itself: 'He looked for justice, but behold, bloodshed; for righteousness, but behold, a cry' (Is 5:7). God looks for and expects justice; but it is not what he gets. And it would be very odd if God made people sin and then punished them for it, though such oddity is not beyond the capacity of some theologians. The main prophetic view is that sin is not from God: 'I am very angry with the nations that are at ease; for while I was angry but a little they furthered the disaster' (Zc 1:15). That is to say, God was quite angry with Israel; but other nations made things much worse than he would have done. This certainly complicates any moralistic view; for now, the innocent suffer the onslaughts of evil men; and such events conflict with what God wants.

It has sometimes been held that there is a deterministic view of the divine will in the prophets: but I think such a thing is impossible to find, without a great deal of special pleading and an omission of many contrary texts. The determinist might call in aid Isaiah 48:3: 'The former things I declared of old . . . then suddenly I did them and they came to pass.' Certainly, Deutero-Isaiah has the strongest doctrine to be found in this part of the Bible of the divine determination of events. But all that is said is that God declares that he will bring specific things to pass; and then he does. This is hardly a doctrine of determinism. It does not say that God decrees everything that happens; only that what he promises to do, he has the power to do and will do. That is quite different. The texts that might support a total divine determination of events are few, vague and fail by a long way to give an unambiguous statement of such a doctrine. On the other hand, the texts that deny it are many and fairly direct.

Jonah 3:10 gives a clear statement: 'When God saw what [the people of Nineveh] did, how they turned from their evil way, God repented of the evil which he had said he would do to them; and he did not do it.' God changed his mind in response to the penitence of those people. He did the same when King Hezekiah repented, and let him live, when he had promised that he would die. And God said to Jeremiah, 'If at any time I declare concerning a nation or a kingdom that I will pluck up and break down and destroy it, and if that nation . . . turns from its evil, I will repent of the evil that I intended to do to it' (Jr 18:7–8). There are many other examples: but the message seems clear, that it is a perfection in God that he stands always ready to change his mind, depending on what his people do. I find it most odd that Peter Geach fails to notice these passages, on behalf of some scholastic notion of divine immutability.[6] For it is at the heart of the prophetic message that, though God threatens death and destruction, yet he stands ready to change his mind, if the people will only repent. What is the point of preaching, if they cannot? And what is the justification of punishing? The God of the prophets is one who responds to what his people do; and that means that he himself does not ordain everything. Nor can he ensure that everything that happens is the due moral consequence of some earlier act.

Perhaps the strongest expression of the independence of human action from God is to be found in Jeremiah 32:35: 'They built the high places of Baal in the valley of the son of Hinnom, to offer up their sons and daughters to Molech, though I did not command them, nor did it enter into my mind, that they should do this.' Even allowing for prophetic hyperbole, people are here clearly spoken of as doing things which had not even entered God's mind; a notable qualification on omniscience, in its scholastic sense.

On this view, God certainly takes the initiative, very often; he does not just wait to see what happens. 'Before you were born I consecrated you: I appointed you a prophet to the nations' (Jr 1:5). He has a special vocation for particular people. But they can refuse to respond, and they often do. God says, 'Why, when I came, was there no man? When I called, was there no one to answer?' (Is 50:2). So the divine plans can be frustrated. Nevertheless, God can use even the disobedience of men for his own purposes: 'Ah Assyria, the rod of my anger . . . against a godless nation I send him . . . but he does not so intend and his mind does not so think' (Is 10:5–7). God's causal power extends not only over the weather, where it is often in evidence, but also over the minds of men. He can make people give confusing advice to foil their plans (Is 19:14). 'The Lord has poured out upon you a spirit of deep sleep, and has closed your eyes' (Is 29:10), he says to the false prophets. On the other hand, he can also raise human capacities to new heights of creativity, strength and wisdom: 'The spirit of the Lord shall rest upon him, the spirit of wisdom and understanding, the spirit of counsel and might' (Is 11:2). And in the end, he will place his own law in the hearts of men, giving them clear and immediate knowledge of him (Jr 31:31).

This is rather a complex picture of God, as one who takes the initiative in particular historical events; who responds to creatures, co-operating with them or obstructing their plans: who sets before them moral demands and shapes events so that sin eventually destroys itself and order is drawn out of chaos and his ultimate good purpose is realized; but who does all this in ways which do not deny the freedom of human wills. It is perhaps an attractive view; but it has major problems.

On the interactionist view, God does some things; and he can do whatever he wants. So eventually he will ensure that he gets what he wants: 'I will plant them upon their land and they shall never again be plucked up out of the land which I have given them' (Am

9:15). But now the problem is, why does God act on some occasions and not on others? If he can sometimes cause it to rain in answer to prayer, why does he not do so always, or at least on more occasions? 'My thoughts are not your thoughts,' says the Lord (Is 55:8); but the excuse wears thin after a while. If God can strike the enemies of Israel with panic and confusion (Zc 12:4) and build a wall of fire around Jerusalem to protect his people (Zc 2:5), why does he not do so? Such thoughts as these no doubt led to the third view of divine action, the catastrophist view.

This view contrasts strongly with the idea that God is moralistically at work in everything that happens: an idea expressed by Amos' question, 'Does disaster strike a city unless the Lord sends it?' (Am 3:6). But it does not suggest that God acts intermittently, in some events and not others. Rather, it supposes that 'Thou hast hid thy face from us and hast delivered us into the hand of our iniquities' (Is 64:7). God does not act at all in the present time. In the far past he made himself known in mighty acts, 'when thou didst terrible things which we looked not for' (Is 64:3); when he divided the sea and spoke from the mountain. And there is a coming day of the Lord when God will again decisively act in catastrophic judgement upon all nations. 'Behold the day of the Lord comes, cruel with wrath and fierce anger . . . the sun will be dark at its rising and the moon will not shed its light' (Is 13:9–10). The mountains will be flattened and a great road will be built through the wilderness so that all Israelites in exile can return to Jerusalem, where God will rule in glory on Mount Zion; and 'there shall be continuous day, not day and not night' (Zc 14:7). Unless there is an obscure prophecy of neon street-lighting, it is apparent that this is a use of cosmic imagery to refer to such things as the Persian defeat of Babylon and the rebuilding of the Temple. The literalization of such passages by some twentieth-century Western Christians is truly extraordinary; for in them God is pictured as tearing the sky apart to get through to the earth, melting the mountains as he treads on them (Mi 1:4) and miraculously making the Temple mound higher than Mount Everest (Mi 4:1). What they are doing is to take some parts of the metaphors literally and overlook the others. It is more consistent to take it all as metaphor; but it still presumably represents some catastrophic future event. It is not surprising that interpretations vacillate between seeing this as a complete transformation of the universe, an end of history as we understand it, and seeing it as symbolic of the political triumph of Israel in the near future. Either way, the difficulty is that Israel did not triumph; the return of the exiles from Babylon was a rather half-hearted and unspectacular affair, by all accounts; and the universe went on.

It is not just a modern process of demythologization which may interpret catastrophism as a symbol of hope for the realization in future of God's purposes. It was perhaps always meant to be a mythic symbol of the historical triumph of those largely hidden purposes; of faith in a God who says, 'What I have determined will be done' (Is 14:24). The delay of God's action was a great problem for the prophets, living as they did at a time of military disasters and social anarchy, punctuated by brief periods of insecure peace. So they swung from moralism to catastrophism, from seeing God as whistling up the Assyrians as a punishment for sin (Is 7:18), to fantasies of a miraculous destruction of all the nations of the world in the Valley of Jehoshaphat (Jl 3:1). But, though not in any coherently worked-out manner, they kept returning to the interactionist view of a God who shapes and uses human plans, being always present to initiate, to respond and to weave the actions of creatures to his own developing moral purposes.

These strands of thought about divine action can be drawn together to give an underlying conception of the power which shapes human history. From the moralistic strand, we can take the insight that what God requires is social justice and fidelity. As Amos puts it, 'I hate, I despise your feasts and I take no delight in your solemn assemblies . . . but let justice roll down like waters and righteousness like an everflowing stream' (Am 5:21–24). But one must remember that the Torah is not a universal set of rational moral principles for the whole world. It sets out a detailed, living and developing way of communal life, whose function is precisely to set this people apart from all others. For an orthodox Jew, it is not permissible to abstract the commands and ordinances of the Law from their context in the history of the patriarchs. They have a history and a particularity which makes them parts of one organic form of the good life, which belongs to the story of this people. For the prophets morality cannot be disentangled from a particular special vocation which God gives this people. The close interweaving of morality and history which gives rise to the distinctive notion of moral vocation is essential to the prophetic view.

From the interactionist strand, we can take the claim that God is both an initiating and responsive will, disclosing his plans to the prophets, working them out through the warrior-liberators of Israel and judging and blessing the acts of his people. And from the catastrophist strand we can see how God is regarded as the almighty God, who made heaven and earth, and for whom nothing is too hard (Jr 32:37); whose purpose will finally be realized. The final idea is of a moral, purposive, responsive and sovereign will. As we have seen, this is not worked out in one consistent view. The interactionist view seems to be the central core, with the others stressing the moral and eschatalogical aspects in extreme forms. But their interest is not to present a theoretical and systematic view; and subsequent reflection needed to develop these ideas in further ways. Perhaps we could say that there is not just one 'biblical view', though there is a set of closely related views, which can provide the basis for subsequent development of the idea of a moral, interactive but ultimately sovereign power which shapes the future and makes specific demands on human lives.

Is this God omnipotent? The point has often been made, and surprisingly by Peter Geach, given his attitude to divine temporality, that the philosophical notion of 'being able to do anything non-self-contradictory' does not occur in Scripture.[7] But God is said to be the maker of heaven and earth – I believe the Bible is unclear as to whether it is shaped out of pre-existent chaotic matter or not – and it is said that nothing is too hard for him. He is certainly regarded as having power over all created things; he is, in Macquarrie's phrase, a monarchical God, a God primarily of power and might.[8] I do not think one should stretch this so far as to ask what sorts of world God might have made; whether he could have made any world at all, or one without suffering. That question is not raised. So one has a slightly restricted notion of omnipotence. God has incomparably great power, and he can bring about whatever he wants on earth. If he is an interactionist God, however, then he leaves some creatures free, within limits that he no doubt sets. That will naturally limit the exercise of his power: but not of course his possession of it. Whether God is limited by the necessities of his own nature, or in what ways, is simply not discussed; though

I cannot resist one mischievous use of a text: 'I, I am he who blots out your transgressions for my own sake' (Is 43:25); or, as it may be translated, because of who I am. God has a nature; he is 'gracious and merciful, slow to anger and abounding in steadfast love' (Jl 2:13); and that nature is unchangeable. It seems to me a logical truth that God has a nature, and so is logically limited in being unable to act against it, in practice; as Geach puts it, God cannot sin.[9] Once that point is conceded, and we admit also that we cannot know the divine essence, we are committed to saying that there may be necessities in God we know nothing of. However, this is never explored in the prophets – though it is not without interest that it became a major feature of debate in Islam.

Is this God omniscient? Jeremiah locates him everywhere, though at other points God sends his angels out to discover what is going on. He does know the secrets of all hearts; yet, as I have noted, people can take him by surprise. The future is open to prayer. And if he can change his mind, presumably he cannot predict that before he does it. This is in line with the general doctrine that God is everlasting (OLAM), that is, he exists for uncountable time; 'I am there at the beginning and at the end' (Is 41:4). The existence of prophecy shows that God can bring about what he intends; but it does not show that he intends everything; and that seems not to be the prophetic doctrine.

Is this God perfectly good? Not in the sense, often used in modern philosophy, that he would never willingly cause harm. He demands justice and punishes sin; he will at last destroy evil utterly (there is no doctrine of endless suffering in the prophets; although the fire never dies out, the bodies on it are already dead (Is 66:24)). Moreover, Deutero-Isaiah is at pains to stress that God says, 'I form light and create darkness, I make weal and create woe' (Is 45:7). The prophets seem to say three things about God's goodness. First, he himself is wholly just (Ps 119:137–8). Second, he demands righteousness of us (Dt 30:16). And third, he offers love, fulfilment and delight to those who turn to him and love him (Jr 32:40–41). Some Christian preachers espouse a misleading idea when they take God's Fatherhood to be an always tender, unconditionally forgiving, universal intimacy. For the prophets, God was the source of all, evil as well as good. In his active interaction with Israel, he demanded justice and promised to bring about good on certain

95

strict conditions. He punished ruthlessly, and is primarily an object of fear and awe. It is fashionable, and Jüngel has encouraged the fashion with a well-developed theological argument, to see God as a suffering, always sympathetic, striving and immanent power within the world, or even within human minds.[10] The monarchical god of the prophets remains demanding, judgemental and sovereign – though not distant or tyrannical. A more realistic idea of what is meant by God's goodness might be given by paying some attention to the idea of the sovereign will who shapes the world that he has brought to be towards the realization of particular moral purposes, by interaction with independent wills and the partly creative, partly destructive powers which were implicit in creation itself.

The contrasts between this view of God and that found in the Indian traditions are obvious. Action is not taken to be of itself an imperfection; so the Lord is conceived as active Will rather than contemplative Self. This Will works itself out in history, seeking to realize specific purposes. And it imposes moral demands on people, as they are to help in that process of realization in time. Nevertheless, there are equally clear analogies between the glorious Lord of Vedanta, in his causal and effected state, and the God of Abraham, Isaac and Jacob. Both reveal themselves in verbal form to seers or prophets. Both can take bodily forms for the benefit of their devotees. Both declare the ultimate purpose of human life to lie in relationship to itself. And both lay down moral and social requirements – the Torah and the Dharma – within which the religious life must normally be lived. Both are compassionate, merciful and gracious, and promise fulfilment to those who submit to them in devotion.

The element which is very prominent in Vedanta, and seems at first to be lacking in the Hebrew Bible, is the doctrine of the 'higher Brahman', Brahman beyond qualities, radically qualifying the understanding of the Lord of the world in an agnostic direction. But is this element of dual-aspect theism indeed absent in the Bible? The orthodox rabbinic interpretation has never thought so. Whenever the prophets speak of that which causes the future and their own experiences, they speak of the great King, Father and Judge of Israel. They speak in metaphor, and refuse to provide any abstract, conceptual or literal account of God as a disembodied will or person. Metaphor is in some ways a better safeguard of the divine mystery than the ambiguous coherence of an abstract philosophical doctrine of God. In their untranslatability, metaphors give us symbols, appropriate for us, of something beyond human imaging; and their clear literal falsity and lack of literal translation expresses the incapacity of the human mind to penetrate the divine reality in its essential nature.[11]

In fact the doctrine of the final unknowability of God is enshrined in the Bible. Moses asks the name of God, which would reveal to him the nature of God; and he is simply told, '*Ehyeh aser ehyeh*', 'I am what I am' or 'I will be what I will'.[12] That is just a way of saying that God's nature is known fully only to himself. The Shekinah, the cloud of divine glory, is inaccessible, so that no man may see God and live.[13] God reveals the Torah, what is to be done and something of what will be. But he does not declare his own being openly; and the reticence of the Bible about the essential nature of the divine being is a way of saying that it is beyond our comprehension. The central symbol of Israelite religion, the Ark of the Covenant, contained in its innermost shrine only a wooden chest containing the tablets of the Torah. There was no image or idol, no physical representation of God. God demands; he acts and brings all things to be in dynamic creativity. But what he is in himself is indescribable. The Bible is quite consistent therefore in never describing him, except in terms of his appearances in vision or his effects in the storm and the whispering voice.

Thus, although the Bible contains no explicit philosophical reflection on the ineffability of God, the whole Jewish tradition is one which deeply treasures the doctrine of divine transcendence of all concepts and images. One may dispute for a lifetime about the minutiae of the Torah; but of God in himself one must be silent. Even the name of God, expressed in the Tetragrammaton, the four Hebrew letters, J$_{\text{HVH}}$, was left unpronounced for hundreds of years, in an attempt to preserve the sense of the utter mystery and transcendence of the divine being. It is therefore not simply the influence of neo-Platonic or Aristotelian philosophy which led theologians such as Maimonides to develop a doctrine of divine incomprehensibility. They *were* using the tools of a newly rediscovered Greek tradition of thought. But they were using them to bring out elements of the biblical tradition which are in danger of being lost if one attends only to the vivid metaphors; and, even worse, if one begins to take those metaphors literally. When one sees that the Bible is, quite consistently, silent about what cannot be said; and that it refuses to translate its metaphors for God in any way, except with the reminder that we are to make no images of God at all; then one may recognize in the Hebrew Bible a similar doctrine of dual-aspect theism to that which can be found in the Indian traditions. But it was left for Maimonides, that great theologian of the orthodox tradition, to express this similarity in an especially striking way, and to make clear once and for all the completely non-anthropomorphic character of the orthodox Jewish doctrine of God.

5

Maimonides: the Unknowable God

The twelfth-century Spanish philosopher and theologian Moses Maimonides has had an enormous influence on the development of Judaism. In his major philosophical work, *The Guide for the Perplexed*, he sets out a view of the nature of God which combines traditional Jewish piety with an Aristotelian metaphysics. This synthesis, derived from the Muslim commentators on Aristotle, was to exert a great influence on Christian theology, too.[1] Thus the three great Semitic religions, Judaism, Christianity and Islam, after about the twelfth century, came to share a very similar conception of God. It was not a new view, since its major elements had been present in the tradition from the earliest times. But the terms in which it was formulated – using the newly rediscovered works of Aristotle – now came to be standardized in a particular way. One problem for the modern interpreter is whether the view itself can be disentangled from its Aristotelian conceptual framework, which has to a large extent been superseded by developments in the physical sciences. The fact that the view parallels in a remarkable way the quite distinct Indian modes of thought about Brahman suggests it *is* capable of being formulated in rather different philosophical terminologies. Thus Aristotle's metaphysics was rather a useful tool than a basic determining factor in the formulation of the classical Semitic concept of God.

Maimonides has no time at all for anthropomorphic views of God. Indeed, his rejection of the belief that God is in any way like a human person is, if anything, too extreme. God is, he says, 'He who is everlasting, constant and in no way subject to change; immutable in his essence, and as he consists of nothing but his essence, he is mutable in no way whatsoever; not mutable in his relation to other things, for there is no relation whatever existing between him and any other being'(23). We seem to be back in the world of Vedanta; and this sentence would not be out of place in either Sankara or Ramanuja. God is immutable and without qualities (that is what 'consisting of nothing but his essence' means), and free from all contact with the finite world. He is eternal, simple and unconditioned; free from qualities and relations; existing from himself alone in an entirely unique manner.

Nor does Maimonides think that this is only a doctrine for the sophisticated, while the simple must be taught a more anthropomorphic doctrine. On the contrary, 'All must be taught by simple authority that God is incorporeal; that there is no similarity in any way whatsoever between him and his creatures . . . The difference between them . . . is absolute'(49). But now, if any terms are used of God at all, they must be terms which trade on some sort of similarity between God and other things. For he cannot be ostensively defined; he cannot be pointed to. He must be identified by description; and how can one have a description that could not, in principle, apply to anything else? It is possible to have a uniquely identifying description. For example, the phrase 'Creator of everything other than itself' is uniquely identifying. It cannot be true of more than one thing – though of course it does not follow that there actually exists such a thing. One could construct other uniquely identifying descriptions. But they will all use terms which apply to classes of object, not only to God. In the description I have mentioned, God is implicitly referred to as 'a thing' which is 'different from' other things, and which 'causes to exist' all other things. One is using the concepts of thing, identity and cause. If one takes the assertion of total dissimilarity seriously, one will have to say that 'cause' here means something quite different from what it means in other contexts. Indeed, Maimonides does say that such terms are used 'homonymously' of God and other things. That is, they have quite a different meaning, and just happen to sound the same. But that is clearly absurd, for then 'creator' could mean 'destroyer' or, indeed, 'red cabbage', and all sense would be lost.

There may be a difference; but there must be some reason why the term 'cause' is used, rather than a term such as 'dustbin'. Clearly, it is because the world is seen to be not self-existent, to be dependent for its existence on something else. The world is an 'effect'; but that entails that there exists something upon which it depends. Perhaps there is hardly anything you can say about that thing which is accurate. As Maimonides puts it, 'In relation to God, what we consider to be a state of perfection is in truth the highest degree of imperfection. If, however, men were to think that these human perfections were absent in God, they would consider him as imperfect'(35).

On one interpretation, he is saying that we consider certain things to be perfections. We may be quite wrong; or, even if we are right, relative to human life, it is most unlikely that these would be absolute perfections, for very different sorts of beings. But we have to ascribe them to God, even while knowing that we do so wrongly; for we have to believe that God is perfect; and that is the only way we can conceive perfection. Yet if we do not mean by 'perfect' the sorts of things we ordinarily mean by it, what could we possibly mean by saying that God is perfect?[2]

If we assert that God is perfect, we must at least believe that God is superior to human beings in some assignable ways. There is nothing to stop us adding that he is so superior that we cannot truly imagine what he is like. Thus he is much more powerful than any human being. That is straightforwardly true; he can do many more things. In one sense, then, it is literally true that God can do more things than I can. But at once the agnostic qualification arises: 'But does God at all act in the way that I do?' Are we really comparing like with like? I do not suppose that God will perform actions in the way that I do, by having learned certain physical or mental capacities and skills. What it is like for God to act or have power, I have no idea, and this is the difficulty Maimonides is striving with.

It is as if we start enriching our concepts in certain ways; speaking of greater and greater degrees of power and wisdom and knowledge; extrapolating from our own case to envisage more and more powerful beings. But at a certain stage the whole process implodes upon itself, because we have stretched our understanding so far that it no longer has anything upon which to get a mental grip. Then we might say, 'There is something wholly inconceivable by me. But I can point towards it by expanding my understanding in a certain direction; and then admitting defeat.' Now is this different from saying that God could be anything at all, or nothing, if he is wholly inconceivable? I think it is. For it is saying that there is a reality which cannot be described; but which can be pointed towards as the imagined completion of a line drawn in a certain direction towards infinity.[3]

Maimonides is quite clear that God is 'above all kinds of deficiency, above all affections . . . not subject to external influence'(50). The central clue is that God is above, higher than, not less than, all conditioned and imperfect things of the world. He is free from limitation. That means that, in thinking of God one progressively removes conditions or restrictions from the things one knows, in a way which seems to increase, not decrease, their perfection.

It is obviously better to be able to do more things rather than fewer. It is thus false that God can do fewer things than I can, that his power is more limited by circumstance. If he has capacity, it must be maximally possessed. We do not know what this would be, since all powers we know are limited. But we can meaningfully say that God is much more powerful than any finite being; and also that his power is radically unlike that of any finite being in its nature. Thus Maimonides says, 'All perfections must really exist in God, and none of them must be in any way a mere potentiality'(78). This lack of potentiality is what marks God off as quite different in kind from any finite, changing thing. But it may seem that such a God is beyond any possibility of human knowledge and description.

It is vital to remember that Maimonides accepts entirely the revelation of the Torah by God to Moses. Thus he does not doubt at all the ascriptions to Jahweh of almightiness, omniscience, sovereignty and righteousness that the Hebrew Bible contains. The question that remains for the philosopher is whether these ascriptions are to be taken literally, as referring to a person, in some fairly recognizable sense. Maimonides' answer to that question is a resounding 'no'. These attributes are ascribed to God on authority; but we actually have no idea of what they mean. He goes further in this regard than almost any other Semitic theologian. 'The negative attributes of God are the true attributes'(81), he says. And again, 'God has no positive attributes'(82). This is not simple negation; for we can correctly ascribe to God wisdom, might and knowledge. Moreover, on the basis of prophetic inspiration, we can ascribe to God a dynamic and creative power. The Hebrew God is not conceived as a 'Witness', after the manner of the Upanishads, but as 'Dynamic Will', at the heart of the finite world. That is the self-revelation of God; but even it must be denied of him, as we understand it.

'By affirming anything of God, you are removed from him in two respects . . . whatever you affirm is only a perfection in relation to us . . . and he does not possess anything superadded to his essence'(84). The emphasis is on the complete incomprehensibility of God. There are no concepts at all which can adequately express his being; he is wholly other. Yet Maimonides gives to negation a sort of positive function. The activity of negating attributes is 'necessary to direct the mind to the truths which we must believe concerning God'(82). What are those truths? That God is 'a being that is incorporeal, most simple, whose existence is absolute and not due to any cause, to whose perfect essence nothing can be superadded, and whose perfection consists in the absence of all defects . . . he has nothing in common with creatures . . . he gives the universe duration and preserves its necessary arrangement'(83). But not all of these attributes are purely negative. God is not spatial; he is not complex; he has no defect; he is not like any creature; he has no cause; he is not conditioned by anything else. Still, God *is* something; he is not non-existent. And he is in fact the *cause* and sustainer of all, and more *perfect* than any created thing, lacking impermanence, dependence and transience, with their attendant chain of ills.

How can Maimonides say that 'by each additional negative attribute you advance towards knowledge of God'(84)? Only if there is something which can in some sense be known. The paradox is glaring. Even in stating this view, God must be said to be existent, knowable, cause and perfect. Thus he says, 'God's existence is absolute . . . we comprehend only the fact that he exists, not his essence'(82). But then we do *know* that he exists. What, then, is Maimonides denying? 'When we say that that essence which is called "God" is a substance with many properties . . . we apply that name to an object which does not at all exist'(89). What it comes down to is that the way in which we represent God to ourselves cannot be adequate to the divine reality. We must think of God in that way – as holy Creator. But he is not as we represent him to be, even in the most recondite and stretched meanings of those concepts.

This view, as it stands, is incoherent. For how could one possibly say that God in himself was unlike any concept we could form of him? If we do not speak at all, then we cannot even assert the existence of anything. But if we assert its existence, we have said something which we understand as like the existence of other things, in however 'stretched' a fashion. What Maimonides has confused, perhaps, is the question of what a word means with the question of whether we can imagine or represent to ourselves the object which a word stands for. The confusion is easy to understand, especially if one has a theory of meaning according to which the meaning of a word is the object it stands for. Then one will not know what it means unless one knows what it stands for; and Maimonides wished to deny the possibility of real human knowledge of the essence of God. Therefore he was committed, it seemed, to saying that we cannot know the meanings of the terms we apply to God.

The problem is eased if we have a different account of meaning.[4] Take the keyword 'cause', for instance. We might find it impossible to say what that word stands for; citing a number of examples will not be giving the meaning, though it may illustrate or teach the meaning, in certain circumstances. One way to give the meaning of 'cause' is to provide a definition – 'that which brings about another thing'. We may not know just what this 'bringing about' consists in. Indeed, the history of philosophical debate shows that we probably cannot get a fully adequate account of it. But we can get a complex of ideas about dependence, origination and so on within which the idea of 'cause' makes sense, even though we cannot agree on precise definitions.

There must be some contexts in which talk about causes has a primary set of uses. So we can talk about the causes of cancer, of sunlight on grass and so on. We have a whole conceptual framework within which we can speak of the influence of one thing on another, and the sort of observable correlations which lead us to erect a 'theory of causality', to act as an explanatory framework for inter-preting and making sense of our world and our experience of it. Kant was correct in thinking that the idea of causality is one basic concept which we use to make sense of the world, a category of experience.[5]

When we have such a concept, its use is not rigidly bound to the precise set of examples which have delimited its use so far. It is essential to useful concepts that they are indefinitely extendable to new and unforeseen contexts. The idea of cause may extend and change, as new theoretical schemes develop, and we engage in new forms of interaction with our environment, which require new explanatory schemes to make sense of them. We cannot place limits on the use of the idea in advance. Moreover, the word 'cause' does not have to refer to a specific thing or entity that is observable or even imaginable. We can meaningfully say, 'This event is so extraordinary that it clearly has a cause; but I have no idea what sort of thing could cause it'. We are here employing the idea of dependence and origination in a context where a relation of causality is being asserted, though one has no idea of what sort of thing can fill one of the two places in the relation of cause and effect (except, of course, that the unknown 'thing' brings into being the observed effect).

Can we not say of the universe as a whole, meaningfully if not truly, that it has the character of 'having been brought into being', or of being dependent on something beyond itself; of not being self-existent? Then we could speak of a cause of the universe, without being able to imagine what could fill the causal space in the bivalent relation. We could say that God is a cause; that is, it is true that he brings about the universe, without knowing anything else about God except what is implied by that assertion itself. We can use the word without being able to imagine what it is like for God to cause the world.[6]

This is still a little disingenuous. For we want to say more about God than that he brings about the world, as water might bring about wetness of skin. We wish to say that the world originates through will, not by accident or unconsciously. And, astonishingly, Maimonides writes: 'God performs actions similar to such of our actions as originate in certain qualities'(76). He is trying to be agnostic, in denying that God has qualities which are actually similar to any human qualities. He means to assert only that certain events in the world are such that they are similar to those produced by human actions. We can say that the world is intelligible and purposively ordered; and that events occur in it which seem to show purposive will and direction (in the history of Israel, specifically). To understand those features of the world, we can say that they are 'as if' purposively caused by an active God, even though we know there is no such substance with attributes.[7] Unfortunately, Maimonides' agnosticism deserts him at the crucial moment, and he slips into saying, 'God performs actions'. How could it be otherwise, if one is to say anything at all?

Again, he writes, 'The knowledge of the works of God is the knowledge of his attributes'(75); and 'All the actions of God emanate from his essence'(72). The analogy he appeals to is of a fire which burns unchangingly, while producing many varied effects. When we speak of the attributes of God, we really seek only 'to express qualities of actions emanating from him'(89). Still, the actions are emanating from something; and, being actions, they are thought of as being consciously intended. How can a wholly changeless being emanate actions? The truth is that, if we really have to think of God in a certain way – as a rational agent – then we cannot at the same time think of him in some other way. We cannot say, at the same time and in the same sense, 'There is no God', and 'There is a God'. True, we can say these things in different senses – there is no literally human-shaped God; but there is a Creator of all. Those differences do, however, need to be spelled out.

What Maimonides can perhaps do is to argue that, though we have to *think of* God as a personal agent, we can also say that he is not one, that our thoughts are totally inadequate to his reality. But why should Maimonides say that? It seems that he is chiefly influenced by a certain sort of causal argument, deriving, in his case, from Aristotle's *Metaphysics*.[8] He says, 'As regards a being whose existence is not due to any cause . . . existence and essence are perfectly identical'(89). As the cause of all change, God must himself be beyond change. And he cannot be composed of parts, which in some way would be the causes of his compositive existence. As wholly underived, God must be absolutely simple, beyond composition and limitation of any sort. 'God is one simple substance, without any composition or plurality of elements'(69). If that does indeed follow from a correct analysis of primary causality, then one has good reason for denying that any words which imply complexity or change of any sort in God, or dependence of any sort (even by relation) can properly apply to God.

But this is not simply a piece of abstract metaphysics. And in fact these parts of Aristotle's own thought may to some extent be taken as expressions of an underlying contemplative vision, which Aristotle preserved from his teacher at the Athenian Academy, Plato.[9] The idea of a wholly unconditioned reality, beyond change and decay, not coming into being or passing away, perfect in bliss and knowledge, is not simply the result of an austere metaphysical argument, a rather insecure inference from a set of ambiguous data. It is an idea which arises in the course of a life of contemplation, the best and highest kind of life, for Aristotle as for Plato. For Judaism, too, the apophatic ideal exists as a central part of the religious tradition.

From the Hebrew Bible one has the idea of the imageless God beyond even the highest heaven, whose purposes cannot possibly be defeated and whose faithfulness is assured. Although at some times this God may be approached in a very personalistic way, in prayer, the Hebrew tradition, like most others, is aware that God is always beyond our images of him. It is this sense of 'beyondness' and supreme perfection, always drawing one towards deeper knowledge yet never fully comprehended, which is the religious root of the idea of the unconditioned God. The idea is not itself directly revealed; but it comes to be seen both as a rational supposition underlying belief in an omnipotent Creator, and also as an idea which extends and deepens the practice of prayer and the attempt to evoke an awareness of the presence of God in all things and at all times. This is not an idea, therefore, which is due to some primitive Aristotelian theory about the necessity of having a prime mover to turn the outer sphere of the heavens.[10] It is a more basic idea, which Aristotle's metaphysical vocabulary seeks to enshrine in one particular way; but which is also enshrined in the very different vocabulary of Indian speculative metaphysics.

Maimonides spells out the nature of God in a series of paradoxes, which parallel the similar set of contrasts to be found in the Vedantic doctrine of a higher and a lower Brahman.

He characterizes God as eternal, in the sense of timeless. God is incapable of change or of being changed. Nothing can cause him to be or to cease to be. As creator of time, he is beyond all time; and as originator of all, nothing stands behind or beyond him which could cause or change him. However, God's eternity is not a blank and static endurance; it is beyond every temporal characterization, even 'enduring'. Thus we cannot speak of it as it is in itself. The operative force of 'eternity' is to stress that God's own being is beyond all that we can say. There is that in God – indeed, it is his essential nature – which is beyond time and restriction, though he is that from which all temporal relations arise.

God is also said to be without relation to anything, because 'When we speak of a relation between two things, these belong to the same kind . . . between one hundred cubits and the heat of pepper there is no relation'(72). God is different in kind from all finite things. He has no positive attributes, and no similarity to anything. Relations can, however, be ascribed to God 'less strictly'(72). What they say is precisely that God is absolutely and fully existent. He does not just happen to exist; and he is different in kind from any created thing. Yet from him all created things flow. Not only is he their cause; in being fully existent and the source of all existence, he is the exemplar of all things, which are in some unimaginable way contained in him primordially.

Finally, God is simple. In him there is no plurality or complexity, no distinguishable attributes. He is pure undifferentiatable unity. Yet in him all perfections exist in unconditioned fullness.

Thus we have a set of paradoxes, quite consciously articulated. God is eternal; but he is the cause of all things, bringing them into being one after another. God is totally unlike anything else; yet he is the most truly existent, indeed absolutely existent, and the exemplary cause of all. God is wholly simple; yet he contains all perfections, in a fully realized way. The first part of each paradox may seem to be wholly negative – God is not temporal, not like anything, not complex. But the second part seems quite positive – God is cause, existent and perfect. Both parts must be taken together, to generate the notion of a quite unique category of being whose fullness of reality is beyond our comprehension, but of which our world is a derived and imperfect shadow. How is language being used here? Not in a straightforward descriptive manner.

If one tries to envisage a simple, unique, independent and immutable being, it is almost impossible not to think of a sort of isolated point, self-contained and without relation to the universe of time and change. But although Maimonides does speak of God as 'separate from the universe and in no contact whatever with it'(119), there is no doubt that he believes God to be the Creator of all, whose 'rule and providence . . . exist in all parts of the universe'(119). Taken as descriptive statements, these propositions would simply form a contradiction. But are they to be taken as description?

One indication that they should not be is given by the statement, 'His existence and that of any other being differ totally . . . the term existence is applied to both homonymously'(49). That is to say, the expression, 'There is a self-existent' has a quite different sense from such expressions as 'There is a chair in the room'. It is rather misleading to call this a homonymous use, as if it was just an accident that the same sounds were used in conveying quite a different and unconnected meaning. There is, after all, some reason why it is said that God exists, rather than that there is no God (though there is no 'substance with attributes'). But it is true that the sense in which we very often use 'exist' is something like: 'has a position in space and time; is causally affectable by other things in space and time; and is observable in principle'. That is at least a central case of the use of the verb 'exists'. However, we can also properly say that dreams exist, and they are not causally related to other substances or clearly locatable in space. Nevertheless, they only exist 'in the mind', as objects of consciousness. We might say 'Numbers exist'; but that means that there are relationships between numbers, which we can discover; it does not mean that there are somehow observable entities called numbers.

The sense of 'God exists' is not given by any of these cases. Maimonides' point is that it is quite a unique sense of 'exist' that is being used. 'God has absolute existence'(71). And perhaps a more productive approach would be to ask why anyone should say, 'A simple immutable being exists'. What is being done by the use of such an expression?[11] Certainly, one can speak of identifying such a being by description, by constructing a uniquely defining expression. But one could never establish its existence by observation; so what is meant by asserting its existence?

Such expressions are never used on their own, in isolation from any context. They belong essentially to the primary context of religious worship and practice. As far as Maimonides was concerned, Moses had received a series of revelations from God which laid down how the Israelites should live and the blessings they could hope for as a result. In visions, dreams, auditions and spirit-inspired utterances, the prophets had spoken the words of

God. By their miracles and prophecies, they had shown that God has power over the world and over the future. At this level, God appears to his chosen servants in special ways. He appears in the Hebrew Bible in a human form, clothed in rainbow-coloured light, surrounded by spiritual beings. But he does not announce philosophical propositions about himself. God is one who appears to the prophets, declaring that he knows the secrets of all hearts and has power over all things. The Jewish faith is built upon claims that God has thus revealed himself, not upon some abstract argument. Maimonides was far from denying that. On the contrary, as an orthodox Jew, he accepted it unreservedly. Yet as one reflects on these revelations, one has to face the questions: what sort of being is this God? And how does he stand in relation to the universe of which we know by investigation?

It is very clear that God has immense knowledge and power. But, if he is the Creator of all things, he cannot be confined to a particular locatable body within space. It is natural then to think of him as a supernatural personal agent, having direct and immediate knowledge of all things and direct and unmediated power to control all things. He is conceived as an agent, with purposes and even desires for the world. Yet the nature of his relation to the world is vastly different from ours. We find ourselves in specific environments, with specific characters and in a particular social context. We learn our abilities slowly; and they are given by our physical environment and also by the sort of society within which we live. We have to come to know what capacities our bodies have – how fast we can run, how well we can sing, how clearly we can think. All such capacities are dependent on the state of our brains and bodies. They depend in innumerable ways upon things other than ourselves. We work out our purposes within a given context, which both constrains us and offers opportunities for creative change.

We cannot think of God as being constrained in that way by a physical world, for he creates the world. He is not constrained by any social context, for he is the one and only God. He does not have to discover his abilities by effort and experiment. God does not have to develop his capacities by reacting to various stimuli and making a particular creative response to the data he is presented with, from within a particular community of knowledge and a particular tradition, as human persons do. Moreover, God's power is unlimited and he has knowledge of the innermost thoughts and feelings of all beings; in these respects, too, he is quite unlike human persons, which are essentially limited in ability and cannot know the inner thoughts of others directly or infallibly. What is left, then, of the notion of rational agency in the case of God? Only the notion that he brings things about intentionally, in virtue of his perfect knowledge of all things. But this is simply a very abstract form of anthropomorphism. And there is no dispute that anthropomorphic or, as I have called them, anthropophanic images of God are properly used in the Jewish tradition. The question is, do we thereby have an adequate idea of God? Or is something important lacking from such a view?

There is something lacking, which is of vital significance; and that is the acceptance that all our concepts of God are mediating images of that which lies beyond all limiting conditions. The idea of God as the supreme cosmic agent, as the creative will lying at the heart of reality, is indeed part of the Jewish tradition. But what can be misleading is the thought that God is an object with properties; or the thought that we have grasped what he is in himself, in his essential nature. These are our dominant matrices for thinking of God, which specify our reactive attitudes to our total environment. But that which we react to is not an object which can be truly grasped by our minds at all. These are our mediating images for the unconditioned. It is fundamental to the Jewish understanding of God that we do not see him as he is; we hear his commands, his promises, and feel the strengthening of his presence; but he is himself absolutely different from our images and thoughts. In making this point so strongly, Maimonides is only bringing out philosophically what is fundamental to the ultimate reticence about God which permeates the Hebrew Bible. The dialectical method Maimonides adopts is to affirm perfection and deny limitation; so that at every stage there is a dynamism of movement which accepts neither unqualified affirmation nor sheer negation. It is basic to Maimonides' thought that there exists both the revelatory paradigm given in Scripture and the mediating insight which always passes beyond it, and yet returns to find an appropriate reactive response to the many experiences we undergo.

At the level of negative attribution, it is said that God cannot be changed; is not related to others, has no accidental properties; is not similar to anything. Even here, not every negation is equally applicable to God. It is the negations of change, complexity, relation, accident and similarity which are ascribed. The negations all operate in one way, towards eliminating finitude and dependence from the idea of God.

This gives the clue to what is being done in making such assertions. The words are being used as 'logical operators', which tell one to do something, just as the logical operator '=' does not mean anything descriptive.[12] It tells you to complete a certain mathematical operation, to complete a calculation. What are you being told to do when you are told that 'God is simple'? You are told to remove all complexity from your thought of God. Similarly, you are to remove all plurality, all transiency; all dependence and contingency. You are to move progressively towards an ideal of unity, simplicity, self-existence, independence and unconditioned reality. You can never arrive at such an ideal, in the sense of comprehending what it could be, coming across it or having some sort of direct intuition of it. The philosophers of this apophatic tradition are agreed that one cannot intuit, and know that one is intuiting, a purely simple being. For how can the complex embrace the utterly simple? How could human knowledge, in its essential finitude, grasp an actual infinity?

Thus when one affirms, 'There is an unconditioned reality', one is saying that there is an asymptotic ideal which guides one's thought to eliminate all conditions from one's concept of God.[13] But when all conditions are eliminated, there is nothing left to think. One may as well speak of nothing; and here we remember the Buddhist notion of the void, or emptiness, as the ultimate idea of the unconditioned.

So the asymptotic ideal must stand in a continuing dialectical tension with the revealed images of a particular tradition. Only when it does so can it have sufficient form and definiteness to move the heart and will, and yet preserve a basic sense of the mystery and infinity of the Divine. The major contribution of Maimonides to the Jewish idea of God is to enshrine at its heart this sense of mystery and to root it in a general sense of the contingency of the finite world.

As one reflects on what it is to exist, one recognizes the dependent existence of all finite things, the fact that they receive existence from a source beyond themselves; or, at the very least, that they do not account for their own existence. With this recognition comes the formation of the idea of a self-existent reality, one which does not depend for its existence on another thing, which has the source of its being in itself alone. This is the notion of an existence beyond all conditioning and determining factors; and it functions as a sort of completion of the idea of a fully existent being.

At the same time, this sense of full existence is that of something which lacks nothing which is possible to existence; so it does not change – which would entail a lack at one time relative to other times. It is beyond even the possibility of impairment or loss; and so it is simple, in not being divisible into smaller separable elements which could cease to cohere, in principle.

This being is the source of all dependent existence, contributing from its own essential nature all that is necessary to existence, at every moment of time. And, as the supreme cause, it must in some sense contain within itself all possible values that could ever come to be in the finite world, in order to account for their existence. The source of existence must contain sufficient reality to account for dependent existence; and in that sense it must be perfect, containing in a different and higher form all values which could ever be instantiated.

The formation of this idea of God is correlative with the arising of the idea of our world as *derived and limited in existence and in value*.[14] Such an idea arouses the notion of a reality absolutely different in kind from all finite beings, yet underlying the finite world as its underived source, unlimited in existence and in value. The arising of the idea of the world as dependent and conditioned is also the arising of the correlative idea of the Unconditioned Origin of all things. This is the primal religious vision which language about God seeks to evoke and articulate. If it is not evoked, religion remains at the level of belief in the existence of further, admittedly spectacular, finite facts. The Jewish prophetic experience, for example, would be that of a cosmic monarch, giving orders and imposing life-tasks on people, and enforcing them by various sanctions to make sure that his demands are carried out in the end. But such an interpretation would entirely miss the *religious* force of these images.

When the prophets declare the moral demands of Jahweh, they

are not relaying the privately narrated commands of a hidden
celestial despot. They are seeking to evoke the vision of a unique
reality which demands righteousness and justice as the proper
response to it. It would hardly be enough to say that the Unconditioned Origin was directly disclosed; that, on its own, would be
much too abstract to convey anything to believers. Indeed, taken
on its own, it does not give very much to believe in. It is essential
that there is some finite manifestation, by which the unconditioned
can be mediated in particular ways. But if one bears firmly in mind
that God is supreme in existence and in value, then a confrontation
with God is an encounter with that which is most fully real, and is
the source of all other reality; and with that which is of supreme
worth, and thus the proper object of our reverence and love. On
the one hand, this cannot be regarded by the believer as just a
constructed or imaginary ideal, which we might decide to strive for.
It has a sort of reality which is wholly beyond illusion or the threat
of change and non-being. On the other hand, it is not just a brute
fact, to be dispassionately accepted as the result of some inference
or argument. It is a reality which is supremely desirable and the
source of all other desirable things. Thus it is, in the end, the only
proper object of our striving, the goal of all our activity; that which
we rightly revere and desire as we see it mediated through aspects
of the finite world.

What the prophets to is to reveal some particular aspect of this
goal, suited to a particular people at a particular time and place;
to show what a true perception of it requires of us, if we are truly to
revere and love it. The Torah teaches us how to live, by showing
to us something of the self-existent supreme value of the Real – in
the language of the Bible, by showing us the faithfulness, righteousness and mercy of almighty God. Under that forceful image of the
mountain-god, El Shaddai, we may so order our lives that we
achieve a proper relation to the origin, exemplar and goal of our
lives. All this is particularized in the disclosures given through the
prophets of Israel. But, Maimonides reminds us, we must always
deny that we have grasped the essence of the Divine. He has shown
himself to us; and his words are true. That is, the propositions in
which they are formed provide us with an understanding which can
– if interpreted rightly – lead to an adequate grasp of the divine
nature for our condition. Yet it must always be asserted that God

himself is beyond any possibility of being grasped by propositional formulations at all. It is in this carefully qualified sense that only negative attributions are adequate to God, from our standpoint.

In the end, then, there is not a great dichotomy between the 'God of the philosophers' and the God of Abraham, Isaac and Jacob.[15] No doubt the early patriarchs of Israel did not write books of apophatic theology. But why should we therefore think that their religious ideas were crude, materialistic and literalist? May we not suppose that, from the first, the religious sense included the element of the iconic vision which is aware of the transcendence of the Divine; of 'mediation' as a characteristic of all religious symbols and concepts; and of a sense of the unconditioned as already present in intimations, so readily and universally available, of the dependence and imperfection of all finite things? To put the point more strongly, it seems most unlikely that so many thousands of years ago any clear distinction could have been made between 'literal' and 'metaphorical' truths. But where a distinction does not yet exist, it is wrong to assume that all assertions must have fallen on one – the literal – side of the distinction which was later drawn. It seems highly likely that early religious worshippers did not really think that their god was in a wooden box, so that he was destroyed when the box was destroyed. It may be argued, then, that philosophers such as Maimonides are only bringing out what has always been implicit in the tradition; and the orthodox are right in accepting these accounts as needful qualifications of any anthropomorphic imagery in their faith.

The distinction, properly made, is between the vivid, direct and intense experience of overwhelming value and reality which comes to some exceptional souls as a vision of God; and the operational qualifiers which have to be made to prevent one thinking that one has thereby grasped God or understood fully what he is. It is most important to grasp the extent to which agnosticism lies at the heart of orthodoxy. If God is truly far beyond our images of him, then the dogmatic arrogance that one has the final and fully adequate truth about God is removed as a possibility for the orthodox. The fundamental error into which some religious believers fall is to take as ultimate matters which are secondary or culture-relative. Though one may treasure a tradition of revealed images, and believe them to be indeed revealed by God, the way in which one asserts and affirms them is bound to be modified if one stresses the ineffability of the ultimate object of one's faith. Thus an orthodoxy which is not merely conventional or superficial actually contains resources of great tolerance and understanding of other traditions, as it recalls constantly that God cannot be bound either by the forms of our thought or by the laws which he makes binding on us.

The similarity between this developed Semitic idea of God and the Vedantic idea of Brahman is striking. Maimonides' view is remarkable for its assertion of the total unknowability and otherness of God: 'It can be proved that God is separate from the universe and is in no contact whatever with it'(119). It may be thought that this view is at the furthest possible remove from 'Indian monism', which asserts that all is Brahman. But we can see that it is not. In fact, this definition of God comes very close to Sankara's character-ization of Brahman as without form, unknowable by reflection, as free from all relationships to the illusory world. Like Sankara, Maimonides too can move easily to anthropomorphic-sounding descriptions of God, as acting, caring for creatures and having all perfections. Thus the essence of God must be distinguished from that of which we can have knowledge, God as he is revealed to us in his actions in the world for the sake of our salvation.

The same dual-aspect doctrine exists as in Vedanta and the more positive forms of Buddhism. We have already noted that the same fiduciary structure exists in these different traditions. Now we can see the same presentation of the iconic vision, with its dialectic of unity and distinctness, transcendent self-sufficiency and manifest creative action. It is in response to this vision that the religious path of self-transcendence is worked out; and here it seems that one can find a distinctive and common characteristic of religious belief, as it is found in its most reflective presentations within the world faiths.

6

Al-Ghazzali and the God of Unveiled Light

The foundation of Islam is the Koran; and the claim the Koran makes for itself is quite uncompromising: 'This book is revealed by Allah, the Mighty One, the All-knowing' (40:1). In common with Vedic Hinduism and Judaism, it claims to be based upon a direct verbal revelation from God himself; to be, indeed, 'a transcript of our eternal book' (43:1). Christianity and Buddhism also depend upon the teachings of individuals, whose words are recorded in written form. But the status of those teachings, while it may be very high, or even held by some to be infallibly recorded, is not quite that of a direct verbal revelation to the transcriber. The words of Jesus and of Gautama which were selected for the written record were so selected by an indirect historical process of oral tradition and editorial selection. And their lives are as important for revealing the truth as their words. While that may be true in Islam, Vedanta and orthodox Judaism, it is less readily admitted by orthodox believers, who tend to hold that the exact words in Arabic, Sanskrit or Hebrew were chosen by God himself.

In a series of visions, the angel Gabriel recited the Koran piece by piece to Mohammed, who memorized it; and who always disclaimed any personal poetic or imaginative ability, ascribing the words to divine inspiration alone. Their beauty and hypnotic thematic repetition have always been appealed to by Muslims as proof of divine authorship. Thus Islam is far from being a religion built upon reflection on the nature of the world and its cause. It is built upon the prophetic warning of a coming Day of Judgement, when those who care for the joys of this life only will taste the fire of hell for ever; and those who practise compassion, mercy and faith in God will be raised to the joys of paradise. People are called to respond to the declaration of this prophecy with submission. And,

117

it is said, 'Allah misleads whom he will and guides whom he pleases'(74:31). He 'leaves in error whom he will and guides those who repent and have faith'(13:25). Islam therefore claims to be a direct revelation from God which summons men to submit or turn away, and thereby tests them to make clear their standing on the Day of Resurrection, when all without exception will come to judgement.

The attributes of Allah are set out clearly and repeatedly in the Koran. He is 'the compassionate, the merciful, Lord of Creation, King of the Judgement Day' (1:1). He is wise and all-knowing (76:29). He is self-sufficient (64:3) and has power over all things (18:41). He is ruthless in judgement, but merciful to those who repent. The central concern in speaking of Allah is the concern with judgement. To be the judge of all the earth, Allah needs to know the secrets of all hearts, and he needs to have power over all things in order to raise the dead to life and ensure their destiny in paradise or hell. The things that are said of Allah are those things which are relevant to human conduct and destiny. None of our acts or thoughts will fail to have their effect; that judgement will surely come; and it is right for us to turn from the things of this world, which are 'but a sport and a pastime'(57:30), and to submit in faith to the will of Allah.

One can see here a similarity of structure even with Buddhism, which seems to know nothing at all of Allah. Buddhists do not think of one imminent Judgement or of a Day of Resurrection. But they do believe that all the acts of human beings will have their due reward, for good or ill. Commitment to the things of this world will ensnare us in a cycle of unending ills. And compassion and prayer, even taking refuge in the Enlightened One, who has passed beyond the confines of space and time, will offer us deliverance from this impermanent realm of sorrow.

Allah is conceived in what seems to be a very personalistic and voluntaristic way. 'No misfortune befalls except by Allah's will'(64:9), and 'he hurls his thunderbolts at whom he pleases'(11:9). Allah will raise all people from the dead, and those who enter paradise will spend their time in praising and glorifying him, who created all things by his mere will and pleasure. I have suggested that there is little basis for a predestinarian view in the Hebrew Bible. But there is much greater basis for one in the Koran, where it is said that 'every misfortune that befalls the earth . . . is ordained before we bring it into being'(57:21); and that 'We have made all things according to a fixed decree'(54:44). Naturally enough, the overall view is complex enough to generate endless arguments.[1] One must take account of texts such as: 'If a misfortune befalls you, it is the fruit of your own labours' (42:28). And one must bear in mind the clear teaching that Allah is both just and merciful – which implies that he leaves repentance in the sphere of each human will, even though no one could will without his sustaining co-operation ('You cannot will, except by the will of Allah'(81:29)). Yet however much Allah leaves to human freedom, there is no doubt that he is the sovereign Will; that is the basic paradigm model for conceiving 'the Most High, the Supreme One' (42:1).

All this seems very different from the Indian traditions, where the model of a personal will is often so attenuated as to disappear; and instead one has the model of a law of karma, and of the liberated state not as one of delighting in paradise, but of transcending all finite goods completely, in a union with unconditioned being. Once again, however, the polarities of personal-impersonal, of identity-otherness and of world-affirmation and world-denial, turn out to exist within each tradition, and to allow many possibilities of convergent interpretation. We have seen how, within Buddhism, the figure of the Bodhisattva may come to have the aspect of a personal saviour; and how nirvana and *samsara*, having been seen to be aspects of one reality, may lead one to affirm the finite world in so far as it is the manifestation of nirvana or of Suchness. Similarly, within Islam, the very personalistic idea of Allah and the rather concrete picture of paradise as consisting of reclining on couches attended by dark-eyed houris may both be supplemented in such a way that they are in fact significantly transformed. Nor is such supplementation some sort of heretical or marginal stream of thought. It is best represented by the eleventh-century figure who is generally taken to be the reconciler of orthodoxy and the Sufi movement within Islam, and to be one of the intellectual pillars, perhaps the greatest theologian, of orthodox Sunni Islam. This is Al-Ghazzali, who develops a view of Allah from within the orthodox tradition which is as well placed as any to be called the classical Muslim view of God. His small work, *The Niche for Lights*, gives a fascinating account of some of the more esoteric aspects of his view, as well as bringing out its main features.

The book is commenting upon a very famous passage from sura 24 of the Koran, which runs as follows: 'Allah is the light of the heavens and the earth. His light may be compared to a niche that enshrines a lamp, the lamp within a crystal of starlike brilliance. It is lit from a blessed olive tree neither eastern nor western. Its very oil would almost shine forth, though no fire touched it. Light upon light; Allah guides to His light whom He will' (24:34). The following sentence says, 'Allah coins metaphors for men'; and this passage has been taken as heavily symbolic of sacred mysteries by generations of commentators. Ghazzali's interpretation is itself highly metaphorical and difficult; but certain features of it reveal its close alignment with the dual-aspect doctrine we have found in each religious tradition so far.

It is often said that Islam sets Allah and creation in complete opposition to one another, as creator to created, self-sufficient to wholly dependent. Yet Ghazzali says, 'There is nothing in existence save Allah alone' (1, 6); and that sounds like the fullest form of monism. 'Each several thing other than Allah is,' he says, 'when considered in and by itself, pure not-being.' What he is doing is to focus on the aspect of the dependent nature of things which means that they would be wholly non-existent were it not for the will of Allah. Each thing depends so totally upon Allah that, but for his will, it could not be. 'If he decrees a thing, he need only say, "Be", and it is' (40:68). Since all is thus directly willed by Allah, it can be said to be an aspect of his own will, which is his own being. 'All existence is, exclusively, his aspect' (1, 6). This is, of course, just to say that nothing exists independently of Allah; and everything that is derives immediately from the being of Allah. What can one then say but that it is a self-manifestation of Allah himself? The total dualism of stressing a radical otherness between Allah and the world is transformed into a form of monism, when one sees that nothing can be truly independent of Allah, and all existence owes all it is to him alone, without contributing anything of its own by virtue of which it might claim to be distinct or different. Its difference lies solely in its derivativeness; the fact that it exists is due solely to Allah.

When Ghazzali comes to speak of the being of Allah, he says, 'It is kindled and fed in itself, from itself and for itself' (1, 7). It is not derived from another; it does not exist for the sake of another ('Allah does not need you, but you need him'; Koran 47:38); and it is wholly self-sufficient. 'He is prior to everything and above everything; he makes everything manifest' (1, 8). Although Allah does not need to create, he makes creation manifest by a sort of 'radiation from above downwards' (1, 7). In fact, in one passage in the Koran, there is a remarkable echo of Vedanta, when it is said, 'Know that the life of this world is but a sport and a pastime' (57:20). One needs to counterbalance that with 44:34: 'It was not in sport that We created . . . We created to reveal the truth.' Nevertheless, Allah did not *need* to reveal truth to anyone; any point there is in creation is not something that discloses a lack in Allah. Rather, creation manifests the abundance of his glory. As Ghazzali puts it, 'There is not a single thing in this world of sense that is not a symbol of something in yonder one' (2, 1). The whole finite world is a derivative and incomplete echo of the fullness of the divine life. It is like the light given off by a pure and brilliant source. Seen in its true aspect, 'The gross lower world becomes . . . like a transparent glass shade . . . a stepping-stone to the world supernal'(2, 4).

One can thus speak of the creating light as 'the goal of goals, the last object of spiritual search' (1, 7). And those who have ascended to knowledge of that light, 'on their return from their ascent . . . confess with one voice that they saw nought existent there save the One Real . . . the plurality of things fell away in its entirety . . . there remained nothing with them save Allah' (1, 6). They did not see Allah and other things, but Allah only. Ghazzali is at once careful to state that he does not mean that these souls have become identified with Allah. 'That had not been actual identity,' he says, 'but only something resembling identity.' But it is clear that the line between this sort of experience of the one fully self-existent being and an experience of union with the Self of bliss and knowledge of which Vedanta speaks is a thin line of theological orthodoxy. It is not something which the experience itself could reveal.

Ghazzali goes even further towards similarity with Indian traditions when he says, 'When this state prevails it is called . . . Extinction'. Again, he does not mean that the soul has literally ceased to exist. But 'the soul has become extinct to itself . . . unconscious of itself'. In a metaphor, this can be called identity; in reality it is unification, he says. The soul is so filled with the glory of the reality it contemplates that it is no longer conscious of itself as different at all. The transparent crystal, filled with the dazzling radiance of rainbow light, shows nothing of itself, in its complete embodiment of that light. Still, it is a finite refraction in the end, and thus light's vehicle, not light's source. Moreover, even as a reflective vehicle, it owes its being entirely to another. This, too, increases the sense of total submission to that which is beyond, and to a sense of the extinction of awareness of self.

Ghazzali has gone as far as he could to include the extremity of the Sufi experience of oneness with the Divine within the orthodoxy of Islam. One can see how the mystic Al-Hallaj came to say, 'I am the Real', in the intensity of such experience.[2] And, interestingly, the possibility of such pure experience of the divine self, together with the possibility of a total submission of the faithful will to the divine Will, is not so far removed from the notion of 'incarnation' as some Muslims may believe. However, Mohammed's testimony is that men remain men only, and Allah is distinct. In the end, no confusion of human and divine is allowed. Ghazzali protects this insight by saying, 'To bear relationship to what is imperfect carries with it imperfection . . . He transcends relation' (2, 2). Like Maimonides, he holds that God is so perfect that he cannot really be compared to any finite thing. 'He is too absolutely great to be called greater or most great by way of relation or comparison' (1, 6). Allah's perfect reality remains alone and unique. He is one and incomparable.

In fact, Ghazzali goes so far in stressing God's utter difference from all finite things that it becomes increasingly difficult to say how Allah is related to the world as Creator and Judge at all. He distinguishes, referring to a tradition that Allah veils His light by ten thousand veils, between various levels of insight with regard to the being of Allah. At the lowest level are those who are veiled with darkness. Then come those who are veiled with a mixture of darkness and light; and the highest of these are 'those who are veiled by light divine mixed with darkness of intelligence' (3, 2). Human reason, with its analytic concepts and categories, interprets the light divine so that they 'worship a deity that hears, sees, and has knowledge, power, will, life . . . whose conception of these attributes is relative to their own. Thus they say, in regard to his will, that it is contingent, like ours; that it is a demanding and purposing, like ours.' That is one level of understanding; and, on its own level, it is not a lie. Yet it is far from being an adequate representation of the truth. It views Allah as a cosmic but finally contingent, and presumably disembodied, will.

There is another level, where Allah is veiled with light alone, and which itself however, contains three sub-divisions. First, there are those who 'avoid denoting him by attributes altogether, and denote him simply by reference to his creation' (3, 3). He is that, whatever it is, which is sufficient to bring about a world like this. But we do not say that he is like us in having or being a contingent will. Secondly, there are those who say that the Lord is 'he who communicates motion to the outermost sphere' of the heavens. In Aristotelian terms, he is the prime mover, the source of all change, who is not himself changed in any way.[3] Then, thirdly, there are those who say that 'the Lord is the Obeyed-One . . . the universal Mover indirectly and by way of command only'. This is highly difficult to interpret.[4] But it implies that Allah does not directly cause change. He commands, and all his commands are obeyed by subsidiary spiritual principles or beings. I do not think that Ghazzali is really speaking of different spiritual beings here, but of some sort of gradation within the Godhead itself. He says, 'The presence of the Godhead is not the same as the presence of the Merciful One, nor the Sovereign Lordship' (2, 3). And here he is certainly not speaking of three different beings; but of God, understood by us in quite different ways. So perhaps he has in mind a sort of purgation of the intellect, by which we progressively remove concepts and images of God from our minds. We move from a contingent will to a non-anthropomorphic cause; then to a cosmic cause; and finally to one who is not really a cause, in the sense of a related being, at all; but who generates the universe by command only, in a quite inconceivable way.

Even that, however, is not the end of the ascent to understanding God. On the last and highest level are those few who penetrate all veils to gaze upon Allah himself, 'those who attain pure unity and perfection' (3, 4). They at last perceive that 'the relation of this Obeyed-One to the Real Existence is as the relation of the sun to essential light'. The sun is a particular place where light manifests itself. So the ultimate cause of the universe is still a particular cause;

and its essential being is beyond that particular manifestation of it. If we seek to probe to that essential nature, we find 'an existent who transcends all that is comprehensible . . . transcendent of and separate from every characterization'. One still speaks of this essential nature as existent, as transcendent and as ungraspable by concepts. This is a claim to knowledge; and it is the culmination of a way of spiritual experience, at the terminus of which lies a state in which 'nothing remains any more save the One, the Real . . . All perishes but his countenance . . . becomes the experience of the soul' (3, 4).

What is remarkable about all this is that Ghazzali remains and is accepted as a philosopher within the orthodox Sunni tradition of Islam. He is not some sort of aberrant mystic. Like Maimonides, he finds that when he presses the quest for understanding the nature of God, he comes to a place where concepts fail of application, but where it seems to make sense to speak of a possible object of experience, knowledge and bliss. When you press the difference of God to its uttermost, and find that 'nothing remains save the One', you have obliterated all difference. We might even say that where one arrives at the incomprehensible, one can no longer say that any ground for asserting difference or identity remains. Finally, the God who is beyond any relation whatsoever turns out to be 'closer to man than the vein of his neck' (50:12). It is no longer better to say that he is far away than that he is near at hand; for the very stressing of difference obliterates all spatial distinctions and separations.

I would be extremely hesitant to offer any precise interpretation of Ghazzali's views. But I suggest that the general tenor of this thought is unmistakable. The God of whom no image can be made is ultimately a god who cannot be confined to any precise set of human concepts. How, then, can one avoid saying that anything goes? At that point one must return to the practice and the context which gives these concepts sense. The life of Islam is a life of submission to the revelation of the Koran, to the worship of Allah and a preparation for judgement. In becoming a Muslim one joins a community built on the Shari'a, the laws of justice and piety; and within that community speaking of Allah and of the will of Allah has its primary place and function. This is not to say that religious terms can be understood solely in terms of some function they have in maintaining a form of social life. But it is the community which defines how the terms are used regulatively to sustain a typical or paradigm set of attitudes.

The Muslim lives before Allah; in the consciousness of one who sees all and who has power over everything in heaven and earth; who will judge with severity, rewarding each according to his works; but who is merciful to those who repent and submit to him. This is a matter of living in accordance with a metaphor; the metaphor of the all-wise, all-powerful judge.[5] But one has to face the question: is there such a judge? And will we face a judgement and an eternity of paradise or hell? If one does not probe the idea too closely, it certainly makes sense to speak of an all-powerful judge. We just take human knowledge, power and mercy and think of them as hugely extended. Even the simplest believer realizes, however, that this judge is invisible and really rather unlike human beings, since he must be beyond the physical universe and related to it in a unique way to have total knowledge and power over it. So we begin to qualify. We say, 'If you think of there being such a judge, you will be able to explain what will happen in the future, to your life, at least after death. Also, you will respond to the things that happen to you now in a particular way, as if in the face of a witness and judge of conduct.' There are two elements present here; the reaction to all that happens now; and the belief that certain things will happen in future, which we can explain by saying that Allah, the perfect Judge, brings them about. Allah is, then, both a reactive model to help you respond to your experiences now in a certain way; and a predictive model giving rise to certain expectations about the future.[6]

This model is based on revelation; and it leaves many questions unresolved. Why does Allah have the character he has? What brings him into being? How can we be sure he will always know everything, that nothing will overpower him? The ordinary believer need not raise these questions; yet they do not just arise from idle curiosity. They arise from a desire to know more of Allah, the source of our life, and thus to react to him properly. It is at this point that contingency is denied of the ultimate source of our life. For what is contingent is in the end inexplicable; and we do not wish to say that Allah just happens to be there, though he might well have been otherwise, or might not have been at all. So we say that Allah is uniquely self-subsistent; he depends on nothing else for his being. If this is so, then all principles of being are contained in him; he is the source and origin of all qualities. There can be no perfection or value which does not take its origin from him; and so he is the highest value as well as the originative being.

By reflection, we quickly progress from the idea of a very wise and powerful mind to the idea of a necessary and perfect source of all. But this idea is so far beyond our imagination that we have to say that we cannot imagine such a being at all; we can only say that the concept of such a being is implicit in our revealed images of Allah. It shows those images to be always inadequate to the reality underlying them, but not to be false or misleading in themselves. Nor is this just an intellectual overlay on a vividly metaphorical religious base. It is essential to the religious form of apprehension that we should see that God cannot be confined to any image, not even to a revealed image. Islam has been consistent in denying any possibility of making an image of God. All we have are words, and they do not show the divine reality; they may express it, but words are essentially communicative and indirect; they do not and cannot carry the divine essence. The idea of the essential hiddenness of God is part of Islam; God shows us only what is required for us to live well. We have the Book of God, but not the Being of God, within our grasp.[7]

In the end, can Islam really be called a form of dualism, opposing God and the world as two essentially distinct realities? God is not another object over against the world, of the same sort. And the world has no essential existence apart from God. Thus the universe is the only existent of its own sort and God is a different category of existent. So to say God *and* the world exist is rather like saying that a pound of rice and a highest prime number exist. Would that be a form of dualism? If the world exists only in total dependence on God, it might be better to say that the world manifests (the will of) God, and so in a sense is God, under the aspect of space and time. It is the finite manifestation of infinity, and so a form of monism after all. The world is limited, imperfect and derived and God is not. Yet even monists agree that is so, and see the world as the contingent and conditioned aspect of God.[8]

We have seen how that supreme monist, Sankara, insists on distinguishing the Real, perfect and untouched by evil and imperfection, from the Unreal, realm of delusion and transience. Now we see that the two quite different forms of reality posited by dualists, the infinite and the finite, are not just distinct and separate. The finite, for Ghazzali, exists in total dependence on the infinite; all that it is depends upon Allah. Thus the world is the direct manifestation of Allah and his will. The more we stress dependence, the more we tend to unity, to the view that the finite manifests, in its own form, part of the nature of the unbounded origin of all. Perhaps, then, it is a misleading opposition that we make between cosmological dualism – saying that God and the world are quite different – and cosmological monism – saying that God and the world together form one reality. We rather need to distinguish the sense in which we use such words, and say that the infinite is different in kind, absolutely different, from the finite. Yet the finite is the manifestation or appearance of the infinite, and is thus the same reality seen under a different aspect. The ultimate distinction, then, is that between reality and appearance; and that is neither the assertion that there are two distinct things nor the assertion that there is only one thing. We might prefer to say that there is really only one thing; but it appears under the aspect of qualification, modification and plurality.

However difficult a concept it may be, it seems that the religious traditions considered so far agree that we must see in the ultimate reality – which we may call 'God', the ultimate focus of creative being and value – a duality of aspect. The primal aspect of God is that in which he is free from contact, the absolute One. He is not dependent on anything else, and so he is unchangeable, indivisible and unlimited in existence and value. This is the *ousia* or essence of God, complete, indivisible and unchanging. It enters into no causal relations with anything; it is, in Ghazzali's terminology, 'an existent ... transcendent of and separate from every characterization'.

But that is not all one can say of God. Indeed, to say that alone is impossible, for it would be incomprehensible altogether and irrelevant to us. There is another aspect of the divine Being; and we may call this the qualified aspect; the *energeia*[9] or activity of the same God. Without changing at all, God manifests his simple nature in time and creativity, as Ruler and Judge of all things, as 'Lord of Creation' (Sura 1,1). Time does not add anything to eternity; and it would be a category mistake to speak of the primal and qualified God additively, as though together they had more reality than they had alone. The world causes no change in the divine essence; it reflects that essence or manifests it in part and sequentially. Time can proceed even without beginning or end, in an ever-creative and changing process; yet the divine essence will not be changed one iota. Of course, the qualified God will continually change – judging, revealing, warning, showing compassion. But all these things will manifest only what he changelessly is. New values will come into existence and pass away, in the cosmos; but they will not affect the reality of that being beyond all contact, and transcendent of all such changes. The changeless perfection of God is mirrored in the world, but not changed or modified by it in any way. Nevertheless, God is modified, in his qualified aspect; and in that aspect he continually enters into the suffering and joy of his creatures. But such passions do not belong to his essential being.

A modern parallel to this doctrine can be found in the philosophical work of Whitehead, who distinguished between the primordial and the consequential nature of God. God's primordial nature is changeless, constituted of a primal act of evaluation of all eternal objects. But God's consequential nature is constantly changing, as it responds to the continual creative advance of the world.[10] However, Whitehead's view is significantly different from that to be found in the classical authors I am considering. On his view, the primordial nature is abstract and not fully real; whereas on the classical view God's primal nature is the only truly real, the only self-existent reality, from which all other existence flows. For Whitehead, God's consequential nature is a continual reception of the many creative acts of creatures, who are the real foci of creativity in the universe. But for the classical view, the qualified aspect of God is still causally primary; it is the source of all change. Creativity flows from it, and is not a superior universal principle. And creatures have only a derived creativity, always dependent on the permissive will of God.

Despite these differences, Whitehead's process philosophy does help to bring out the importance of temporality, creativity and plurality in a religious view. Perhaps the classical theistic view has sometimes ignored these aspects in its concern to emphasize the eternity and impassibility of God, thus devaluing to some extent the material world and the possibilities for creative change it presents. Such a charge is a difficult one to bring against Islam, however, which has always been primarily a social and politically aware faith. Given the constraints which lack of technological skill placed upon traditional Islamic cultures, they were very much concerned with enjoying life in this world in a just and ordered society. Nevertheless, it is precisely in Islam that Al-Ghazzali developed his views of the divine nature; and they express that aspect of Islamic thought which has consistently refused to represent the divine Being in any art form. God is both free from contact and he will judge the people of the earth in accordance with their deeds – and thus react to what they do. What looks like a sheer contradiction must be taken as an assertion of dual-aspect theism – that the God who is supremely one and in himself supremely simple yet possesses another aspect, according to which it may be rightly said that he is related in creation, warning, judgement and compassion to creatures.

In the religious traditions examined so far, there are in fact four divisions that can be made in the divine Being. First, there is the level of complete unknowability, denied by Ramanuja, but affirmed by Sankara, by Buddhaghosa and apparently, however strangely, by both Maimonides and Al-Ghazzali. Below that is the level of the 'higher Brahman', the Lord of bliss, knowledge and unlimited existence, who is not tainted by contact with the world, but who contains in himself an infinite number of excellences. On the third level, as it were, is the qualified Brahman, Brahman as causal and effected, the glorious Lord or, in Buddhist tradition, the body of bliss. For Maimonides and Al-Ghazzali, this is God as Lord of creation, Lord of the glorious throne and the Father of Israel. And lastly is the *nirmana-kaya*, the body of flesh, of the earthly Buddha, or the *avatar* of Vishnu who represents God in human form. Jews and Muslims do not accept doctrines either of an ascent of man to the Divine such as is found in Buddhism, or of a descent of God to man such as is found in Vishnaism. Yet the Hebrew Bible contains accounts of the appearances of God in human form; and even the Koran, though in general less overt, speaks of Allah as seated on a throne, and so as, in some sense, capable of manifesting in human form. Without diminishing these differences, there is a commonly accepted view that the Divine can be expressed in human form, even if no image can be made of that form.

It is clear that the manifestations of God in human form by no means express the whole reality of the Divine. They are precisely forms which the believer may encounter, expressing a reality beyond themselves. It is in Christianity that one finds the strongest doctrine that God is expressed, not only in human appearance, but in a fully human life. In Islam the metaphorical nature of talk of the feet, throne and speech of Allah is most clearly apparent. Yet, though Christians insist that Christ is really a man, they do not believe that God turned wholly into a man; he continued to be the Ruler of the universe, in a reality far transcending human capacities. Thus all traditions are agreed that the divine Being cannot be fully and in every respect manifested in human form or reality.

What is not so often realized is that the idea of God as the compassionate Lord of creation is also an idea which the classical theologians take to express a reality transcending it. Such an idea is true at the level of human understanding, just as a human form may truly represent God to human perception. But one must also see that there is a level beyond. Belief in God, for orthodox Islam as for orthodox Judaism and Vedanta – and Christianity, as we shall see – is not just belief that there is a very powerful, wise and knowledgeable person behind the universe. God is not an object at all, and there are no concepts which can encompass his nature, as the imageless and unconditioned one. The basic religious core of the idea is that God is always beyond; he transcends every limitation of thought and being. The highest revelation remains a symbol, pointing beyond itself, to be responded to and cast aside. It is essential to religious discernment that one both defines one's total reactive response by a revelatory symbol; and that one negates the symbol, if understood as comprehending the nature of the revealer. One must both climb the ladder and throw it away; for the point of the ladder was to bring the mind to a new viewpoint, not to be revered as a sacred idol. How is the viewpoint reached? By climbing – that is, by using a symbol to specify a set of distinctive attitudes (to God as compassionate Judge, for example). But it is equally important that these symbols do not become seen as wholly adequate and definitive. They are revealed in a certain context of history; but the inner dynamic of faith leads one to transcend them and to transcend every thought-construct as definitive of God.

So one has first of all the level of revealed symbols, culturally

conditioned and expressing many particularities of temperament
and social ideal. By reflection one moves to the level of philosophical
concept – the systematization of images and their integration within
wider spheres of knowledge. Here one may get the disembodied
person or the self-existent perfect one as a concept. This is unlikely
to be an object of piety, but its presence prevents real idolatry
and explores the sense of basic reality and supremacy and all-
embracingness which is part of the revealed truth. Finally one has
the abandonment of all concepts, not in a simple negation, but as
a denial of the final adequacy of human understanding, a way of
saying, 'This is as much as we can understand; the reality is far
beyond', hidden in the cloud of dazzling light.

One must continually move back and forwards between these
levels. On the level of symbols alone, religious piety tends to be
naïve, exclusively intolerant and over-dogmatic ('This is the only
way'). On the level of abstract concept alone, one has a rather
abstruse and dispassionate, remote God to whom it is difficult to
relate; and religion tends to be seen primarily as a matter of argument, theory and metaphysical speculation. On the level of negation
alone, everything tends to disappear into an opaque cloud of indifference; where nothing can be said, nothing matters, and the most
absurd contradictions are as acceptable as the most profound paradoxes. One needs the devotional symbols, the metaphysical concepts
and the apophatic ideals to stand together in continually reactive
interrelation. On this view, the apophatic is not the final truth.
Taken alone, it can hardly be said to be true at all. Each level has
its appropriate form of truth – as symbol, as concept and as asymptotic ideal.

The classical tradition itself was more able to speak of the
complete, immutable and simple reality as the one truly Real,
because virtually all those who wrote in that tradition viewed time
as itself in some sense closed or completed. Of course the Vedantins
thought time was without beginning or end; yet it consisted, they
said, of endlessly recurring identical cycles of time; and in that sense
nothing completely new could ever happen. The Jewish, and even
more, the Muslim, philosophers believed that time had begun and
could be viewed by God as completed; it was in principle a closed
and finite series; so God could be aware of it 'all at once', or without
succession in his knowledge. Thus the Koran can say, 'We have

planned the actions of all men' (6:104); and 'We know those who have gone before you and those who will come hereafter' (15:21). It can read as if Allah knows everything that will ever happen in time, and has planned all things in the future even before time begins. 'He knows what is before and behind men' (2:255); and 'We have predestined for hell many jinn and many men' (7:177). Similar views will be found defended in Aquinas. Of course it is perfectly possible to interpret such passages in a metaphorical sense, without being committed to complete foreknowledge of everything or a total determination of every detail of creation by Allah. However one interprets such passages, it is logically much easier to regard God as wholly immutable if one believes that the time series, being essentially complete, can in principle be seen as a whole, timelessly by God.[11] Dual-aspect theism then becomes the view that God in himself is wholly immutable, knowing creatures by knowing his own essence and the eternal decrees it contains. But this immutability is expressed temporally, in the form of a knowing, acting Lord; as indeed he is so far as creatures are concerned. Time is indeed the 'moving image of eternity',[12] where it can be seen as a temporal manifestation of eternity, essentially complete and in that sense unchanging. Nevertheless, the problem remains that, even in a 'closed time', finite action and knowledge add something to a purely infinite God.

Suppose one asks the question, 'Can really new things happen in time? Can God do creatively new things and therefore come to know things he has never known before?' The prospect of an endless and non-cyclic time opens up new dimensions to the problem of dual-aspect theism. One would have to say more clearly that the temporal, causal Lord of creation is real, and changes in respect of his actions and his knowledge of particular events in the finite world. Yet this reality could still be taken as a manifestation of an unchanging reality beyond it. And perhaps Al-Ghazzali offers a clue to this problem in saying that the relation of the One Real to the 'Obeyed-One' is like the relation of light to the sun. If God in himself is not an object, then we cannot really think of him as possessing knowledge or as a causal agent in any way we can understand. We might say that this aspect of God, which is the self-existent aspect and the foundation of all other reality whatsoever, is immutably and completely perfect, but is wholly beyond objectification. He cannot be changeless in respect of his knowledge of the finite world, in all its details. If he has changeless knowledge, it must be of his own archetypal essence; and if he has changeless power, it must be in respect of the self-existence which ensures that he immutably possesses all excellences, indivisibly and incorruptibly.

All orthodox traditions agree that God is immutable and eternal. But the notion of 'eternity' is very complex, and at least three rather different concepts of eternity can be posited. The first is the concept of exclusive eternity, where the eternal has no relation to any time at all. Al-Ghazzali may speak as though he accepts that view; but in fact of course the eternity of Allah is manifested in the finite world. It is not correct to say that it is merely separate and wholly self-contained; for all the world exists by its will. A second concept is that of inclusive eternity, where the eternal is seen as emanating time and reabsorbing it; so that all time progressively reveals it and is in the end consummated in a completed eternity.[13] Here, the eternal is a sort of timeless summation of completed time. That may be near the view the classical theologians actually took, with their closed view of time. But there is a third possibility, the concept of dynamic eternity. The eternal endlessly expresses itself in dynamic openness. It remains changeless in creativity, wisdom, omnipotence and omniscience – knowing all things that are actual, yet possessing a dynamic aspect which is in its finite aspect incomplete, while being complete in not lacking being and in possessing it unlimitedly.

On this third view, there is an endless time, in which creative action manifests itself in infinite ways. Yet the divine nature never changes; its creative expressions and responses simply specify that nature in endlessly new ways. Moreover, the immutable nature is not merely abstract; and it is not merely that which is common to the flux of the manifold. It has a self-existent, fundamental and originative character, an infinite fullness which no finite changes can diminish or augment. The finite derives from and participates in it. That which is beyond each finite reality is complete in its own being, needing nothing else to exist in the fullest sense. The dynamism of endless creativity does not fill a gap in the divine nature. But in another sense it introduces new, finite, qualities. These do not make the divine nature more perfect or more real; they are not necessary to it; nor do they in any way imperil it or involve it in imperfection. The eternal is free from all contact; yet the endlessly creative and compassionate Lord is a true manifestation in time of the ineffable nature of that which lies beyond. He is a finite manifestation of changeless light. Allah is, as Al-Ghazzali puts it, an unbounded ocean of light which in itself is not augmented or diminished. But through its ten thousand veils it shines in an endless variety of forms. The light in its essential nature does not change; yet by its own power it manifests all the forms of the heavens and the earth.

The attribution of such a duality of aspect to the One Real can be traced, as I have sought to show, in Vedanta, Mahayana and Judaism as well as in this strand of orthodox Muslim thought. While Islam can seem utterly opposed especially to Hindu forms of worship, at least in one of its foremost theologians it preserves the view that the Supreme Reality is beyond all our conceptual restrictions. The way to union with that reality shows a strong operative similarity to that found in other traditions also. It is in that apophatic movement of the mind, which is also a purifying of the will of all attachments to finite goals and images, that the end of the religious life is accomplished. 'Light upon light: Allah guides to his light whom he will.'

Thomas Aquinas: the Idea of Subsistent Being

The classical Christian idea of God is found, at least in its basic and essential tenets, in virtually all the early Christian theologians. It reached its paradigm formulation in the work of Thomas Aquinas, who, until very recently, was the official philosopher of the Roman Catholic Church.[1] But it is found in the theologians of Eastern Orthodoxy and Anglicanism, too, and the great Reformed theologians qualify it rather than rejecting it outright. At any rate, Aquinas is a theologian and philosopher of the highest stature; his Christian orthodoxy is impeccable; and the doctrine of God he expounded both epitomizes a thousand years of consistent theological development and exerted a huge influence on his successors, especially in the Catholic tradition.

The key text for Aquinas' view is to be found in the *Summa Theologiae*, Articles 2–11, which deal specifically with the existence and attributes of God. In other works he amplified but did not fundamentally modify the views he takes in that book. Aquinas begins his whole discussion of God by saying, 'We cannot know what God is, but only what he is not' (1a, 3, intro.). This blunt phrase sets the scene for Aquinas' discussion of God's nature, and places an agnostic qualifier on everything that is said about God. So he sets out to discover 'the ways in which God does not exist'.[2] His aim is to define God as a quite unique category of object – if, indeed, the word 'object' is at all in place here. He does of course believe that God exists and even that his existence can be demonstrated. It can be shown, he claims, that there is a cause of the world, which must have certain characteristics to account for the nature of its effects. It must contain in actuality all that it could ever bring to be, though in a higher manner. It must be immutable and necessary, for only thus could change and contingency find a finally adequate basis and explanation. We can say, then, that God is a cause, that he is immutable and necessary, purposive and containing all perfections. But how much does this really tell us positively about God?

Aquinas' task is to rule out from his account of God everything which is inappropriate to him. And the first thing to go is composition. 'In God', he says, 'there can be no potentiality.' There can be nothing which at one time is not and at some future time will come to be. Nothing can come to be in God, for he is changelessly all that he is. He is not even logically capable of change; for such a logical capability would be a form of potentiality; it would be an unrealized possibility, even if it was never to be realized in fact. The completely unrestricted perfection of God therefore requires that potentiality does not exist in him.

Thus God cannot be a material body, extended in space. Then it could be divided up; there is something that could happen to it to change it. God actually exists, then, without even the logical possibility of change; he cannot be or contain anything material. Neither can he be a disembodied mind. Minds are in continual change — thoughts, feelings, decisions, sensations succeed one another continuously. At this point (1a, 3, 2), Aquinas accepts Aristotle's dictum that it is matter which makes forms particular, which makes this chair different from that exactly similar chair.[3] If there is no matter, then there cannot be individual chairs at all, but only what we might call one unindividualized essence of chairness. If God is not in any respect material, there is a sense in which he cannot be an individual, a particular case either of mind or of Godness, of which there might in principle be other cases, perhaps in other universes. He must be, uniquely, a form 'not assumed by material things', but which 'itself subsists as a thing . . . and is thus individual of itself'. God is a subsistent form or nature and not a particular case of such a nature. He is more like a universal, subsisting of itself alone, than he is like a particular individual; though he is not a universal, considered as something which might be shared by many particulars.

In a philosophical world which is not inclined to think that things instantiate real essences anyway, this idea of God as a subsistent essence is likely to seem doubly incoherent. In the first place, there are no forms at all; in the second place, the idea of a form without embodiment taxes the intellect too far. It is interesting to note, however, that Aquinas never sympathizes with the view that God is a disembodied mind or person, a rational agent of some exalted sort. His model of God was of a being beyond all change of any sort, purely actual and the most perfect good. This is an essentially Platonic idea of God as a pure form, without any mixture of material elements. 'God is to be identified with his own essence or nature' (1a, 3, 3). This is not quite uniquely true of God. It would be true of any subsistent form; it is just to say that subsistent forms (such as angels?) are, as such, intrinsically individual. But it follows that God does not possess a number of properties which may be added to him or taken away, which he may or may not possess. That which makes him God is simply his essential nature itself, indivisibly and unchangeably actual. We may speak of God as having various properties – of wisdom, goodness, power and so forth. But 'the diversity this implies is not to be attributed to God himself, but to the way in which we conceive him'.

God is not only identical with his essence. He is also to be identified with his existence: 'The substance of God is therefore his existence' (1a, 3, 4). For what could cause God to exist? There is nothing other than God which could bring him into being; for he is the first cause. Nor could he bring himself into being, which is absurd. Perhaps, then, he just pops into being, quite uncaused? But that would be to render the whole nature of things ultimately arbitrary. Why should a subsistent form of just this nature exist at all? The only intelligible view is to say that it is not the sort of being which could logically be caused. God either always is or he never is. But if you say he always is, that means that God's actual existence is part of, or is identical with, his nature. That nature carries its existence with it. Once again, many modern philosophers would find this incomprehensible. They would argue that one may specify the nature of a thing completely; and one can still ask, 'But is there an X?' How can a mere description of something entail its existence? Of course it is not the description which entails existence; it is the objective nature itself. This is no magic charm, which conjures out of mere words the reality of God. What is being said is that there is a unique form of existent, such that it is 'its very nature to exist' (1a, 3, 4). We are not to think of an abstract nature forcing itself to exist. We are to think of a unique existent which, being wholly incapable of change, cannot fail to be.[4] But, we feel compelled to ask, might it not fail ever to have been? After all, I can say, 'There is no X' quite consistently, whatever X may be. What I can *say*, however, is beside the point. The point is that Aquinas wishes to speak of 'the act of existing' (*actum essendi*) as having its own unique sort of actuality. God is the pure act of being, which cannot be separated from that which defines what he is; it is his nature.

It is usual, in post-Fregean philosophy, to analyse 'existence' in terms of the existential quantifier; to say 'there is an x', where x is some predicate expression, descriptive of some object.[5] This is helpful logically, for the purposes of logical symbolism, but it does not really resolve any philosophical problems. For what does 'there is a' mean? The meaning is extremely complex, and can vary from 'there is a prime number between 11 and 14', 'there is a chair in the room' to 'there is a God'. We can use the same symbolism in each case, but does it have the same meaning? We need to spell the meaning out each time in terms of its context. So 'there is a chair' will contextually imply that if I go there, I will see it and so on. It will imply that it will attract or repel other solid objects in the vicinity. I need not spell all these things out, or even know what they all are. My phrase will carry a host of implications, depending on what sort of things chairs are and how I can know whether they exist or not. And if I say, 'There is a prime number', I must understand what a prime number is (which I learn from mathematics books) and know how to decide when it is correct to say there is one.

Now if I say, 'There is a God', I must first understand what God is – and for Aquinas, God is a subsistent form, the pure act of being, fully actual cause of all derived beings. How do I decide whether there is one? There are no observational or computational techniques that can help me. It is established by argument, as far as philosophy goes, from the universe, seen as derived. But this cannot be an inductive argument to the existence of another object. So different is God's form of being from anything of which we can form any idea that we must say that 'God does not belong to a genus' (1a, 3, 5). Since his nature is to exist, and (following Aristotle) existence is not a genus, God does not have a nature which can be defined in any other way. This is a very obscure notion, since in one sense God must belong to the class of 'pure acts of being', even though that is a necessarily one-member class. What I think Aquinas means is that one cannot define something as belonging to the nature of God, prior to his actual existence. He is indefinable, in that his nature cannot be broken up into smaller elements, which can be used as an analysis of the divine Being. His Being is absolutely indefinable by analysis into simpler terms.

But is God not known as the cause of his effects, and thus belonging to the class of causes? No; for we cannot say what a cause is and then say that God is a being who happens to instantiate causality. Rather God's definition is given uniquely by his unrestricted form of existing. He does not instantiate a prior form of causality. The form of causality derives whatever reality it has entirely from the pure act of being, which is prior to all forms. There would be no forms at all without the act of being. In the case of God, existence precedes essence – or, more exactly, it is identical with a quite unique essence from which all more restricted essences derive by limitation and particularization. In saying that God does not belong to a class, Aquinas is saying that the being of God does not conform to some prior nature, to a pre-existent world of forms, which sets conceptual limits on his being – as the forms set constraints on Plato's Demiurge in the *Timaeus*.[6] Rather, all natures derive from the act of pure being, without which no natures would even be possible. As he says, 'Actual existence takes precedence of potential existence' (1a, 3, 1). Though we can say 'God is not', even to form an idea of God entails that God is logically possible; and that entails that something is actual, even in the world of which it is said, 'God is not'. There can thus be no null class of possibilities; and, since God either exists in every possible world or not at all, in that sense God necessarily exists.

Aquinas does not think that one can demonstrate the divine existence just by this consideration.[7] After all, we cannot really tell whether the concept of such a God is really coherent, and so really possible, or not. We have no direct apprehension of the divine essence, and our concepts do not straightforwardly apply to it. So we cannot be sure they are coherent, or that they point to something truly, though always inadequately. But it should be clear that what Aquinas means by a 'demonstration' of God's existence is not an inductive argument from the nature of the world to the likelihood of there being a designer or creator of it. The world is not evidence for God – a seventeenth-century notion quite foreign to Aquinas – from which a cause could be probabilistically inferred. Rather, as in Aristotle, the mind achieves identity with universal essences, via the senses, in all intellective knowing.[8] In so doing, the mind can apprehend the necessary dependence of all forms upon one supreme originative and self-existent form. It does not apprehend God, who is beyond; but it apprehends the dependence of the intelligible realm upon a self-existent pure form, the ultimately non-participating, in which all else participates. God is not inferred; but is apprehended as in and through all intelligible structures. This is a 'demonstration', in the sense of making clear, expounding, showing how essences are completed in the wholly actual essence, not itself graspable by the mind, though one can say *that* it must be, if there is to be an intelligible world of essences at all. We can see that there must be such a necessary being, since other actual essences are incomplete and dependent and imperfect and not fully intelligible. What we discern is the incompleteness and the necessity of completion. This is not an abstractly intellectual argument; it requires a vision of the completion of the world in a self-existent Ideal. It is already a form of self-transcendence, which is realized existentially in worship, transcendence towards the Ideal. The reason to which God's existence can be made evident is not ordinary human reason as we might think of it today. It is the fully developed capacity of the intellectual understanding to apprehend the true natures of things and thus to apprehend their dependence on one perfect form or essence. In this interpretation of reason, there is already that idea of *ascesis*, of self-transcendence towards the supremely real, which is the expression of the religious form of life, the understanding of sensory existence as both a fall from and a sacrament of the good and the real. So this is not simply an abstract intellectual exercise. The Aristotelian philosophy is used to validate the object of contemplative worship by locating it at the apex of a general coherent metaphysical scheme.[9]

The point of the exercise of 'demonstrating God' is not to win an argument, but to evoke in the mind a faint idea of a form of being which is far beyond our comprehension, but which we may in some sense discern as 'the immortal hidden in the real', the unconditioned mediated in the conditioned, and the fully self-existent foundation of all finite reality. The Five Ways only make sense when some such vision is presupposed.[10] What they articulate conceptually is the sense of the unconditioned – not a discrete mental feeling, but an innate directionality implicit in our conceptual response to the world as a patterned unity, mediating meanings. This disposition is given particular form in the teachings of the prophets and seers, who teach ways of life in which this religious response can be channelled to human flourishing. This vision is not dependent upon the Aristotelian philosophy in which Aquinas expounds it; indeed, it antedates that philosophy, and even Platonism is only one form of its expression. The sense of the absolute simplicity of God, which is fundamental to Aquinas' account of the divine Being, is the sense that God is not a thing which happens to possess existence. He is '*esse subsistens*', the act of ceaseless and unrestricted being. As Dionysius puts it, remaining 'in one single, ceaseless and transcendent act', it 'produces in infinite ways an infinite number of other powers' (*On the Divine Names*, 1, 5). 'From its oneness it becomes manifold while yet remaining within itself' (*On the Divine Names* 2, 11). It is the light of Al-Ghazzali, which remains constant while found in a myriad particular forms.

However, Aquinas recognizes that 'in the material world simpleness implies imperfection'. So he insists that construing God as the pure act of being is compatible with perfection. More than that, it entails perfection. For 'things are called perfect when they have achieved actuality' (1a, 4, 2); and God is completely actual. 'The perfections of everything exist in God' (1a, 4, 2); because the cause must, he assumes, be at least as perfect as any of its effects. These perfections, diverse and opposed in themselves, 'pre-exist as one in God', in a higher manner (*eminentiorem modum*). All created things receive their existence from God, and he is the unrestricted act of existence itself. Thus Aquinas can say that, in a way, creatures resemble God – all that they are derives, in an incomplete and imperfect way, from the unconditioned reality of subsistent being. But he refuses to say that God resembles creatures in any way; for there is nothing in God which actually has a qualitative likeness to the complex and finite things of the universe. This one-way resemblance is, he suggests, like that between a portrait and a man – between two things of different categories, one of which is in a way an expression of the other. The example is not wholly convincing, since men do have some similarities to portraits (two eyes, a nose and so on). But one may see how finite things may express infinite being, without there being anything in God which is a sort of shadow-copy of what is in the world. Divine perfection, then, is nothing like human perfection. It is a fullness of being from which all particular perfections flow, in which they participate and which they partially express.

What Aquinas means by saying that God is good is certainly not that he is morally commendable, or that he acts benevolently. Again he follows Aristotle in saying that 'the goodness of a thing consists in its being desirable' (1a, 5, 1). He supposes that the supremely actual is supremely desirable. So God, as supremely actual, is that at which all things aim, as they strive towards fuller actuality. He is that in which all desires can rest satisfied; for he is the consummation of complete actuality, leaving nothing further to be desired.

It is an important part of Aquinas' view of God that God is not only the first cause; he is also the final cause of all things. It is quite inadequate to think of God just starting everything going, and then playing no further part in what happens. As complete actuality, he is the final cause, that at which all things aim, as their own completion.[11] It is in this sense, as the final object of all desire, that God is primarily said to be good, 'what is desired from it being a share in resembling it' (1a, 6, 1). He is the first source of every perfection things desire, and is also the ultimate goal of all things; he is the 'pattern, source and goal of all goodness' (1a, 6, 4). Thus, as supremely actual, God is free from all potentiality and restriction; he is perfect in being. As perfect, he is supremely desirable and so supremely good. One can see how far the problem of suffering is from threatening this notion of divine goodness. God is neither good in the sense of having a choice between selfishness and altruism and freely choosing the latter; nor good in the sense of always seeking to protect creatures from harm. He is good as being the source of all perfections and the goal of all rightly ordered desires. Evil does exist, as a sort of defect of being, to some extent inevitable in any finite world; but compounded by the free choice of finite wills and so a contingent consequence of their proper, though misused, perfection. Problems remain which are vast enough, to be sure; but at least we are delivered from the idea of the perpetually fussing yet strangely incapable heavenly welfare officer.

Since God is subsistent existence and pure form, he is infinite, not being restricted in any way by matter. If it is objected that God is not for example a stone, and is therefore limited by only being one thing among others, Aquinas replies that divine existence is infinite, for it is incapable of being acquired by anything, or of being set alongside another thing of the same sort (1a, 7, 1). It is precisely and uniquely, infinite existence, unrestricted and unoriginated existence. Of course it sets all finite existences outside itself. But that does not limit it. On the contrary, it makes clear just what is meant by an infinite form of being. It excludes everything finite. Yet Aquinas is clear that it is the pattern, source and goal of everything finite, so far as such things truly participate in being. He is 'active in everything' (1a, 8, 1), as the only ultimate agent of all finite effects. 'During the whole period of a thing's existence, therefore, God must be present to it.' As perfect and infinite, God is above everything. Yet 'as causing their existence he also exists in everything'. The finite world is not part of God, it is quite distinct from him; as different as finite and infinite. Yet it only exists because of him and so he can be said to be everywhere 'in substance, power and presence', as the present cause of existence. He 'exists wholly in each and every thing' (1a, 8, 3), since his being is simple and indivisible.

In what sense, then, is God outside the universe? Aquinas says, 'Just as the soul exists wholly everywhere in the body, so God exists wholly in each and every thing' (1a, 8, 2). Yet he denies that God can be thought of as the soul of the world (1a, 3, 8); as pure form, he cannot enter into composition with anything, so as to make one whole, as soul and body form one person. Aquinas refuses to allow that God and the world can form one type of being, logically prior to the Being of God as Subsistent Existence. The world derives wholly from God, is sustained by him and will return to him. God is unaffected by what happens in the world. But it is not accurate to regard him as outside the world. He could exist alone, no doubt. But if there is any finite reality, he is substantially present in every part of it.

That God is immutable follows immediately from his having no potentiality for change. He cannot acquire anything, since he is already infinite and comprehends in himself the whole plenitude of perfections. Accordingly, he is also eternal, possessing his being perfectly and wholly, and thus without the continual acquisition and loss that belongs to temporality. There is no before and after, no successiveness in God. We must think of God's life, not as a succession of events, but as a *nunc stans*, an enduring now, or a *tota simul*, wholly possessed in one ceaseless act. God does not vary from present to past to future. Yet 'his eternity includes all times' (1a, 13, 2); it does not exclude them. Just as God is wholly present in every space, so he must be wholly present at every time. He is not absent from any time. Yet his nature is beyond all times, as immutably and perfectly possessed. For Aquinas, God is fundamentally *'ipsum esse subsistens omnibus modis indeterminatum'* (1a, 11, 4), being of itself subsistent and undetermined or unlimited in every possible way.

We can see here a virtually complete operative identity with the Vedantic idea of Brahman. Brahman is the Witness beyond change, and God is pure and ceaseless act. The paradigm metaphor is different. Yet both are beyond change and contact, and are to be found whole and entire in every part of the finite world. Indeed, Aquinas is forced to include relations to the finite as a basic part of his view, because of the idea of incarnation which lies at the heart of orthodox Christianity. Jesus Christ unites in himself the divine nature and human nature in one *hypostasis* or 'person'. On naïve understandings of the incarnation, God changed by becoming man. But Aquinas firmly denies this: 'The mystery of the incarnation was not completed through God being changed in any way from the state in which he had been from eternity, but through his having united himself to the creatures in a new way, or rather through having united it to himself' (3, 1, 1). The immutable God unites human nature to himself in one *hypostasis;* but those natures remain quite distinct. One is immutable, impassible and infinite; the other is changing, suffering and limited in various ways (by being born, dying and so on). Taking human nature does not add anything to the divine nature: 'since the divine Person is infinite, no addition can be made to it . . . not God but man is perfected' (3, 3, 1). Moreover, the divine nature cannot experience what the human nature experiences; 'What is impassible cannot suffer. Consequently, Christ's passion did not concern his Godhead' (3, 46, 12). Nevertheless, it can truly be said that God suffered, not because of the divine nature, but by reason of the human nature. 'Christ's passion belongs to the *suppositum* of the divine nature by reason of the passible nature assumed, but not on account of the impassible divine nature.'

One finds here, in a particularly striking form, the duality of aspect which we have found as a feature of all accounts of the unconditioned origin of the finite world. There is one being with two natures: one of them simple, impassible and infinite; the other complex, passionate and dependent. One can see that it would be wholly misleading for Aquinas to say that the divine nature was simple and leave it at that. Surprising and paradoxical as it seems, in the Christian view God has both a divine nature and a human nature; we might say, both an infinite and a finite nature. These are unconfused and yet not wholly separate. The divine nature is wholly beyond change; it is what is ontologically primary; it suffuses the finite nature and transforms its being, in knowledge and bliss (Jesus has perfect knowledge of God from a human point of view, and shares the beatific vision from the very first moment of his existence in the womb, according to Aquinas). It would be a heresy, the heresy of Nestorius, to say that Jesus was just a man who lived in perfect unity of will with God. He is truly God; which is to say that his human nature is assumed by the Word, the second person of the Trinity. Christians cannot shrink from saying, therefore, that God includes the finite in his own being, even if not in his own essential nature. There can be no clearer presentation of dual-aspect theism than this. The infinite assumes the finite, which is indeed wholly its own creation, but without in any way being changed in its divine nature.

What is meant by 'assumption' is left suitably vague; it is indeed a mystery beyond rational analysis, for the orthodox. And one can see it as just the same mystery as that upon which Sankara insists on the cosmic scale when he speaks of the one Brahman, which is both unqualified and qualified, and in its essential nature beyond name and form entirely. Moreover, for Aquinas, who believes that the faithful will have their bodies raised from death and will live with God in the communion of saints for ever, time must be regarded as endless. This heaven and earth may come to an end, but bodies will continue to be in space and time of some sort; and thus time is infinite at one end, even if it once began. That means that the immutability of God must be endlessly associated with a mutable aspect, as the risen and glorified Christ will always

145

continue to reign in the Kingdom. It is not the case that all temporal things will return to the eternal, into a forever completed immutable condition. An endless time can never be completed; so the completeness of the divine nature is the completeness which belongs properly to infinite being, and it is compatible with the sort of incompleteness which belongs to endless embodied existence, which will be forever united with, assumed into, the Being of God.

For Aquinas, the human nature of Jesus is forever united to the divine nature: 'The human nature is the instrument of the divine action and the human action receives power from the divine nature' (3, 43, 2). Moreover, all the redeemed will be embraced within the humanity of Christ, as one body with him as its Head, and so will in a sense be granted the grace of *theosis*, or assumption, by adoption, into the divine nature. Finite and created human persons can be sharers in the divine nature, under the Kingship of one human nature which is substantially and indefectibly united to the divine nature in one *hypostasis*. In a real sense, for the Christian vision as for the Vedantic, God is the Self of all, as Christ is the Head of the mystical body which is his Church. And God shows himself truly in the person of a glorified Lord, having a perfect human nature as the instrument of his action. For all that, God himself remains always beyond even the human comprehension of Jesus; though he can be truly known, he cannot be perfectly known, or comprehended, by any human nature, however perfect. What Aquinas says of God is that 'we know about his relation to creatures – that he is the cause of them all; about the difference between him and them – that nothing created is in him; that his lack of such things is not a deficiency in him but due to his transcendence' (1a, 12, 12). God is known in a threefold aspect – as cause of all; as utterly different from all created things; and as infinitely more perfect than any or all of them. Because of these facts, even Jesus can say that 'my Father . . . is greater than I' (Jn 14:27), referring to the infinite distinction between his human nature and the divine nature which united the human to itself without confusion.

Aquinas rejects the opinion of Maimonides, already noted, that we can only truly speak of God in negative terms. For, he says, words 'do say what God is' but they 'fail to represent adequately what he is' (1a, 13, 2). We speak of God in so far as creatures represent him, seeing them as imperfect representations of something in itself unknown. Our words apply properly to God; but their *modum significandi*, the way they signify to us, is appropriate only to creatures. In this way, 'God' is an operational word (*nomen operationis*); we use it in seeing the working of divine providence in the world; yet it refers to the divine nature, one and simple. In the end, he follows ancient tradition in saying that 'He who Is' is the most adequate name for God, since it 'fixes on no aspect of being but stands open to all and refers to him as to an infinite ocean of being' (1a, 13, 11).

It is possible to argue that Aquinas has simply been misled by Aristotelian philosophy; by a mythology of subsistent forms and essences, by a Greek devaluation of the material and temporal, and by a neo-Platonic negative theology which owes little or nothing to the Bible.[12] Of course it is true that Aquinas, like Maimonides and Al-Ghazzali, used the terminology provided by Greek philosophy to give a reflective account of the concept of God. If that whole mode of thinking is rejected, these things would have to be put in another way. Yet the central Christian doctrines of the incarnation and atonement require something very like Aquinas' view. It is hardly possible to have a satisfactory doctrine of the incarnation if one insists, for example, that God is a supreme rational agent, with knowledge and power much greater than the human, yet similar in kind. For then the relation of the divine mind and the human mind in the person of Jesus becomes impossible to manage. One has to think of a continual interaction of two minds in the same body; and it is hard to escape a very unsatisfactory sort of dualism, whereby one mind simply controls the other as some sort of puppet. Aquinas' account avoids this difficulty by making God and man different in kind; so Jesus becomes the finite instrument of the infinite indeed; but that is totally unlike one person being the slave of another much more powerful person. The humanity retains its own proper nature and autonomy. Its unity with the divine is not the negation but the fulfilment of something that all may hope for, in a lesser degree: the liberation of human life by its becoming a vehicle for manifesting the 'infinite ocean of being' which is God.

Similarly the atonement can seem rigidly legalistic if one views it as one person requiring another person (Jesus) to suffer for the sins of yet other persons. On the Thomist account the passion of the human nature of Jesus, freely offered, must also be seen as the suffering of God, in his human nature; and it is only in that aspect that Jesus' death can atone for the sins of the whole world. It is God himself who suffers; and yet the divine nature remains beyond all imperfection and grief. It is thus God himself who pays the price or suffers the consequence of sin, not just some innocent human being. And in that unique way he removes all that stands between human beings and their fulfilment in God. Now this doctrine remains obscure, a mystery of faith. But it can only be held at all if one has some view of God which does not make him simply another person, however exalted, distinct from the human person of Jesus or of any other creature. Here again we may discern that dialectical tension of distinctness (the infinite being wholly unlike the finite) and unity (the divine and human natures being united in Christ) which is a fundamental characterization of the Divine in each tradition we have examined. The very real differences between religious traditions are differences in the ways this complex dialectical tension is worked out; yet the underlying structure remains discernibly similar. That infinite, unlimited and unconditioned ocean of being beyond and untouched by the finite is also mediated in the finite, in the wisdom and beauty of the heavens, in the majesty and awesomeness of the moral law, in the inspired teachings of saints and visionaries, and in the souls of men and women.

It is worth recalling that the work of Aquinas is not just a speculative metaphysical enterprise. Like the theologians of the other orthodox traditions we have been dealing with, he accepts revelation as the source of his faith. It is not that he takes the work of Aristotle, recently recovered from the works of his Arabic translators, and squeezes Christian doctrines into it at any price. He does take the work of Aristotle as philosophically definitive; but his references are as often to Dionysius and to the Fathers who stood in a more Platonic tradition. That tradition in turn became so powerful because it offered a way in which the central New Testament teachings could be built into a coherent interpretative framework for understanding the universe. Of course the search for a coherent explanatory scheme was important. Yet the decisive factor was the life of faith itself, built in response to the revelatory matrix of the life of Jesus, who was taken to be the mediator of the infinite in the realm of the finite.

The distinctiveness of the Christian position is that the mediation does not take place in the history of a people (Judaism); through the words of an inspired book (Islam); through a man who by his own effort became one with the unconditioned (Buddhism); or through avatars who took only the appearance of humanity (Vishnaism); but in a human person who was believed to be united to God from the first moment of his life. Again, these are not to be taken as wholly exclusive paradigms, but as controlling matrices with many complex, subordinate and complementary elements. From the Christian fundamental paradigm flow a great number of consequent differences, which depend upon the uniqueness of the one person of Jesus and the role of the Church as the mediation of that uniqueness, in turn, to each succeeding age.

The differences are real and important. But it is equally important to discern the similarity of structure and concern. The infinite is mediated, not for speculative enrichment, but for the liberation of humanity from its limiting conditions. In the case of Christianity, the limitations of human existence are primarily those of death and lack of knowledge of God. The cause is sin or failure to rely wholly on God. The goal is the beatific vision, a fulfilment of a whole human life in the communal vision of God. The means is faith in the redeeming incarnation of God in the person of Jesus. And the revelatory matrix of the whole process is the life, death and resurrection of Jesus. It is this life, as it was first perceived by the apostles, and is now proclaimed by word and sacrament, which is potent to evoke an experience of the unlimited reality and bliss of unconditioned being, in and through that particular human person.

One can see the nature of religious faith clearly delineated in the believer's response to the revelation of God in the person of Jesus Christ. First of all is the vision of a reality of absolute worth in Jesus, which leads one to see him (as he is presented in the believing community) as the icon or image of God, the being unlimited in reality and value. This vision, which of course only comes to some people and is not based on inference or argument, leads immediately to a second element of faith. For the vision of a perfectly mediating life leads one to see one's own life as bound to failure, illusion, alienation and futility. In Christian language, it 'convicts of sin'; and, as one believes oneself to see the true goal of human selfhood, so there occurs a reorientation of one's view of one's own existence. The given revelation is not only about an objective reality other than oneself; it is also, and at the same time, a revelation of the disordered nature of one's own personal life. The third element of faith, when properly carried through, is the personal submission to the supreme reality which has been discerned in Jesus; the preparedness to let oneself be confronted and changed by the divine power that is seen in him. And this naturally leads to the fourth element, which is the adoption of a personal discipline of life, in which all things are ordered to the one final goal of complete union with the Divine, or conformity to the pattern of the life of Christ.

These four elements, of vision, self-understanding, submission and self-discipline, together constitute the response of faith. It is not at all a dispassionate, theoretical or speculative response to some sort of probabilistic inference. It is essentially self-involving, reactive and transformative; and though one would hope that one's faith was reasonably grounded, it is entirely inappropriate to think of measuring it out in some precise proportion to objectively accumulated evidence.[13] The structure of vision and commitment has a peremptory and yet commissive character which is quite different from that of a tentative speculation founded on the careful collection of all relevant clues. It may, of course, be doubted whether much original scientific speculation has that patient and tentative character. But at least in the natural sciences one would admit the relevance of careful checking procedures and controlled experiment. Though one may, by analogy, speak of religious commitment as an 'experiment of faith', which may confirm or disconfirm belief, yet the procedures regarded as appropriate are very different. One cannot conduct experiments on God; and it is not appropriate to seek to test one's faith in the most difficult possible conditions.[14] There is no compelling reason why all rational human activity should conform to one pattern or scientific method, however. So one may propose that religious faith has its own proper structure and place in human life.

The philosopher may seek to bring out the structure of the response of faith and to integrate it within a wider view of the nature of reality. That is what Aquinas did; and he naturally used the best available philosophical tools of his time, in the new and rather radical philosophy of Aristotle, so far as he knew it from the Arabic translations. If one rejects that philosophy, one might say that it is all founded on a vast philosophical mistake. Perhaps there are no forms or natures in things. Perhaps talk of a self-subsistent form is meaningless. Perhaps the whole Aristotelian view of knowledge and metaphysics is simply obsolete. Would that mean that the notion of God as '*esse subsistens*' would collapse? I do not think so. On the contrary, it seems an absurd suggestion that the whole neo-Platonic vision which is found in Plotinus and Pseudo-Dionysius arises from a philosophical mistake; as if thousands of people had been misled by a false step in philosophy. Philosophy does not have that sort of influence. It is rather that Plato himself was stumblingly trying to formulate a primal vision in terms which were by no means fixed and rigid. A similar vision is found in the Upanishads, as we have seen, and in Buddhist thought. The terminologies are different – and again, I am not saying that those differences are unimportant. Yet the conceptual tools are precisely tools, known to be inadequate and to point beyond themselves by those who used them.[15]

The vision which the philosophers are attempting to conceptualize, by putting it within a framework which can embrace all well-attested knowledge of the world in one more or less coherent scheme is the iconic vision of the finite as the image of the infinite. Aquinas captures the main elements of this vision when he characterizes God, in the early articles of the *Summa Theologiae*, under the threefold aspect of perfect and utterly distinct cause of all. The element of distinctness points to that which is always beyond, unique in kind and complete in its own infinite reality. The term '*esse subsistens*' attempts to capture this sense of utter difference of category and unrestricted being; but it is an intentional misuse of language to make '*esse*' into a substantive term.[16] It tries to point to that by which all things have being, but which is not itself limited in existence in any way. The element of causality points to the fact that this is an existent reality; we live in response to it, and all derives from it; it is the source and goal of all finite being. The element of perfection, or maximal intrinsic value, points to the fact that what appears and is present in all things by its substance, presence and power, is nevertheless always beyond, as an Ideal which draws us on asymptotically; being present in all finite values, it draws from us reverence for its inexhaustible fecundity of value and love for the delight it gives as we contemplate it. God is the self-existent Ideal – not just an ideal without being, and not just the source of all derived being, without value; but the congruence of ultimate value and reality in one transcending infinity.

This primal vision may be expressed in many conceptual schemes, which all share the dialectical opposition between unity and difference, which is mediated within a particular tradition by a dominant matrix. It is not enough, therefore, to judge Aquinas' view of God in terms of either Platonic or Aristotelian philosophy. The classical doctrine is a formulation in the best available philosophical terms (by which I simply mean the most general and adequate conceptual framework available) of the basic iconic vision. It is found in different forms in the main religious traditions. It is this vision which can help us to see the fundamental structure of the religious form of life.

8

The Dual-Aspect Doctrine of God

I have spoken of the iconic vision as the discernment of the infinite in and through the finite; and I have suggested that this vision is what makes the religious form of life distinctive, at least from an epistemological point of view. But what difference does it really make to see the infinite in the finite, to posit a complete, underived ocean of being? Is it more than an aesthetic play, a weaving of poetic fancy over the indifferent facts of our world as disclosed by the natural sciences? It is important to see that religion is not attempting to posit another object which we may one day come across. And it is not attempting to communicate a purely dispassionate or theoretical vision of how things are. Religion is primarily concerned with the transformation of the self, by appropriate response to that which is most truly real. It is not so much an attempt to see the world differently as to be in the world in a different manner. The vision is not primarily of another thing; but of oneself, as transfigured by the infinite. This is a creative work to be wrought within the self, as it seeks to act in accordance with a true vision of its own being. Thus, in the Christian scheme, it is not enough to see the human and divine united objectively in the person of Jesus. One must die with him to rise with him; and that is to adopt a role which makes possible a particular vision of the world. In the Muslim scheme, similarly, it is not enough to see the Koran as portraying objectively the revelation of the will of Allah. One must submit to that will in one's own life and live in the sight of Allah.

The matrix of one's own tradition provides the exemplary role which will in turn give shape to one's apprehension of and response to all finite objects and events. It is my self which must become an icon of the self-manifesting God. I can indeed see him as the glorified

Lord whom I can revere as over against me. I can see him as the one who is hidden in all finite things, and thus see Christ in every other person, as an object of reverence and care. But I must also, and first of all, allow Christ to live in me, transforming my mind into the likeness of his until I can say, with Paul, 'Not I live, but Christ lives in me' (Ga 12:20). Or, in other traditions, I must allow the Buddha-nature to grow in me; I must let the true Self come to realization in me; I must let the Torah grow in my heart and soul, until I am filled with the spirit of God; or I must submit my life wholly to Allah, until 'all perishes save his countenance,' and his will is perfectly worked out through my obedience.

It is vitally important that this is not seen as a takeover of a human self by a superhuman controller. In some way the Self must be my 'true' self, not its conqueror. And yet it must not be that too familiar self so bound up with ignorance and imperfection which I so often and naturally call 'me'. So the dialectic of identity and otherness begins. The search for myself is also the flight from myself. As I deny myself by negating attachment to finite things and desires, I also seek self-fulfilment by striving for greater perfection and bliss. In this always difficult and finely judged process, what I actually seek is self-transcendence, in which I discover the deepest resources of myself by being lost in another, by being open to that existent Ideal which opens itself infinitely before me. That Self manifests itself in me and transforms me, so that I become an icon of the Self of all. The distinctness must remain; and this is the side the great monotheistic Semitic traditions emphasize. But so must the unity; and that is the great contribution of India to the religious thought of humankind.

Because this is a regulative and dynamic process, an infinite journey of the self into God, God can never be simply objectified. He is both the asymptotic goal, which will never be finally attained; the unlimited source of endless being; and the one who is never far away, but reveals himself to Christians in the ultimate mystery of 'Christ in you, the hope of glory to come' (Col 1:27), and to others in operatively similar fashion, 'nearer than the vein of the neck' (Koran 50:12), known as 'a light within the heart' (Brihad. Up. 4, 3, 7). So if we see our own finite selves as deriving from the unlimited ocean of being, we will both relativize the finite things by which our lives are bounded, and yet take them as sacramental of a presence, a demand and a hope which lies always beyond and yet is truly manifested in those wills which are open to his creative power.

The iconic vision is primarily a vision of the self, or the adoption of a way of life which is defined by a regulative ideal of human authenticity, that understanding of oneself which is also an appropriate way of relating to the limiting conditions of one's existence. Secondarily, it is a way of responding to all finite things, as understood in the light of a set of concepts which derive from the dominant revelatory matrix of the tradition. And this necessitates in the end a philosophical working-out of a coherent conceptual framework within which the religious form of life and other well-established forms of human knowledge can form an integrated unity. It is this which the philosophers attempt – not to construct an abstract and theoretical idea of a remote and ineffectual God; but to conceptualize the symbols of faith which must finally relate to the nature of the world as a whole.

Philosophical fashions come and go; but the classical concept of God has an enduring validity. It presents the idea of God as infinite being, knowledge and bliss. This divine nature is 'unpierced by evil', impassible and unchanged by the world. It is importantly unlike Whitehead's primordial nature of God, with which it may seem to bear a superficial resemblance.[1] For Whitehead speaks of that nature as abstract and unknowing, whereas the divine nature has knowledge and completeness, being fully actual of itself, having no lack and not being dependent on the world in any way. Nor is the divine nature abstracted artificially from the concrete temporal process of multiple knowing and acting selves. It is self-existent and simple, not containing internal complexities, and thus utterly distinct from the complex world of name and form. Yet it is an essential part of the classical concept that God both causes and enters into finitude and an endlessly creative temporality, ever realizing new values in time. His infinity is a dynamic creativity, an unlimited ceaseless act. As Aquinas says, 'the very nature of God is goodness . . . it belongs to the essence of goodness to communicate itself to others' (*ST* 3, 1, 1). Thus there are always endlessly finite expressions of the infinite nature of God. He does not change in his essential being, *qua* pure form; thus no creatures can enter into the eternal nature itself (which would change it by increase). Yet creatures can be united with God, in that temporal sovereign nature which expresses the eternal in time. And there is a unity of the divine nature (*ousia*) and its temporal expression (*energeia*); though a unique form of unity, unparalleled elsewhere, by which we are able truly to say that the infinite, and not another, is what is expressed in time. Dual-aspect theism is the classical view; it is present in every major religious tradition. To see the temporal as the image of eternity and to pursue the path of self-transcendence in relation to it is perhaps the central clue to understanding the religious form of life.

For dual-aspect theism, the immutable nature of God cannot be considered as an abstraction from the concrete reality of his causal agency, as though it was an abstract form, always embodied in a particular agent. God, in his essential nature, is beyond the category of agency; he is not an object, not even an object which is the supreme rational agent. He does manifest as such an object, so far as the world of space and time is concerned. Yet that is not his essential nature. That nature is complete, immutable, infinite and fully actual. As Plotinus puts it, 'It is sufficient to itself . . . neither indigent with reference to itself, nor with reference to any other thing' (*Ennead* 6, 9, 6).[2] It is not just one aspect of a reality which is only complete when both aspects are taken together. 'It does not seek after anything in order that it may be . . . what addition can be made to it external to itself?' (ibid.).

Nevertheless, 'The nature of the One is generative of all things' (6, 9, 3); and 'It is the fountain of the most excellent things, a power generating being, abiding in itself without diminution, and not subsisting in its progeny' (6, 9, 5). The infinite nature of God does give rise to all finite things, yet without itself changing, being added to or diminished in any way. Dionysius says, 'Power produces in infinite ways an infinite number of other existent powers' (*On the Divine Names*, 8, 2). 'He becomes all things in all . . . while yet remaining in himself . . . in that one ceaseless act wherein his life consists' (9, 5).

Remarkably, Dionysius does allow himself to speak of a divine 'yearning', 'overflowing from the Good into creation and once again returning to the Good' (4, 14). 'The divine desire . . . allowed him not to remain unfruitful in himself, but moved him to . . . the production of the unvierse' (4, 10, 10). Yet this is no lack or need in God. 'The Creator of the universe . . . is through the excessive yearning of his goodness, transported outside of himself in his providential activities . . . and so is drawn from his transcendent throne . . . to dwell within the heart of all things . . . whereby he yet stays within himself' (4, 13). The creation is like an emanation or overflow from the divine goodness; but again the divine essence must remain unchanged in itself. He contains all things in himself in a simple manner and knows them in himself, not from external things, but as they exist in him 'in a causal manner'. The doctrine is summed up in the paradoxical phrase, 'From its Oneness it becomes manifold while yet remaining within itself' (2, 11).

The paradox is uncomfortably like a contradiction. The One, being changeless, cannot become at all; and yet it *becomes* manifold – while remaining indivisibly one. A paradox, properly speaking, consists of two apparently conflicting statements, each of which one can see to be true, but which one is unable to place within one coherent theory. If mere contradiciton is to be avoided, it is essential that each statement should be true of something under a certain aspect, or from a certain point of view. Then one can say that one has two rather different points of view of the same subject, saving the contradiction (which occurs only when one says conflicting things of the same subject in the same respect). But one is unable to embrace them within one wider explanatory theory (and thus one saves the mystery, affirming that the subject, taken in its wholeness, is beyond the understanding of the human mind). We can say certain true things of it; but we can never form a whole, coherent comprehension of it, as it stands beyond the limits of human thought-forms.

Paradox is actually quite welcome in speaking of God; for it might well be said that a God we could fully comprehend would hardly be God.[3] We might expect God to be beyond human comprehension. And we might welcome the sense of mystery, as that which goes beyond our highest intellectual endeavours. Yet it cannot simply contradict our intellectual efforts. So it is important that we can draw attention to the different aspects under which one is speaking of God, when one says, both that he is changelessly one and that he becomes manifold through his goodness.

What is needed is to ask why one speaks of God in this double way. My suggestion has been that it arises out of the dialectical tension between reality and manifestation, difference and identity, which constitutes the iconic vision. And that in turn is what evokes the response of self-transcendence, when it is mediated in a specific revelatory matrix. Thus one speaks of the compassionate Lord or the merciful Creator, as the manifested form of God to which we respond in devotion or internalization through mental discipline. And one speaks of the infinite ocean of being (*pelagus substantiae infinitum*) in a vain attempt to free the Being of God from all limitations and suggest to the mind his limitless self-existence and perfection. The believer wishes to say of God that his Being is self-sufficient, not standing in need of anything, indestructible, the source of limitless value and changeless in its perfections. It is for that reason that one cannot say he needs the world to complete his full actuality. Unfortunately, this leads to the conclusion that God in his essential nature cannot really be related to the world at all by any form of dependence whatsoever.

When the qualified aspect is taken on its own, one has the idea of a contingent God, to some extent at the mercy of the world, an object over against me who might conceivably change or cease to exist, who needs me as much as I need him. But when the unqualified aspect is taken on its own, one has the idea of a totally isolated and unrelated God, to whom the world makes no difference at all and who therefore cannot be moved by or respond to what happens in it in any way. Classical theism has therefore insisted that both these aspects must be said to be aspects of one unitary being, whose essential nature is the reality underlying the appearances of the qualified and related nature. It is extraordinarily difficult to decide whether this is a coherent notion; since one main point of it is to say that human understanding cannot comprehend the manner in which these two are aspects of one being, and yet it understands enough to affirm each aspect in its due place. It is quite essential, however, to accept the necessity of each aspect, and not simply to reduce one to an improper form of the other.

Can we say that God is complete in his infinite nature and yet endlessly incomplete in his finite nature, which is the instrumental agent and enjoyer and the primary creative cause of the finite world? I have tried to show how the five orthodox traditions with which I have dealt are all committed to a distinction of this sort. I think it is possible that all these traditions have understressed the extent to which creativity, passionate responsivity and spontaneity might enter into the nature of God. In the twentieth century, people often find it hard to accept a view that God does not enter into the sufferings of the world, or that he cannot be changed by any human approaches to him.[4] At the same time, they often dislike other aspects of an anthropomorphic idea of God – as that he is a moral tyrant or an interfering busybody, always prying into the private affairs of everyone else.[5] So one finds ideas of a rather humble, suffering and meek God, perhaps making suggestions that people may care to follow up, but rarely judging in fury or imperiously commanding. To recover an adequate sense of God, as expounded in the great religious traditions of the world, it is important to stress both the ability of God to respond creatively to events in the finite world and the complete transcendence of God over any of our categories of thought. The dialectic must remain between the compassionate Lord and Saviour of the world, and the eternal, immutable and fully actual unlimited ocean of being who remains unmoved by all things infinite, but is their ultimate foundation.

The dual-aspect view attempts to do this by distinguishing two modes in which God exists. These modes cannot be confused with one another, and yet they must be said to be modes of one and the same being, and not just to parallel one another by some sort of similarity. God, in one aspect, is the unlimited actual awareness of supreme bliss. In this aspect, he is wholly beyond change; the world makes no difference to him. He is not a mere abstraction, unaware and potential until realized in finite actualities. In his divine nature, he is fully actual and aware. God, in another aspect, is the unlimited source of creative spontaneity, the supreme agent and enjoyer of endlessly novel temporal succession. Thus God necessarily exists in two modes, one fully actual, the other creatively actualizing. The creative Will of Semitic revelation is the manifestation or temporal appearance of the eternal Self to which Vedanta testifies. The relation between these modes is that the fully actual infinite mode manifests in the temporal, creatively actualizing mode. It does so by inner necessity, but not out of any lack or need – rather, as Aquinas puts it, out of the superfluity of its essential self-expressing goodness.

God necessarily manifests himself as the dynamically infinite, his actual infinity remaining unchanged. 'From its Oneness it becomes manifold while yet remaining within itself.' In this manifestation, not everything is necessarily determined to be what it is – otherwise creative contingency would be impossible. God necessarily determines that there are particulars and that they necessarily possess specific characteristics, including most centrally that of creativity. He thus is necessarily the causal basis of finite appearances, including finite expressions of his own being, which are dynamically undetermined; that is, undetermined in respect of their freedom of creative expression.[6] What is necessary, then, is the infinite being, simple and changeless, completed awareness and bliss; and its self-expression in a dynamically and always uncompleted creative agent.

In his necessary finite self-expression, God also relates himself to other beings; beings drawn from nothingness to reach inclusion in his own fullness of existence. It is in respect of this divine relatedness that the polarities of the faith structure emerge most clearly. There seems to be an almost irresistible tendency, at least among philosophers in the orthodox traditions, to magnify the infinite mode of the divine Being at the expense of the finite. When this is done, it becomes extremely difficult to give any adequate account of divine revelation, salvation, personal relationship or action in the world. For all these things imply some element of divine response to finite events which would obviously have had to be other than it actually is if the world had been different (as it could have been, if it is truly contingent). In the most extreme case of Buddhism, all these elements can be eliminated, so that one must simply work for one's own liberation in a sort of heroic spiritual isolation. It is noteworthy that many Buddhist traditions qualify this rigorous stance by finding space for an eternal Buddha-nature which can be realized in compassionate saviours (the Bodhisattvas) who continually help their devotees to attain liberation. I suppose that the other extreme is represented by orthodox Christianity, which sees Jesus Christ as a unique historical action by God to save human beings by grace alone. Again, however, one can see the qualifications which insist that God does not change by becoming incarnate; that all changes in relation to God are actually changes in human nature and understanding; and that good works, sincere penitence and resolute faith are necessary to salvation.

It may seem that the truth is not to be found at either extreme. Nor is it to be found at some carefully balanced point in the middle.

It may rather be that the human mind needs continually to swing in dialectical movement between one pole of understanding and the other, in endless search for greater understanding. If God is bimodal, in a way beyond the competence of the human mind adequately to comprehend, then this is what one might expect, and one mark of religious understanding will be the perception of the need for permanent qualification, without the loss of that basic vision and response which gives force to religious concepts. It is perhaps largely for this reason that there is sometimes said to be an intelligibility gap between believers and unbelievers.[7] It is rarely true that believers and unbelievers understand one another perfectly, but disagree about whether there is such an object as God or not. Unbelievers most often cannot see why believers seem driven to speak so paradoxically about their God, at one time saying something that seems comprehensible yet false; and at another time saying something that is just incomprehensible.

That need for paradox, I have suggested, derives from the basic nature of the iconic vision, wherein the ideas of manifestation and hiddenness, finite and infinite are held together in tension. And that vision in turn already evinces a beginning of the self-transcending response, because it is already the adoption of a complex reaction of submission and fulfilment which generates the distinctive character of religious faith. In other words, this is not a purely theoretical matter, of seeing things in a rather odd way. It is a matter of the adoption of a mode of being which can only be spelled out by the religious use of concepts, the use of them to sponsor that vision and specify that response. The adoption of that mode is not something which can be decided at an intellectual level; and thus the scope of reason is to achieve such understanding as may be possible and to outline the religious doctrine as clearly as possible, in its relation to other forms of human knowledge. It may thereby remove obstacles to faith (or strengthen them, for some) or enable one to achieve a richer understanding of what one already believes. But, like most important matters of human decision, reasons will in the end seem to be fairly finely balanced, and decisions, where they exist, must just be taken as honestly as one can. Since this is the case, what is most important is to bring out the distinctive character of religious commitment; to make clear that it is neither some sort of irrational leap of blind faith nor some compelling inference. It is a matter of fundamental vision and response, specified by concepts which cannot be assimilated to non-religious categories without changing their meaning.[8] In this sense, the religious form of life is basic and inexponable. And though it is neither universally adopted nor necessary to adopt, for the believer it is a form of life which brings out the true nature and goal of human existence in a world in which that goal is hidden and obscured by all the ambiguities of self-will. There is, nevertheless, a sense in which religious beliefs can be justified. In the concluding chapter I will try to sketch the extent to which, and the way in which, rational argumentation can and should play a part in one's decision about whether or not to adopt such a form of life, in one of its many particular historical specifications.

In *Rational Theology and the Creativity of God* I developed a bimodal view of God; and the basic analogy I used was that of the character of a person and the acts which realize that character. I suggested that it is the 'character' or nature of God which is necessary and immutable, while he is a causal agent, expressing this character in creatively free relation to the universe which he has brought into being. I added that this necessary nature must include the limitless range of archetypes of form and value upon which the intelligibility of the world is patterned, and which limit the particular acts of God. The nature of God thus includes the exemplary forms of all possible worlds. I did, however, suggest (p. 165) that these properties were 'themselves uncaused, uncausing and unconscious'. They are objects of his everlasting awareness; but it is God, *qua* individual causal agent, who is the first cause and experient of the world.

This form of expression may be misleading, and I would point to its qualification at page 233, where I said: 'One may wish to preserve the possibility of a more purely internalized triad within the divine Being, of the self-existent, the exemplary Ideal and the appreciative awareness of it.' While stressing the incomprehensibility of the divine Being in itself, I did wish to preserve the possibility that there could be a form of awareness of archetypal ideals within the Godhead. The ideals are themselves unconscious; but there is an eternal awareness of them, which is quite unlike any sort of awareness we can imagine. Moreover, since the divine Being is necessarily the origin of the finite world, I would wish to make it clear that the relation between the eternal Godhead and the qualified agency of God is one of necessary generation – it is therefore not a relation of 'creation', in the sense of something freely or temporally brought about. But what is generated – most importantly, the qualified nature of God himself – is not necessary in all its details. It is precisely the necessary generation of a temporal source of spontaneous freedom which captures, so far as may be, the relation of identity which holds between the two aspects – the 'nature' or *ousia* and the activities or *energeia* – of the divine Being.

The dual-aspect view which I have found at the base of each main religious tradition is, therefore, a view which is expressed in one form in my earlier work. My criticisms there of Aquinas and various other theologians of the classical tradition is that they tended to stress the eternal aspect to the exclusion of the temporal. Thus they were not able to develop an adequate doctrine of the creativity of God, and left the devotional aspects of theism almost incomprehensible, in terms of the official view. How can one ask things of a changeless God or hope that he will respond to one's actions and devotions when he cannot even acquire any new knowledge at all? A dual-aspect doctrine is alone, I think, able to deal with these problems, and expound a doctrine adequate both to the requirements of personal devotion and to the root perception of the infinity of God which underlies the fundamental religious response of self-transcendence.

I would therefore now regard this volume as effecting a completion of the notions of God which are to be found in *The Concept of God* and in *Rational Theology and the Creativity of God*. If the three volumes are taken together, while they contain many differences of detail, they will, I think, provide an overall view in which each volume complements the others.

9

Faith and Reason

The five major religious traditions that have been considered in these chapters are all scriptural traditions. In the form in which they now exist, they appeal to an authoritative canon of Scripture which defines the faith they profess. The orthodox traditions all tend to ascribe to this Scripture an infallibility which derives either from direct dictation by God or from a miraculously preserved remembrance of the teachings of the original founder of the community. It is obvious that these claims to infallibility cannot all be true. The doctrine of rebirth, for example, is quite different from the hope for the resurrection of the body; and the desire for release from all finite things is quite different from the hope for a messianic rule of God in a transfigured world. It is not enough to make a claim for infallibility, however often the claim is repeated with conviction. It does not seem possible that any informed person should simply point without argument to a particular Scripture and say, 'This is infallible; all the others are mistaken in at least some respects'. It is possible that, since all these Scriptures are concerned with similar sorts of material, and can be shown to have been formed in rather similar ways, bearing the marks of their own cultures very distinctly, all the Scriptures contain errors or partialities of one sort or another. Yet it is also possible that one alone is inerrantly true. If so, one needs to have good reasons for selecting that Scripture as privileged. Thus one cannot avoid the question of the reasons there are for adopting a particular religious faith. It is not enough to say that it is the faith of one's ancestors, though that may be one reason, in so far as cultural and historical factors are important in the formulation of a religious tradition.

I do not wish to select one tradition preferentially over the others. What I am concerned to do is bring out the sorts of reason there can be for adopting one tradition of faith. Throughout this book, I have spoken of a basic attitude which I have termed the iconic vision: a vision of the temporal in the light of eternity. And I have spoken of the response of self-transcendence, which sees the finite self as the vehicle of an unlimited and unique reality beyond it, conceived under the analogy of Self or Will. I have suggested that the language of religion attempts to evoke such a vision and portray it in symbolic terms, using a set of concepts available in a specific culture, with all the knowledge of the world available to it and the basic evaluations typical of it. One may speak of the iconic sense as a distinctive form of sensibility which may be possessed and cultivated in different degrees. But I have tried to stress that this vision should not be thought of as some sort of discrete and peculiar mental state. It does not necessarily come in one moment of ecstasy at all – though it may do in some spectacular cases. It is constituted by a general way of seeing one's own existence in the world. It thus depends on the possession of a set of concepts, or a use of concepts, which enable one to adopt that way of seeing. What they provide is a general and reactive interpretation of experience; that is, they specify a way of reacting responsively to any and all of the experiences one encounters, in accordance with a particular pattern. Religious concepts are in this sense regulative concepts;[1] and it is possible to live a religious life with very few intense and dramatic mental feelings, or even with none.

That is because religion, despite Schleiermacher and his spiritual successors, does not consist primarily in having certain feelings, whether of absolute dependence or of numinous awe.[2] Nor is it, as Whitehead once suggested, what a man does with his solitariness[3] – though solitude can be important to many religious believers. I have suggested that a religious form of life may be most helpfully characterized in terms of a fiduciary structure. This is a conceptual structure which presents a view of human existence as conditioned in specific respects. It then propounds a goal of liberation from these restricting conditions. It shows the way to achieve that goal. And it propounds a general doctrine of the nature of ultimate reality, so far as this is necessary to explain how the limitations arose and how they can be overcome. This structure is determined in a particular way by the authoritative teaching which is enshrined in Scripture and preserved in a religious community.

This is at the same time more theoretical and more practical than an account of religion primarily in terms of feelings or inner mental experiences. It is more theoretical, because it presents a theoretical view of the nature of the ultimately real and its relation to human existence. It is more practical, because it is primarily concerned with liberation, as the attainment of a way of being which delivers one from the limiting imperfections of human existence, either now (and usually now to some extent) or hereafter. It is within such a structure that the iconic vision is conceptualized by means of a specific matrix.

In one sense, then, the religious form of life may be thought of as a distinct area of human thought and experience: the articulation of the iconic vision within a structural framework for the pursuit of self-transcendence. If the sorts of reason for religious belief do not relate to this central complex of themes, then they are not religious reasons at all – but perhaps metaphysical or ethical reasons. A metaphysical reason might marshal various arguments to suggest a central picture of the sorts of thing that exist. An ethical reason might seek to show what sorts of practical commitment are rationally justifiable. But a religious reason must be concerned to elucidate an objective goal of human striving and self-understanding, a goal which in its fullest development is seen to derive from an indestructible and perfect source of all, and to give form and direction to a way of self-transcendence. It gives form, by providing an exemplary matrix in terms of which self-transcendence can be understood. It gives direction, by pointing to the direction in which one must strive for such transcendence.

How can one decide whether or not there is such a goal, and what its nature is? Perhaps the first way to approach this question is to give a genetic account, though such an account cannot be adequate in the end as a justification. It can show, however, how such questions of justification arise, and the context in which they must be answered.

If, as one example, one takes the Upanishads, and views them as documents from an ancient culture, on a par with similar documents from other cultures, then one can see in them a complex mingling of many different elements. [4] There are magical spells and charms, concerned to bring about human welfare or fulfil various human desires by the attainment of magical power over natural forces. Associated with this concern with magical power is the development of amazingly complex systems of cosmic correspondence. Using highly imaginative etymologies and word-play, mystic analogies are discerned between words, rites and the systems of the heavens. Secret doctrines are built up, in which initiates are given magical formulae granting power over the corresponding cosmic realities. The ritual is developed in intricate detail, and one discerns a priestly love of elaborate numerological and obscurely symbolic interpretation.

One source of religion is undoubtedly this concern to obtain protection against evil and fulfilment of desires by secret magical means, controlled by a special class of 'holy persons', who are initiated into the obscure charms and rites. This is a popular level of religion, and it is bound up with techniques of folk-healing and fortune-telling which survive in the most secular societies today. In the Hebrew Bible, too, there is plenty of evidence for the casting of oracles (Urim and Thummim) and practices such as exorcism, which Jesus himself used. What such beliefs show is a deeply rooted belief that human existence is at least partly determined by principles and forces which are subject to manipulation by psychic power and which show a psychic, if not a fully personal, dimension in the world to which it is important to relate in the right way. Specially gifted persons, or specially trained persons, can gain insight into these powers or the ability to control them to some extent; so that religion exists as a mechanism of control over hidden psychic powers.[5]

As religion becomes institutionalized, the anarchical claims to psychic power are defined within institutional forms. The rules of priesthood and its ritual are laid down in a rigidly prescribed way, and the emphasis is less on power over the psychic, as on discovering what true welfare is by right relation to the gods, through performance of the sacrificial rites and observances. The emphasis is more on submission or devotion to the gods than on attempts to control them by magical formulae; and the ritual is taken as an external (but essential) sign of inward attitudes. I am not suggesting that this is a straightforward evolutionary process, or that it happens in such a temporal sequence as this may imply. But I do suggest that the latter view can be seen to be a deeper one than the former. The devout offering of scarce food to the gods out of reverence for their bounty is a higher view than the chanting of charms to bring more material wealth. It is higher in a twofold sense: first, it is morally higher, in that it is less self-regarding; second, it is intellectually higher or more subtle, in that one is no longer committed to belief in direct magical causality by wholly unknown mechanisms. The causal connection between offering and petition is very indirect, and is seen to depend on the moral worth of the worshipper, not just on the correct performance of the ritual. There still exists the basic belief, however, in psychic determining factors of human life and in the ability of specially gifted persons to mediate the right relation between most people and these 'gods'. Religion is now a means of mediation between humanity and the still hidden gods.

A further moral and intellectual deepening of thought takes place in the Indian tradition when the self-regarding aspect is abandoned, and one seeks to obtain release from attachment to desires. Moreover, one no longer believes in individual and discrete gods who require the performance of their own special rites. Rather, all the gods are taken to be aspects of one spiritual reality, by increasing union with which one seeks a deeper form of fulfilment. For the tradition of the Upanishads, this is exemplified in the practice of the ascetic sages, the forest-dwellers, who renounce all for the sake of Brahman, the one reality which is the Self of all, and in union with which is eternal bliss. In its highest stage, religion is self-transcendence towards the existent Ideal.

What can be discerned here is the way in which the fully-fledged doctrine of Brahman as the Self of all develops from the logically more primitive forms of Indian religious life. In the Upanishads, all these strands continue to coexist; but the Vedantins at least make it quite clear that the doctrine of liberation by realization of Selfhood is the heart of the Vedic teaching. That doctrine has developed its particular form because of the multi-stranded system within which it originates, with its emphasis on the importance of sacrificial ritual, of devotion to the many gods and on the ascetic path. The many gods lead, by reflection, to monism, of which they are aspects. The ascetic path suggests the relative insignificance of the world. The ritual texts elaborate a series of cosmogenic correspondences, which lead to the cyclic mystical cosmology so prevalent in Indian thought. Finally, the caste system originating, perhaps, in the Aryan conquest of the aboriginal peoples, and validated by the doctrines of karma and rebirth, sets the goal of release from *samsara* as the final goal of human striving.

A similar distinction of levels, always coexisting at every stage of history to which we have access, can be found in the Jewish tradition. The soothsayers and makers of charms were subsumed and institutionalized by Levitical priesthood and their carefully-worked-out rituals of sacrifice. Attempts to use the magical force of Jahweh, as in sending the Ark of the Covenant into battle at the head of the army (1 S 4:3) were replaced by hymns of thanksgiving and praise. The primitive taboos of circumcision and food laws were given a deeper spiritual meaning, and placed within a wider context of Torah as the laws of righteousness and loyalty to God. And the prophetic foretellers of the future became the proclaimers of moral judgement and the dream of restoration for a penitent people. As I have said, this was not an easy one-way process, but more like a continual tension of lower and higher levels of interpretation. But it was the higher level which issued in the great reforms which gave rise to the Hebrew Bible in its present form.

At the highest level, the priestly mediation is itself replaced by an internalization of the major themes of the tradition. After the destruction of the second Temple, external sacrifice disappears entirely and is replaced by the central ideas of atonement and renewal. The idea of one morally demanding God gives rise to a dualistic view of God and the world – God standing against the world in judgement, and the world being desacralized and so made a possible object of study and experiment – an idea to have very fruitful consequences later in European history. The prophetic heritage produces an emphasis on the basic goodness of the world, and the hope for a future transformation and vindication of the just in a resurrection of the flesh (a doctrine probably influenced by Zoroastrian themes).[6] Thus the spiritual goal is seen as one of a relationship to a holy God which is established by the indwelling of his spirit in the heart, when a new covenant will be placed in the heart of every person, and all shall know the Lord.

The central matrix of Judaism, the messianic rule of God in the hearts of his chosen people, is thus, from a human and historical point of view, built up out of a complex of themes which converge on that one dominant image – long-established ritual, social practices and sacred stories developed over many generations. This reminds us that no one can simply start again in religion, constructing a wholly original view of the world and a purely personally discovered way of liberation. Even the greatest religious teacher has his thinking shaped by specific concepts, practices and symbols. Some primitive religions were almost wholly wrong – for example, in thinking that human sacrifice was needed to ensure fertility. Such systems of thought can be so morally barbaric and causally mistaken that they may be called the alchemies of religion. Most ancient religions will contain some elements which now seem morally limited or mistaken as to scientifically established fact. (I am on safe ground in saying this, since every orthodox believer will admit that it is true of every tradition but his own.) But it by no means follows that because we can to some extent trace the historical influences which have gone to shape the definitive canonical form of a religion, we have to understand the present phenomenon solely in terms of its ancient past forms, especially when these forms are expounded in their most primitive guises, morally and evaluatively. Part of what a better understanding of history can do is to free us from the tyranny of a tradition which will usually turn out to be little more than a hundred years old, to be creative in the way in which the great figures of our past whom we revere were creative. For even the great teachers did not just receive entire revelations out of the blue. Each lived in a social historical context which permitted certain revelatory symbols to appear, which are almost unthinkable in very different contexts. Even where visions were involved, as with Mohammed, it is not hard to trace the influence of Jewish and Christian ideas in the concepts of the Koran, or even in the fact that Gabriel, not Krishna, appeared to the Prophet. Similarly, Sakyamuni can only be understood against the background of Hindu practice, to which the new faith was a 'puritan' reaction, rejecting the gods, sacrifice and caste as irrelevant and unhelpful, but retaining the idea of rebirth, asceticism and release as central to its understanding of the world.

The teachers – Zarathustra, Moses, Jesus, Sakyamuni, Mohammed – took existing traditions and – partly because the time was right, because different currents cross-fertilized; and partly by their own extreme piety and sensitivity to God – crystallized them around a new matrix. So Moses was probably a codifier of laws, a visionary and wonder worker; a man of charismatic authority, intense visionary experience, psychic powers and poetic skill. Around his name were gathered that set of traditions now known as the Torah. The historian would doubt that Moses himself codified it; but it is likely that it was ascribed to him because of his immense authority in providing symbols for God.[7] Sakyamuni had very similar personal characteristics, according to accounts of his life. But he lived in a very different context – not among nomadic tribesmen seeking a place to settle, where Egyptian and Sumerian, Canaanite and desert traditions mingled; but within a long ascetic tradition of tropical lassitude, where Persian (Aryan) and Dravidian elements mingled to produce a society of sometimes stifling social rigidity and priestly privilege. Both teachers opposed many religious traditions in their environments. So their teaching arises partly from a meeting of diverse traditions, partly from an opposition to some existing traditions, and partly from an attempt to purify and get to the heart of other traditions, in the light of new situations and opportunities. They are the catalysts for a new creative matrix of faith.

In assessing the acceptability of such a matrix, its whole context must be taken into account. It is always a blind alley, in religion, to try to believe just as our remote ancestors believed. Even apart from the fact that we can never be quite sure what form their faith took, or how they interpreted it, our cultural context will be so different that each age must, in a sense, build the faith anew. But this building cannot be an escape from tradition; that is a different sort of blindness, which assumes an absolute omniscience, removed from the processes of history. We are in history, and we cannot escape it. The point about the past is that it has become – as it could not have been for itself – part of our objective understanding of the world; part of the given data upon which we now proceed. One fundamental reason why we cannot believe as the first believers did is that the record of their beliefs is now part of our consciousness, or at least a possible part, and more likely an actual but unrecognized part. We understand the world from a different place, and our culture will have changed simply through the accumulation of knowledge and its successive appropriations. There will have been generations of reactions to exaggerated emphases, and then counter-reactions to redress the balance. Still involved in this process, we can in some ways see the partialities of the past more clearly; but we can also see that we are hardly likely to be immune from the same defects.[8]

Though one can trace out the possible development of religious traditions in this way, such an account does not answer the question of justification. It does provide considerations which may help one to see how the historical process has developed and made certain adjustments of view necessary. It certainly provides a wider knowledge than might otherwise be available of the claims which need to be assessed. But, in the end, a claim to revealed truth is common to all the traditions I have dealt with. It is those claims which must be subject to the scrutiny of reason, and more or less probable opinions about their genesis and historical context (their diachronic and synchronic structure, as some would say) cannot in themselves compel a decision as to their acceptability. So, having set out such an account, one must proceed to apply certain general criteria of rationality to the various claims which form the corpus of any specific revelatory tradition.

The first and most obvious requirement is that of consistency. It is often possible to avoid a charge of inconsistency by appeal to paradox. Nevertheless, it is important that religious doctrines should not contain self-contradictions; and though this is a minimal requirement, such contradictions can be harder to spot than it may seem. More importantly, religious beliefs should not be inconsistent with other well-established knowledge. Each tradition includes a number of general doctrines about the nature of human existence and destiny. Vedanta has a complicated cosmogony, a doctrine of rebirth and of philosophical monism. Buddhism has a doctrine of causality and of the non-existence of an enduring self. Judaism and Islam have doctrines of a coming Judgement and of the resurrection of the body. Christianity has its doctrines of the Fall and redemption through the unique incarnation of God. These are very general explanatory schemes for understanding human life and must be assessed in accordance with our other knowledge and our general philosophical beliefs.

If elements of these schemes conflict with well-established knowledge in the sciences, for example, then some resolution of that conflict needs to be sought – either a considered rebuttal of the claims of science, or a revision of the scheme. Then, such schemes may have internal difficulties which make them philosophically weak. Naturally, all philosophical systems have their weaknesses; so this may not provide conclusive refutations. But the consonance of a scheme (for instance, of the resurrection of the body) with our explanatory paradigms (theories of personal identity, for example) and with our general overall way of viewing the universe is certainly one important consideration for someone who is wondering whether to accept a revealed body of doctrine. One might also look for a certain integrating power which a religious scheme brings to our knowledge in general – its power to relate diverse phenomena within one illuminating pattern. Other rational requirements may be that a scheme should exhibit simplicity, in the sense of accounting economically for the facts as we see them; adequacy, so that no areas of fact are omitted; and fruitfulness for suggesting new developments of thought and patterns of explanation. It is a counsel of perfection to expect that all these criteria could be clearly met by any general explanatory scheme, whether religious or not. Any decision procedure which involves their use will ineluctably remain a matter for personal judgement and a delicate weighing of various rather diverse factors. They shape no Procrustean bed which threatens to cut all religions down to a preordained size. Yet they remain important factors by which the reasonableness of religious claims must be assessed, in so far as those claims purport to be factual claims about the general nature of the cosmos and the place of human beings within it.

As well as general doctrines, there are specific historical claims to the occurrence of miracles or the immanent end of the world, for example; to a perceived resurrection and return in Judgement. Here general historical considerations will enter, of our other knowledge of history and comparative studies of similar accounts elsewhere. The Eastern traditions sit very loose to history; but in principle the assessment of such historical claims is no different from the assessment of general factual claims about rebirth and so on. Both are asserted on faith; and what one is asking is whether they contradict known facts or require assumptions that we are not in general disposed to admit (about the existence of demons, for example).

The most important doctrines propounded in a tradition are those which analyse the human condition, as sinful or under illusion. It is perhaps these doctrines which speak most powerfully to potential believers. In stories, wisdom sayings and collections of laws, a set of evaluations of human life is given, together with a vision of a proper goal for human life. These can be assessed for their moral insight and also for their ability to make plain the levels of human motivation and self-deception. The lives and doctrines which define the basic evaluations of a religious scheme must, negatively, not contradict our most firmly based ethical views. Positively, they should have the power to generate moral insights which transcend what one previously knew; and disclose an understanding of human life which can enlarge one's self-awareness. Again, there is no objective measure here; just the question of whether one's life is illuminated and shown to be limited by the exposition of these teachings.

Then there are the mental disciplines which are enjoined in pursuit of the goal of liberation. One may accept the testimony of others that the goal can be achieved; but there must be some indications of this in one's own life. It is not a matter of inner mental feelings, but of a growing liberation from greed, hatred, envy and so on, a growth in wisdom, compassion and love.

Finally, there is a claim that life is to be lived in relation to an ultimately real and personal being, whose grace can be felt in experience. Experiences do play an important part here; for in submission to Allah, or in taking refuge in the Buddha, or in giving one's life to Christ, there must be some personal feelings of comfort, love and sustenance which make these claims plausible. Again, one may rely very much on the testimony of others if one's own experiences are rather thin in this area. They are part of the complex picture, but not the whole, and not the foundation either.

One can see how far all this is from seeking evidence for a factual theory. One has indeed to reflect critically; true faith does not have to be blind. Yet faith has a definite structure of commitment to a way of inward response to that which it is believed will bring liberation from sin. If it is asked whether such a commitment is reasonable, that will depend upon whether one thinks humans are in need of liberation; whether the general religious picture of the world is both coherent, consistent with other knowledge and capable of integrating it in an illuminating way; whether the religious goal is an admirable and sensible one; and whether one's mentors in the faith are wise and good – and holy, in living a self-transcending life of moral pre-eminence. Religion is a path to liberation, involving a basic insight into human existence; rules of conduct towards others; a discipline of mind and will; and a goal of peace or self-transcendence in the supremely real. The path is proclaimed on the authority of seers or prophets, who mediate this saving knowledge, claiming it either to be given by the supremely real or to be personally known by their union with that supremely real.

It is not appropriate to seek evidence for the nature of the supremely real. All the evidence lies before one; what is needed is an assessment of its character.[9] It is noteworthy that arguments for God play no role in scriptural texts, except in the very general sense that the heavens may be said to declare the glory of God (Ps 19:1) or the regularities of nature to be a sign of his wisdom and care. This is hardly an argument, however. It is more a symptom of belief. If one asks where the belief comes from, the answer is 'revelation'. It may be said that one must first know there is a God, before one can accept something as a revelation from God. But this is artificially schematic. Of course, to have the idea of something as a revelation, one must have the idea of a being which could reveal – in some sense a personal, active, communicating being. One must have a logical space for possible revelation. But that space can then be filled simply by a prophetic claim to proclaim the mind of God. If the claim meets all the moral and factual tests that can be devised, then its status is as clear as the status of any argument for God on independent grounds would be.

Now what the revelation does is not to say, 'There is a God'. It declares judgement on human conduct, reveals the full despair of the human situation, and calls for repentance and faith – for a turning from worldly life and commitment to a path to liberation. If the religious claim is true, then human beings are under illusion, deluded by the world or blinded by sin. They will not be changed by argument, which is itself a device of illusion. They will be changed only by a secret inner turning to the Real, in response to the proclamation which they hear and are ready to receive with faith. Indeed, if the religious claim is true, God could simply cause all people to believe in him, without any argument at all, if he so chose. 'Do the faithful doubt that Allah, if he pleased, could have guided all mankind?' (Koran 13:31).

God does not do that. In the Indian traditions, the basic reason is due to karma. People are ensnared by desire and must work out their own destinies. They will turn to God and accept his grace only when they are inwardly ready. Thus it is the job of the sages only to keep open the way, to preach the Dharma. People will respond when their karma has so worked out that they are ready. In the Semitic traditions, the reason given is usually that humans must be free to answer the call of God and put their trust in him, or to turn away and harden their hearts. When the message of God is preached to them, they can either respond in penitence or turn away, regarding it as foolishness or offensive to their way of life.

On no view is intelligence the prerequisite of salvation. Faith is the secret response of the heart to the call of God. Only God knows when that call has truly been issued, or when the soul has decisively responded or turned away. This may be all very unsatisfactory for the philosopher, who would like to have good arguments for everything. But if real belief in God is a matter of responding in faith to a secret call, then it is clearly not a matter of argument at all. One would wish to know that belief in God was reasonable; but that is not at all the same as being able to prove it. In fact, if the structure of faith is as I have suggested, proof is not so much out of the question as irrelevant. It would not matter if you proved the existence of God intellectually. What would matter would still be the commitment of faith, the willing response of self-transcendence to the supremely real. It is not quite, as Kant suggested, that knowledge must be denied to make room for faith.[10] It is that faith is quite distinct from intellectual knowledge, and it does not depend upon an independently achieved intellectual knowledge. It does, of course, logically depend upon belief that there is a God to whom one responds, or (in Buddhism) that there is a goal which the enlightened have achieved. But the engendering of that belief is itself the first work of grace. From the religious point of view, the inward assent to such beliefs – which one cannot consciously help – is already the first seed of a positive response, which may or may not develop further, to the hidden presence and activity of God.

The complication is that not all who assent to the existence of God have taken the path of faith; and not all who deny it are wholly precluded from the goal of faith. It would be so easy to divide the world into the good and the bad; to say that all professing Muslims are saved and all unbelievers are damned. Believers do sometimes say that sort of thing; but it shows a remarkable lack of reflection on the compassion of God. For a start, there are thousands of different religious traditions, and many subdivisions even of the five main traditions I have considered here. In a world of sin and illusion, religion itself must partake of that illusory and sinful nature. Thus people can advance far in religion for motives of pride, power over others and straightforward greed. Seeing this, others may be put off religion altogether. There may also be intellectual factors which make religious faith virtually impossible at certain times – in Albania at the present day, for example, one would be unlikely to give Christian faith any credence at all, without an amazing degree of intellectual independence and moral heroism.

In trying to elucidate a basic structure of religious life, common to the great faiths, I have tried to suggest that the two factors of the iconic vision and the self-transcending response are definitive of the religious form of life in its orthodox and purest forms. One cannot isolate these factors and reify a 'pure essence of religion', distinct and apart from all particular religions. Both vision and response have to take a particular form, as shaped by the revelatory matrix classically enshrined in a canonical Scripture. The attitude of any particular person to that matrix will be influenced in many ways – by the history of his culture, his temperament, interests and personal goals. Now suppose that I am brought up in a secular culture to value independence of thought and freedom above all, to regard religious institutions as essentially reactionary and authoritarian, and am trained in a philosophy which is critical of all systems and in a science which limits itself to what is experimentally testable. My predispositions and values are likely to be inimical to the claims of religion, which may well seem to me mere mystery-mongering and obscurantism. Is faith then possible to me in any sense? There are analogies to faith possible for me. I may give my life in the heroic service of others; I may love the beauty of mathematics and pursue truth with utter zeal; I may revel in the beauties of the world and have compassion for its miseries. I may be humble, patient, kind, temperate. The iconic vision has its surrogates, in art, science and morality. I do not systematically pursue a path of liberation or accept the existence of an existent ideal to which I could respond. In that sense faith is not possible for me. Yet, from the religious point of view, within the limitations of my culture, I may be said to be preparing myself for faith by my unselfish response to the values I perceive. For many millions of people, faith in its true sense is impossible. The Indian traditions can say that they are preparing themselves for faith in a subsequent life. The

Semitic traditions have to take another route. It may be said that faith can be imputed to them vicariously (so that the faith of Israel may redeem the world); or that 'we have our own works and you have yours; let there be no argument between us. Allah will bring us all together, for to him we shall return' (Koran 42:13); or that people will be judged by the Law written in their hearts (Rm 2:15). What is in general necessary is that the nearest analogy to a faith-response which is possible in a person's life should be made.[11] Alongside this goes the warning that if a person clearly sees the light and turns from it, that is unbelief. And with that warning goes the admonition to believers that it is not for them to judge when and in what form such a call from God is made in the life of anyone.

On the religious view, faith is a response to one who claims my loyalty by showing the true nature of my present mode of being and the way to salvation. It is not the prudential calculation of the most reasonable way to live in view of the most probable estimate of the nature of the universe (whether or not there is a God). That is why the Indian traditions generally reject the whole procedure of arguing from the world to the existence of a God. Religious faith is not the acceptance of a probable inference. It consists in coming to see oneself as fallen into sin or ignorance, and as posed with a possible way of release or salvation. This requires a reorientation of vision, so that one sees oneself as both alienated from and confronted by that unique reality which is characterized most adequately as unconditioned Self or Will. This vision already embodies the beginning of that response of submission and disciplined striving to achieve a state hard to discern, preferred by few, beyond sense and desire, bringing freedom from sorrow. For my form of engagement determines my form of understanding; and, revelation speaks to the one who is ready to receive it.

The attempt to justify religious belief from some neutral standpoint is surely mistaken.[12] It is rather like trying to justify moral belief by reference to the findings of the natural sciences. Of course those findings are relevant, and may well cause modifications to some of our moral beliefs. But they do not provide a foundation for moral belief. Karl Barth was right in taking his stand on revelation, and holding that it is and must be its own foundation.[13] Where his view was too restrictive was in considering only one tradition of faith, and thus appearing to assume that God only speaks once and in one tradition. One must view religious faith in a much broader perspective to gain an idea of its full range and scope. When that is done, the structure of a distinctive form of religious life does appear. And then it must be judged by the general attempt to construct an integrating framework of factual and evaluative concepts from the whole range of human experience and knowledge. Such judgement must take place; no revelation is or can be immune from rational assessment; and rethinkings of tradition are part of the tradition itself. Reason has its essential part to play, in criticism and integration from as wide a range of data as possible. What it cannot do is assume a neutral dispassionate posture by which the practice of religious faith can itself be justified or found wanting. Religious faith begins from a revealed structure of vision and response. Philosophical reflection may clarify that structure, explore its implications and its relation to other areas of human activity and knowledge and confront it with alternative and critical viewpoints. Faith may be defensible by argument; but it is not held on the basis of reasons, or established by argument.[14] And that is just to say that it is not a dispassionate intellectual inquiry, but a commitment to a way of life founded on a primal vision of the supreme goal of human endeavour.

In religious faith, the natural movement of the mind towards the asymptotic ideal of a reality unconditioned in being and value is met by the mediated disclosure of that reality in the finite world and the self. When the self is transformed by its participation in this reciprocal movement, a religious form of life is born. In the works I have considered, the structure of this form of life is clearly discernible. Beneath the important variety of its doctrinal and cultural matrices, it testifies to a common core of belief about the appropriate relation of human life to its ultimate environing reality, about the need for salvation and the means to attain it.

All this, of course, is said from within the religious perspective. To the unbeliever, it is all deception and wish-fulfilment; the evidence can never be enough. Then the believer will say that it is not a question of evidence, but of vision and commitment. To know the nature of the vision one must come to understand the distinctive use of religious concepts which evoke and sustain it. It cannot be inferred from a distinct logical type of discourse, though of course it must relate to other sorts of discourse, to the facts and to human desires, in intelligible ways. The structure of faith itself, however, is a basic and distinctive mode of human thought and activity. It is a higher-level postulate, not necessary to the basic conditions of existence, but giving a sort of value to human life which, to those who adopt it, seems essential to a worthwhile and adequately perceived life. In the end, the iconic vision and the commitment to self-transcendence must exert their own inexponable claim to human attention. It is within that structure that the quest for a fully rational faith must be continually pursued, and that one's acceptance and interpretation of a particular revelatory tradition must be explored.

Epilogue

This has been an inquiry into God; into the concept of God and what it seeks to evoke or show. It has been by no means an exhaustive account of what humans have thought about God and its cognates, such as 'ultimate reality' or 'the absolute'. But I have attempted to provide an accurate, if sometimes rather blunt and abbreviated, account of what some major philosophers in five rather different religious traditions have said. These are not the only acceptable accounts in those traditions. They are sometimes strongly opposed, whether as being too philosophical, too Aristotelian or too medieval. They are, nevertheless, accounts which have been widely accepted as definitive of an orthodox belief within each tradition, and that gives them a particular importance and centrality. It is perhaps not too surprising that Jewish, Christian and Muslim concepts should turn out to be very similar, since they influenced each other closely through the work of the Arabic translators of Aristotle's works. But it is less commonly remarked that there are strong similarities with Vedanta and even with the 'atheistic' religion of Buddhism.

In drawing attention to these similarities I have not wished to say that it does not matter which tradition one accepts, or to deny that there are also some important dissimilarities. But it is, in my view, significant that within these traditions there are convergences of thought which make it reasonable to speak of them as ultimately concerned with one common object and goal of human existence. I hope that I have written this book in such a way that an adherent of any tradition or none would be able to assent to it, or to dissent from it, on grounds of scholarly study of texts and their interpretation, rather than on sectarian grounds. I suppose the chief criticism to which I am liable is that of over-generalization, of drawing conclusions much too general and doctrinaire from the very various materials I have considered – especially with regard to the semi-technical notions I have introduced of fiduciary structure, iconic vision and the idea of self-transcendence. But it seems to me that these assertions of pattern in various religious forms of life are warranted by the nature of the material; and they do enable the philosopher to draw on a wider range of material than is usual in considering the nature and rationality of religious belief.

There is much more that needs to be said on this matter of the justification of religious belief. What I have said on that issue is more of a propaedeutic than a full analysis of the problem. It has not been my central concern; though indeed it could not be ignored entirely, since questions of the meaning of 'God' and of the grounds for believing in God are closely related. They cannot be considered in complete isolation, any more than any question of meaning can be isolated from the question of what would have to be the case for one to be warranted in asserting something to be true. Nevertheless, my central concern has been with the *idea* of God, and with the primary place of that idea within a religious form of life. It has, correlatively, been with the nature of religious faith which has God, or its cognates, as object.

The work has been in no sense apologetic, on behalf of one set of religious beliefs. I have not even argued for the acceptance of religious belief in general – though I have tried to show how reasonable and reflective accounts of belief can be and have been given. It should be quite possible, however, for someone to accept my analysis and still maintain that all the central ideas of religious faith are illusory, unacceptable or even irrational, by some relatively restricted criterion of rationality which might insist, for example, on empirical evidence for every justifiably assertable proposition.

What, then, has been the point of this work? First, for me, the sheer intellectual interest of following the thoughts, sometimes unfamiliar, of outstanding writers in human history. Second, the attempt to achieve a greater, more comprehensive understanding of the religious traditions of humankind, and of the phenomenon of religion itself. Third, the effort to get clearer about the intellectual roots of some major traditions which have shaped human thought in decisive ways. Fourth, the attempt to see how diverse religions relate to each other – whether they are doomed to endless confrontation or have some ground for greater mutual understanding and interaction in future. And fifth, the continuing pursuit of a more adequate idea of God, in the light of the teachings of some of the greatest spiritual masters in history. I hope these endeavours would prove acceptable to all who are curious about human beings, their thoughts and beliefs, and who have an interest in the varied phenomena of religion. The attempt to understand is itself a chief distinguishing feature of human existence; it is the source of everything that is most worthwhile in life. The attempt to understand what so many have taken to be the ultimate object and goal of human striving is thus, for those fortunate enough to be able to pursue it, an activity of supreme intrinsic interest and importance. It is that inquiry which I have tried to further in my own way.

Notes

References to the page numbers of the major texts discussed in this work are to the following English translations:

SANKARA. References are to *The Vedanta-Sutras*, trans. George Thibaut (Delhi, Motilal Banarsidass 1962), *Sacred Books of the East*, ed. Max Muller, vols. XXXIV and XXXVIII.

RAMANUJA. *The Vedanta-Sutras*, trans. George Thibaut (Delhi, Motilal Banarsidass 1962), *Sacred Books of the East*, ed. Max Muller, vol. XLVIII.

ASVAGHOSA (attributed). *The Awakening of Faith*, trans. Yoshito S. Hakeda (Columbia University Press 1967).

MAIMONIDES. *The Guide for the Perplexed*, trans. Shlomo Pines (University of Chicago Press 1963).

AL-GHAZZALI. *The Niche for Lights*, trans. W. H. T. Gairdner (Pakistan, Sh. Muhammad Ashraf). First published as Monograph XIX by the Royal Asiatic Society, London in 1924; reprinted 1952.

AQUINAS. *Summa Theologiae*, various translators, Blackfriars ed., (Eyre & Spottiswoode 1964).

PREFACE

1 For the classical exposition of phenomenological method, as applied to religion, cf. G. Van der Leeuw, *Religion, in Essence and Manifestation* (Allen & Unwin 1938).

CHAPTER 1: THE VEDANTIC PHILOSOPHY OF SANKARA

1 Thomas Aquinas, *Summa Theologiae*, 1a, 11, 4 and 1a, 13, 11.

2 Descartes, *Meditations on First Philosophy*, IV: 'I am in a sense something intermediate between God and nothing.'

3 Cf. Chandradhar Sharma, *A Critical Survey of Indian Philosophy* (Rider 1960).

4 J. Huxley, *The Perennial Philosophy* (Chatto 1969); S. Radhakrishnan,

The Hindu View of Life (Allen & Unwin 1980) and *Indian Philosophy* (Allen & Unwin 1929).

5 Even the excellent *Dictionary of Religions*, ed. John Hinnells (Penguin 1984), gives a brusque definition of Brahman as 'the abstract, impersonal Absolute'.

6 Karl Potter, *Encyclopedia of Indian Philosophies: Advaita Vedanta up to Sankara* (Princeton University Press 1981). Cf. particularly the bibliographies in the Notes.

7 I. Kant, *Critique of Pure Reason, Transcendental Aesthetic*, first section conclusions (A. 28).

8 Useful books include the following: D. Bohm, *Quantum Theory* (Prentice-Hall 1951); F. Capra, *The Tao of Physics* (Fontana 1983), esp. ch. 4 and 'The New Physics Revisited'; J. Polkinghorne, *The Quantum World* (Longman 1984).

9 Leibniz, *The Monadology*, 54.

10 *Brihadaranyaka* Upanishad, Adhyaya I, Brahmana 3, 27.

11 Aristotle, *Metaphysics*, ch. 12.

12 *Maitri* Upanishad, 6, 1.

13 *Brihadaranyaka* Upanishad, 2, 2, 1, 17.

CHAPTER 2: RAMANUJA AND THE NON-DUALISM OF THE DIFFERENTIATED

1 Cf. Grace Jantzen, *God's World, God's Body* (Darton, Longman & Todd 1984), for an interestingly different use of the 'Body' metaphor.

2 Plotinus, *Ennead*, 3, 8, 8.

3 Isaiah 45:7.

4 Bhagavad Gita 3, 19.

5 J. H. Leuba, *A Psychological Study of Religion*, lists forty-eight definitions of religion.

6 *Isa* Upanishad, 6.

7 Psalm 16:11.

8 Plotinus, *Ennead*, 6, 9, 11.

9 *Isa* Upanishad, 17.

10 *Chandogya* Upanishad, 6, 10, 3.

11 A phrase often misleadingly generalized from Wittgenstein, *Philosophical Investigations*, (Basil Blackwell 1953), 43: 'For a large class of cases – though not for all – in which we employ the word "meaning", it can be defined thus: the meaning of a word is its use in the language.'

12 Cf. Paul Deussen, *The Philosophy of the Upanishads*, trans. A. S. Geden (T. & T. Clark 1906).

CHAPTER 3: BUDDHAGHOSA AND ASVAGHOSA: BUDDHIST ANALOGUES TO GOD

1 H. von Glasenapp, *Buddhism – a Non-Theistic Religion*, trans. 1. Schloegl (New York, G. Bruziller 1966).
2 W. D. Hudson, *A Philosophical Approach to Religion* (Macmillan 1974), p. 16.
3 *Udana*, trans. F. L. Woodward as *Verses of Uplift*, (1948).
4 von Glasenapp, ibid., p. 109.
5 C. Gudmunsen, *Wittgenstein and Buddhism* (Macmillan 1977).
6 Buddhaghosa, *Visuddhimagga*, trans. Pe Maung Tun as *The Path of Purity* (Luzac, Pali Text Soc. 1971).
7 For a discussion of authorship, cf. Peter Gregory, 'The Problem of Theodicy in the Awakening of Faith', in *Religious Studies* 22, i, esp. pp. 63 and 64.
8 S. Dasgupta, *A History of Indian Philosophy*, ch. 10 and 11 esp. (Cambridge University Press 1957).
9 Cf. T. Stcherbatsky, *The Central Conception of Buddhism and the Meaning of the Word 'Dharma'* (Royal Asiatic Soc. 1923), pp. 73–5.
10 An example of a very positive view is: P. D. Mehta, *Early Indian Religious Thought* (Luzac 1956).
11 Cf. 'Suvarnaprabhasa Sutra', ch. 12, trans. R. Robinson, in *Chinese Buddhist Verse* (John Murray 1954), p. 48, for a typical devotional text.
12 L. Kolakowski, *Religion* (Fontana 1982) makes a similar set of distinctions.

CHAPTER 4: IMAGES OF GOD IN THE HEBREW BIBLE

1 Cf. J. S. Chesnut, *The Old Testament Understanding of God* (Westminster Press 1968).
2 For a defence of the untranslatability of metaphor, cf. Janet Martin Soskice, *Metaphor and Religious Language* (Clarendon Press 1985).
3 For many biblical scholars, such an interpretation is forced by historical considerations, as well as by considerations of the nature of language: cf. Alberto Soggin, *A History of Israel* (SCM Press 1984).
4 G. B. Caird, *The Language and Imagery of the Bible* (Duckworth 1980).
5 I. Kant, *Critique of Practical Reason*, Pt. i, Bk. 2, ch. 2, 9.
6 P. T. Geach, *God and the Soul* (Routledge & Kegan Paul 1969), ch. 5.
7 P. T. Geach, *Providence and Evil* (Cambridge University Press 1977), ch. 1.
8 John Macquarrie, *In Search of Deity* (SCM Press 1984), ch. 3.
9 P. T. Geach, *Providence and Evil*, ch. 1.
10 E. Jüngel, *God as the Mystery of the World* (T. & T. Clark 1983).

11 Cf. Janet Martin Soskice, ibid., and I. T. Ramsey, *Models for Divine Activity* (SCM Press 1973).

12 Exodus 3:14.

CHAPTER 5: MAIMONIDES: THE UNKNOWABLE GOD

1 For general studies of the influence of Aristotle on medieval Jewish and Muslim thought, cf. R. Walzer, 'Early Islamic Philosophy', in the *Cambridge History of Later Greek and Early Medieval Philosophy* (Cambridge University Press 1970). Also, F. E. Peters, *Aristotle and the Arabs* (New York University 1968) and C. Shirat, *A History of Jewish Philosophy in the Middle Ages* (CUP 1985).

2 Note J. S. Mill's similar point about God's goodness, in *Autobiography*, ch. 2 (Oxford University Press 1969).

3 Ian Crombie in *New Essays in Philosophical Theology*, ed. Flew and MacIntyre (SCM Press 1955).

4 Many such accounts are available. For a representative modern discussion, cf. *Truth and Meaning*, ed. Evans and McDowall (Clarendon Press 1976).

5 I. Kant, *Critique of Pure Reason, Transcendental Analytic*, Bk. 1.

6 Cf. the discussion by P. T. Geach, *God and the Soul* (Routledge & Kegan Paul 1969).

7 Vaihinger, *The Philosophy of 'As-If'* develops this view, derived from Kant, in some detail (Routledge & Kegan Paul 1966).

8 Aristotle, *Metaphysics*, Bk. 12.

9 Plato, *Republic*, 505.

10 Aristotle, idem.

11 Cf. the approach suggested by D. Z. Phillips, in *Faith and Philosophical Enquiry* (Routledge & Kegan Paul 1970).

12 I. T. Ramsey, *Religious Language* (SCM Press 1957).

13 I. Kant, *Critique of Pure Reason, Transcendental Dialectic*, Bk. 2, ch. 3: 'The Ideal of Pure Reason'.

14 E. L. Mascall speaks of this as 'contuition' – *He Who Is* (Longmans Green 1943).

15 The contrast made so forcibly by B. Pascal in the Memorial – 'God of Abraham, God of Isaac, God of Jacob, not of philosophers and scholars' – a parchment sewn into his clothing, recording an experience of 1654.

CHAPTER 6: AL-GHAZZALI AND THE GOD OF UNVEILED LIGHT

1 Cf. W. Montgomery Watt, *Free Will and Predestination in Early Islam* (Luzac 1948).

2 Al-Hallaj's famous statements, 'Ana'l-Haqq' – 'I am the Real'; cf. Louis Massignon, *The Passion of Al-Hallaj*, vol. ɪ, (Princeton University Press 1982), p. 126.

3 Aristotle, *Metaphysics*, Bk. 12. For general commentaries on Al-Ghazzali, cf. W. Montgomery Watt, *Islamic Philosophy and Theology* (Edinburgh University Press 1985) and *The Faith and Practice of Al-Ghazzali* (Allen & Unwin 1953). On authorship of *Mishkat al-Anwar* (*The Niche for Lights*) Montgomery Watt says, 'This work is genuine, except possibly the last section'. However, it has long been accepted by orthodox Sunni Muslims as an authentic work, and so has been taken to have the authority of the master.

4 The doctrine of the 'obeyed-one' (*muta*) is hotly debated. Cf. the introduction to the Royal Asiatic Society ed. 1924, by W. H. T. Gairdner and R. Nicholson, *The Idea of Personality in Sufism*.

5 The idea of religion as 'living in accordance with a metaphor' is sketched briefly by Wittgenstein, with specific reference to the idea of the Last Judgement, in lectures of which student notes were published as *Lectures and Conversations on Aesthetics, Psychology and Religious Belief* (Basil Blackwell 1966), pp. 53ff.

6 D. Z. Phillips writes helpfully of the reactive function of religious concepts, but apparently denies any predictive force, in *Death and Immortality* (Macmillan 1970).

7 The idea of the hiddenness or utter difference (*mukhalafah*) of God is an important strand of Muslim thought – cf. Fadlou Shehadi, *Ghazzali's Unique Unknowable God* (Leiden, Brill 1964).

8 Even that supreme monist Spinoza distinguishes God, as *natura naturans*, from the world, as *natura naturata* – *Ethics*, Pt. ɪ, prop. 29ff.

9 The distinction of *ousia* and *energeia* became at one time standard in Orthodox theology. Rooted in the work of Gregory of Nazianzus, it was developed by Gregory Palamas (1296–1359). Cf. V. Lossky, *The Mystical Theology of the Eastern Church* (1957).

10 A. N. Whitehead, *Process and Reality* (Cambridge University Press 1929), pp. 521ff.

11 Aquinas, *Summa Theologiae*, 1a, 14, 13.

12 Plato, *Timaeus*, 7.

13 Hegel's view is of this kind – *Phenomenology of Mind*, 780, trans. Sir James Baillie (London 1931).

CHAPTER 7: THOMAS AQUINAS: THE IDEA OF SUBSISTENT BEING

1 Leo XIII, *Aeterni Patris* (1879). While the Pope urged Catholic philosophers to draw their inspiration from Aquinas, this does not entail that they are committed to something called 'Thomism'.

2 David Burrell, *Aquinas: God and Action* (Routledge & Kegan Paul 1979), develops the 'agnostic' account of Thomas at some length.

3 Aristotle, *Metaphysics*, Bk. 7.

4 Aristotle, *Metaphysics*, Bk. 12, 6.

5 It is to Frege that we owe the general quantifier-variable notation. Cf. Michael Dummett, *Frege* (Duckworth 1973), esp. ch. 2.

6 Plato, *Timaeus*, 20.

7 Aquinas, *Summa Theologiae*, 1a, 2, 1.

8 Aristotle, *De Anima*, Bk. 3, 4.

9 David Burrell, *Knowing the Unknowable God* (Notre Dame University of Press 1986), speaks of Aquinas as 'transforming classical philosophy to display divine transcendence' (p. ix).

10 Cf. E. L. Mascall, *He Who Is* (Darton, Longman & Todd 1966); and Garrigou-Lagrange, *Dieu, son Existence at sa nature* (Paris, Gabalsa 1927).

11 Aristotle, *Metaphysics*, 12, 7.

12 Cf. Emil Brunner, *The Christian Doctrine of God*, trans. O. Wyon (Lutterworth 1949), p. 152: 'There is the sharpest contradiction between the Christian and the philosophical idea of God.'

13 So W. K. Clifford's principle: 'It is wrong always, everywhere and for anyone, to believe anything upon insufficient evidence'; 'The Ethics of Belief', in *Lectures and Essays* (Macmillan 1879), vol. 2, p. 186. He speaks as if religious belief must be a result of this sort of dispassionate investigation, but only succeeds in ruling it out of court completely.

14 W. K. Clifford, ibid., p. 183, writes of 'the universal duty of questioning all that we believe'. But while we should not accept beliefs uncritically, we cannot be always questioning commitments that we have made. As he himself says, 'It is our duty to act upon probabilities' (189).

15 Aquinas suspended work on the third part of the *Summa Theologiae* in December 1273, after an experience at Mass, telling his secretary: 'All I have written seems to me like so much straw compared with what I have seen and with what has been revealed to me'.

16 John Macquarrie attempts a similar 'strained use' of language in *Principles of Christian Theology* (SCM Press 1966), ch. 5. Cf. also Paul Tillich's characterization of God as 'Being-itself' in his *Systematic Theology*, pt 2, 1 (James Nisbet 1968).

CHAPTER 8: THE DUAL-ASPECT DOCTRINE OF GOD

1 A. N. Whitehead, *Process and Reality* (Cambridge University Press 1929), pp. 521ff.

2 Cf. Jarozlav Pelikan, *The Christian Tradition* (University of Chicago Press 1974), vol. 2, ch. 5. Plotinus and Dionysius both strongly influenced developing Christian ideas of God.

3 LeComte du Nouy, *Human Destiny* (1947): 'If we could really conceive God we could no longer believe in him because our representation, being human, would inspire us with doubts.'

4 Cf. Dietrich Bonhoeffer, *Letters and Papers from Prison* (SCM Press 1971).

5 Don Cupitt, *Taking Leave of God* (SCM Press 1980), ch. 1, makes this point.

6 C. Hartshorne, *The Logic of Perfection* (Open Court 1962).

7 S. C. Brown, in *Do Religious Claims Make Sense?* (SCM Press 1969) speaks of an intelligibility-gap between believers and unbelievers.

8 D. Z. Phillips, *Faith and Philosophical Enquiry* (Routledge & Kegan Paul 1970), esp. ch. 3.

CHAPTER 9: FAITH AND REASON

1 Cf. L. Wittgenstein, *Lectures and Conversations on Aesthetics, Psychology and Religious Belief* (Basil Blackwell 1966), for an outline of this view. Also K. Ward, *The Concept of God* (Basil Blackwell 1974).

2 F. Schleiermacher, *The Christian Faith* (T. & T. Clark 1928), p. 12.

3 A. N. Whitehead, *Religion in the Making* (Cambridge University Press, 1927), p. 6.

4 A. B. Keith, *The Religion and Philosophy of the Veda* (Harvard University Press 1925), esp. vol. 2, provides a succinct account.

5 Cf. E. B. Tylor, *Primitive Culture* (John Murray 1873).

6 Cf. Rudolf Ott, *Reich Gottes und Menschensohn* (1934). But cf. also the discussion in J. Duchesne-Guillemin, *The Western Response to Zoroaster* (Oxford University Press 1958).

7 Bernhard Anderson, *The Living World of the Old Testament* (Longman 1958), esp. ch. 2.

8 H.-G. Gadamer, *Truth and Method* (Sheed & Ward 1981).

9 Cf. the masterly treatment in J. Wisdom, *Gods*, reprinted in *Logic and Language*, first series, ed. Flew (Basil Blackwell 1963).

10 Kant, *Critique of Pure Reason, Transcendental Doctrine of Method*, sect. A 745.

11 Karl Rahner, *Foundations of Christian Faith* (Seabury 1978), pp. 311–21 on 'anonymous Christians'.

12 D. Z. Phillips, *Faith and Philosophical Enquiry* (Routledge & Kegan Paul 1970), ch. 7.

13 Karl Barth, *Church Dogmatics*, 1, 1, 6 (p. 187), trans. G. W. Bromiley (T. & T. Clark 1975): 'The reality of the Word of God . . . is grounded only in itself. So, too, the knowledge of it by men can consist only in its acknowledgement'.

14 A. Plantinga, 'Reason and Belief in God', in Plantinga and Wolterstorff, *Faith and Rationality* (University of Notre Dame Press 1983).

Bibliography

This is a very selective bibliography of books not explicitly referred to in the text which are yet closely relevant to its major themes. It is not intended to be a list of generally introductory books on the philosophy of religion or religious studies, but only of books actually used in writing, though not mentioned by name.

Askari, H. and Hick, J. (eds.), *The Experience of Religious Diversity* (Aldershot, Gower 1985).

B. Barua, *A History of Pre-Buddhistic Indian Philosophy* (Delhi, Motilal Banarsidass 1970).

S. R. Bhatt, *Studies in Ramanuja Vedanta* (New Delhi 1975).

J. B. Carman, *The Theology of Ramanuja* (Yale University Press 1974).

W. Christian, *Opposition of Religious Doctrines* (Macmillan 1972).

J. Cobb, *Beyond Dialogue: Towards a Mutual Transformation of Christianity and Buddhism* (Philadelphia, Fortress 1982).

E. Conze, *Buddhism: its Essence and Development* (Oxford, Cassirer 1957).

F. Copleston, *Religion and the One* (Search Press 1982).

G. D'Costa, *Theology and Religious Pluralism* (Basil Blackwell 1986).

P. Deussen, *The System of the Vedanta* (New York 1973).

Mircea Eliade, *The Sacred and the Profane* (New York, Harper 1961).

E. Evans-Pritchard, *Theories of Primitive Religion* (Clarendon Press 1965).

B. Griffiths, *Return to the Centre*; and *The Marriage of East and West* (Collins 1978 and 1982).

John Hick, *God and the Universe of Faiths* (Macmillan 1973); *God Has Many Names* (Westminster Press 1982). The Gifford Lectures 1986–7, *An Interpretation of Religion*, are being prepared for publication.

W. Hocking, *Living Religions and a World Faith* (Allen & Unwin 1940).

Karl Jaspers, *The Origin and Goal of History* (Routledge & Kegan Paul 1953).

T. Ling, *A History of Religions East and West* (Macmillan 1968).

J. Lipner, *The Face of Truth* (Macmillan 1986).

E. Lott, *Vedantic Approaches to God* (Macmillan 1980).

Bibliography

K. S. Murty, *Revelation and Reason in Advaita Vedanta* (Delhi 1974).

Rudolf Otto, *Mysticism, East and West* (Macmillan 1970); *The Idea of the Holy* (Oxford University Press 1968).

G. Parrinder, *Avatar and Incarnation* (Faber & Faber 1970).

D. Z. Phillips, *The Concept of Prayer* (Routledge & Kegan Paul 1965).

S. Radhakrishnan, *A Hindu View of Life* (Allen & Unwin 1927).

J. Robinson, *Truth is Two-Eyed* (SCM Press 1985).

B. N. K. Sharma, *The Brahmasutras and their Principal Commentaries* (Bombay, Bharatiya Vidya Bharan 1971).

W. Cantwell Smith, *The Meaning and End of Religion* (Sheldon 1978); *Towards a World Theology* (Macmillan 1980).

G. R. Welbon, *The Buddhist Nirvana and its Western Interpreters* (University of Chicago Press 1968).

Index